LIVING WITH WILDNESS

Living with Wildness

An Alaskan Odyssey

BILL SHERWONIT

UNIVERSITY OF ALASKA PRESS
Fairbanks

Portions of this book have appeared, in slightly different form, in *American Nature Writing 2001*; *Anchorage Daily News*; *Anchorage Press*; *Alaska*; *Appalachia*; *Backpacker*; *Best American Science and Nature Writing 2007*; the *Christian Science Monitor*; *Coast*; *Connecticut Woodlands*; *Danger! True Stories of Trouble and Survival*; *Dark Moon Lilith*; *Earth Beneath, Sky Beyond: Nature and Our Planet*; *ISLE*; *Take Two—They're Small*; *The Best Travel Writing* (2005); and *Travelers' Tales Alaska*.

Printed in China

This publication was printed on paper that meets the minimum requirements for
ANSI/NISO Z39.48-1992 (Permanence of Paper).

Library of Congress Cataloging-in-Publication Data

Sherwonit, Bill, 1950–
    Living with wildness : an Alaskan odyssey / Bill Sherwonit.
       p. cm.
    Includes bibliographical references.
    ISBN-13: 978-1-60223-014-9 (pbk. : alk. paper)
    ISBN-10: 1-60223-014-5 (pbk. : alk. paper)
      1. Natural history—Alaska—Anchorage Region—Anecdotes. 2. Wilderness—
       Alaska—Anchorage Region—Anecdotes. 3. Sherwonit, Bill, 1950- I. Title.
    QH105.A4S54 2007
    508.798'35—dc22

                            2007022673

For my wild teachers, especially human, bear, snake, frog, and chickadee

Contents

Acknowledgments

THE PATH LEADING TO THIS BOOK HAS BEEN LONG AND WINDING. More than a dozen years have passed since I wrote the first essays that would eventually morph into assorted chapters; others I've finished only within the past year or two. Along the way I have received guidance of many different kinds. I'd like to recognize and thank the people who have assisted me the most, but there are many others who nudged me along or helped keep me going in one way or another, and I apologize to any I've somehow forgotten. I owe all of you many, many thanks.

To begin, I wish to acknowledge those who shared their natural history knowledge, often while guiding me in the field, whether the field was an Anchorage-area woodland, alpine meadow, or coastal mudflats, or deeper into the wilds of Cook Inlet, the Chugach Mountains, and beyond. Thanks to Larry Aumiller, Mark Chihuly, Jessy Coltrane, Dave DeLap, Ann Garibaldi, Chris Kleckner, Jerry Kudenov, Smiley Shields, Kristin Simac, Katie Turner, John Wenger, and especially biologist and wildlife manager Rick Sinnott, who invited me along while he looked for cranes and captured bears and who took the time, on more occasions than I can count, to talk about the sometimes wondrous and other times stressful relationship between us humans and the wild neighbors with whom we share the Anchorage-area landscape. I also appreciate those who engaged in conversations that helped broaden my understanding of Alaska's people, places, and wildlife. Foremost among these were the Native peoples of the Bristol Bay region, who discussed their knowledge of the Hairy Man and other wild beings: Myrtle Anelon, Ted Angasan, Elena and John Gumlickpuk, and Sam Stepanoff. Others to thank include Brian Barnes, Neil Barten, Bruce Dinneford, Bob Dittrick, Jim Fall, and Larry Van Daele.

I also must thank the friends who have kept me company and added plea-sure to my wanderings in Anchorage and nearby wilds, particularly William Ashton, Ellen Bielawski, Dulcy Boehle, Jeff Fair, Helene Feiner, Dale Gardner, and the entire Romano-Lax family: Andromeda and Brian and their fast-growing-up kids, Aryeh and Tziporah. Thanks also to Barry and Brian Wallace, with whom I explored the Woods of Trumbull, Connecticut, so many years ago, and who recently re-entered my life after more than three decades. I also extend my appre-ciation to the men with whom I've explored notions of the Wild Man and what it means to be healthily male and wild, most notably William Ashton, Harry Brod, Mike Burwell, Alan Colter, Denny Eagen, Sean Elder, Bob Jacobs, Gordon Jones, Jac Morgan, and Bob Pelz.

Equally important have been the writers who have passed through my life these past dozen years or so. Though I haven't met them, or have only briefly, I have been greatly influenced by the writings and ideas of Robert Bly, Loren Eiseley, Mat-thew Fox, James Hillman, Barry Lopez, Roderick Nash, Paul Shepard, Gary Snyder, Jack Turner, and Terry Tempest Williams. Among those who have helped actively shape my work and/or shared their good company are Wendell Berry, John Daniel, John Haines, Kim Heacox, Ted Hoagland, Nancy Lord, Tom Lyon, Bill McKibben, Robert Michael Pyle, Sherry Simpson, and Tom Walker. I especially celebrate the influence of Carolyn Servid, co-founder of the Island Institute and organizer of the Sitka Symposium with husband Dorik Mechau; my Alaskan hero, Richard (Nels) Nelson; philosopher-essayist-teacher Kathleen Dean Moore, who's become both an inspiration and a long-distance friend; and Scott Russell Sanders, another essay-ist, author, and teacher, who is among the most deeply thoughtful people it's been my pleasure to know, and who has inspired me with his writings, talks, critiques, and occasional company since we first met in 2001.

I must also thank the people who have given me the opportunity to attend various writing workshops and retreats, most notably those at Montana's Envi-ronmental Writing Institute, California's Mesa Refuge, and Oregon's Andrews Experimental Forest. All have both grounded me and lifted me up.

Equally influential, if not more so, are the writers who have moved (and in some instances, continue to move) through my Alaskan days and nights since I became a serious essayist and nature writer in the early 1990s, while sharing ideas, writings, laughter, hopes, and good cheer in one writing forum or another. You may have noticed that some of these folks have been mentioned more than once, which should suggest their importance in my life: Jim Adams, William Ashton, Ellen Bielawski, George Bryson, Amanda Coyne, Nancy Deschu, Jeff Fair,

Lee Goodman, Dan Henry, Marybeth Holleman, Nancy Lord, Jon Nickles, Doug O'Harra, Andromeda Romano-Lax, and Kathy Tarr. Andromeda, in particular, has been a constant source of wisdom and inspiration.

And because reading is such a key element of the writing life, I thank the Earthworms, a group of nature-writing readers who've been digging their way through books since 1994. I appreciate all those who have joined the circle of Worms, but especially the core members (past and present) who have kept the group going all these years: Marilee Clack-Tandee, Dale Gardner, Jon Nickles, Julie Obermeyer, Sue Pope, Sean Smith, and especially Patti Harper, whose good idea gave birth to the Earthworms.

I owe a special debt to University of Alaska Press editor Erica Hill, who enthusiastically embraced this book early on and has helped shepherd it to completion; and to the press's advisory board, especially Pat Partnow, who recognized its value and championed it, while also sharing some of her own writings about Anchorage's wild side and the Alutiiq people's recognition of "hairy men" known as *a'ula'ats* or *a'ula'aqs*. Thanks also to other editors and proofreaders who have helped turn my manuscript into a book: Sue Mitchell at UA Press, Rachel Fudge, and Jennie Goode.

Thanks, finally—and especially—to Dulcy Boehle, with whom I shared eighteen growth-filled years, thirteen of them on Anchorage's Hillside, and who wholeheartedly supported my writing life while we lived together; to my mom, Torie Sherwonit, who joined me in Alaska for the last years of her life and has given me good company on our "wheeling-and-walking" forays along Anchorage's Coastal Trail; to my brother Dave, who has shared a lifelong love for nature and, since I settled here, has traveled from the East Coast to share a few memorable adventures in Alaska's wilds; and to Helene Feiner, my new and much-loved sweetheart, another transplanted easterner and nature-loving sort, who has read my stories, joined me on long walks and in long conversations, and been a valued ally as I continue my journey through the wild places of this miraculous place, my adopted homeland, Alaska.

ONE

Introduction

Coming Home

THE QUESTION WAS A SIMPLE ONE, BUT IT HELD FAR DEEPER implications than I could have imagined when Tom Andrews posed it to me in the spring of 1974: "Would you like to work in Alaska this summer?"

Tom had worked seasonally in Alaska before. Now, about to get a master's degree in economic geology, he'd been hired full time by an Anchorage minerals-exploration company. His first assignment: round up summer help. A classmate of Tom's at the University of Arizona, I happened to be in the right place at the right time. Back then, I would have considered this to be a happy coincidence, a stroke of luck. Now I'm not so sure. The older I get, the less I believe in the notion of coincidences. Things happen for a reason, I like to tell friends. There are no accidents, I say, though I'm not entirely certain that's what I believe either.

Whatever put me at UA in 1974—fate, chance, a guiding spirit, or some grand plan—I answered Tom with an emphatic "Yes!" And with that response, I took an unexpected fork in the trail, one that ultimately brought me to where I live today: Anchorage, best known as Alaska's urban center, but also a place of surprising wildness; and a city that borders one of the state's grandest wilderness areas, Chugach State Park.

Strangely, until Tom popped the question, I had never fantasized about traveling to America's "Last Frontier." And I certainly never imagined that I would someday call Alaska home. Not simply my place of residence, but the place to which I belong. At age twenty-four I knew almost nothing about Alaska, except for the usual stereotypes: that it was a land of Eskimos, polar bears, vast wilderness, and Mount McKinley (which I now know by its Athabascan name, Denali).

In answering yes, I consciously knew only one thing for certain: a great adventure lay ahead. Now I suspect that some deeper, wiser part of me knew a doorway was opening to more than a summer's adventure. In some curious and inexplicable way, I would be coming home, to a place whose wild spirit would touch my own like no other had since my boyhood days in Connecticut. Though I didn't settle here immediately, in time I would establish deep roots—physically, emotionally, and spiritually. I can't imagine living anywhere else, just as I can't imagine a life without writing. Yet both came to me relatively late, during my twenties.

Who can explain such things? But I sense the truth of it. Alaska is every bit as much my homeland as Connecticut, the place where I spent my first eighteen years (and to which I remained closely tied through my mid-twenties). Perhaps it always was.

Connecticut and Alaska make curious bookends to the life I've lived so far. A continent apart, one is among the smallest and most densely populated states, with only small, scattered pockets of wildness. The other is a place of vast wilderness and untamed nature, a place where caribou outnumber people and where thousands of streams and mountains remain unnamed. Connecticut, one of the original thirteen colonies and with deeply rooted Anglo-American traditions. Alaska, the forty-ninth state and still a foreign land to most Americans, separate from the Lower 48 states and much of it geographically closer to Asia. Here you can walk from the Arctic Coast to Bristol Bay—more than seven hundred miles—without intersecting a road or village. And indigenous peoples still follow subsistence lifestyles that reach back thousands of years.

West vs. east. Big vs. little. Sparsely populated frontier vs. densely packed and urbanized New England state. For all of its differences with Alaska, Connecticut set the stage for later dramas. It was there that wild nature—in the form of woods and swamps, frogs and snakes and fish—first touched me deeply. My boyhood days and discoveries put me on a path that would eventually lead me west and north to my second homeland and new understandings of my place in the world.

It surprises me, more than three decades later, that I knew so little about Alaska when I first traveled north. There's so much here that resonates with me: high mountains, abundant grizzly bears and wolves, alpine meadows, northern lights, ice-sculpted fjords, immense wilderness landscapes that seem to stretch forever—and the chance to keep them whole. In my adopted homeland, I may find black bears, bald eagles, or moose calves right outside my door. Chickadees and squirrels are among my closest and dearest neighbors. I can gaze north and see Denali, "The High One," glow in day's first light, watch the aurora pulse in midnight skies, or share the yard with a hawk hunting songbirds.

Besides knowing almost nothing about Alaska, at age twenty-four I didn't clearly understand the importance of wild nature to my life. Or, perhaps better put, I'd gradually forgotten its importance, something I'd intuitively understood as a young boy. In Alaska I have rediscovered my early passions and re-formed primal bonds that connect me to the more-than-human world. Along the way, I have redefined—and continue to explore—what wildness means to me, and its relevance to my life and the larger American culture.

As a nation, we seem to be ever more separated from wild nature. And because of that, our relationship with the Earth and our planet's other beings is increasingly ruinous. How do we stay connected, whole? One answer, given by many others before me but worth repeating over and over, is that we need to pay more attention to the nature—the essence—of the places we inhabit: the seasons and weather, the shape of the land, the natural and human history, the animals and plants. And we must do so wherever we live, from remote backcountry to inner city. Paying attention is an essential step to becoming a true inhabitant, a native; it's part of the practice that poet-essayist-philosopher Gary Snyder so beautifully describes in *The Practice of the Wild.*

Most Americans seem to believe that true wildness is only to be found "out there," in the remote backcountry. By and large, our culture equates the two: wildness equals wilderness. Looking back, that's pretty much how I saw things for much of my young adulthood, especially while living in Tucson and Los Angeles in my twenties; though as a young boy, I innately understood that wildness was right outside the back door. And sometimes even infiltrated our house.

As Jack Turner points out in *The Abstract Wild*, this popular misconception helps to explain why people so often misquote Henry David Thoreau, erroneously substituting "wilderness" in his famous saying "In wildness is the preservation of the world."

Of course wildness and wilderness are not at all the same, a point that Snyder, Turner, Paul Shepard, Wendell Berry, and many other American nature writers have emphatically made in their works, sometimes at great length. (I use the term "nature writers" loosely, to include all those who've written about humans and our relationship with larger nature; some would shudder at being defined this way.)

Wilderness is a place. And, some would argue, an idea. As Roderick Nash explains in his acclaimed work *Wilderness and the American Mind,*

for nomadic hunters and gatherers, who represented our species for most of its existence, "wilderness" had no meaning. Everything natural was simply habitat, and people understood themselves to be part of a seamless living community. Lines began to be drawn with the advent of herding, agriculture, and settlement.... For the first time humans saw themselves as distinct from and, they reasoned, better than the rest of nature. It was tempting to think of themselves as masters and not as members of the life community.

The concept of wilderness thus emerged as a way of thinking about larger nature—the "natural world" as opposed to the civilized human world—with the shift from hunting and gathering to a more pastoral lifestyle some twelve thousand years ago.

For some cultures, of course, nomadic hunting-gathering lifestyles extended deep into the twentieth century. Certainly that was true of Alaska's indigenous peoples, from the Tlingits and Haida of Southeast Alaska to the Inupiat and Nunamiut Eskimos in the state's far northern reaches, and many tribes in between, among them Dena'ina Athabascans who have inhabited Southcentral Alaska—including what is now the Anchorage metropolis—for thousands of years. For these peoples, Alaska's wildlands have been homelands, places they cohabited with other life-forms, places inseparable from their cultural traditions and understandings of themselves.

While no longer nomadic, many Dena'ina and other Native Alaskans continue to experience themselves as part of nature, not separate from it. Thus they struggle with the idea of wilderness and consider it a perplexing Western Euro-American myth—or conceit—that ignores and denies the indigenous way of being in the world.

Nash and other scholars point out that the idea of wilderness has evolved significantly over time. For much of the past twelve thousand years, Westerners imagined wilderness to be a frightening place of savage beasts (and sometimes humans), a wasteland to be avoided, subdued, or exploited for its "natural resources." Nowadays, wilderness is more often romanticized and celebrated than despised or feared. Certainly that is true in the United States, where large pieces of the American landscape have been designated, protected, and yes, managed, as wilderness with a capital W.

Most Americans today would likely describe wilderness areas as places that are pristine and uninhabited by people, with a primeval feel; places where wild animals still roam through forests and deserts and high-alpine tundra unblemished by human touch; and places where they can "return to nature" and escape the stresses and responsibilities of their day-to-day lives. Or something like that. Alaska is rich in such places, with millions of acres preserved as wilderness and millions more that could easily qualify for the capital W.

Wildness, on the other hand, is a quality, a state of being. Perhaps that's why wildness and its root word, "wild," are so hard to define, or pin down. I love Snyder's discussion of the two in *The Practice of the Wild.* "The word *wild*," he writes, "is like a gray fox trotting off through the forest, ducking behind bushes, going in and out of sight." Later he compares its various definitions to "how the Chinese define the term *Dao*, the *way* of Great Nature: eluding analysis, beyond categories, self-organizing, self-informing, playful, surprising, impermanent, insubstantial, independent, complete, orderly, unmediated, freely manifesting, self-authenticating, self-willed, complex, quite simple. Both empty and real at the same time. In some cases we might call it sacred."

Then, considering wildness, Snyder comments, "[I]t is everywhere: ineradicable populations of fungi, moss, mold, yeasts, and such that surround and inhabit us. Deer mice on the back porch, deer bounding across the freeway, pigeons in the park, spiders in the corners. . . . Wilderness may temporarily dwindle, but wildness won't go away."

Even in our high-tech, polluted world of the early twenty-first century, wildness is all around us. And within us. Our bodies, our imaginations, our dreams and emotions and ideas are wild. But in going about our busy, modern lives, we consciously or unconsciously suppress, ignore, deny, or forget our wildness. In adapting to the human-dominated, civilized environment we've built, we become tamed, human ecologist Paul Shepard argues in *The Tender Carnivore* and other writings.

Still, the wild animal remains, waiting for release. And—naturally—it's most easily set free in wild surroundings free of artifice and development. Free, largely, of the human touch. That's why the *feeling* of wildness most deeply resonates within us when we enter wilderness. And for many of us, the longer we stay in the "wilds," the more connected, refreshed, invigorated, and even healed we feel. There's a sense of being at ease, and sometimes even of being one with nature. Something shifts *inside*.

That's what happened, I think, when I came to Alaska in the mid-seventies and spent several summers working deep in the wilderness. Something shifted and opened up. Feelings and understandings I'd had as a youngster were subtly resurrected. My life took a necessary detour to Los Angeles, but I knew I'd return to Alaska. I had to return. And after moving back in 1982, I resumed my wilderness explorations. Over time, I also began to pay more attention to my new homeland: Anchorage and its surroundings. At the same time, I began to explore a literary genre that I'd largely ignored, or, more to the point, that I hadn't been aware of: nature writing and the literature of place.

In my fourth and fifth decades, I've rediscovered how much wondrous wild there is to be found right outside my door, or even inside it, though I live on the edge of Alaska's urban center. It seems that for me, entering the wilderness was a necessary step to recovering this lost, or buried, recognition. And living in Anchorage, I have the advantage of being an urban guy surrounded by wildness. But I also believe that this sense of connection, this love for wild nature, is part of being human. It's alive in us when we're born, no matter where that is. The question, then, is how do we nurture our wildness, rather than subdue and tame it?

In *The Abstract Wild*, Turner argues that "in many inner cities, here [in the United States] and in the developing world, people no longer have a concept of wild nature based on personal experience." I agree wholeheartedly with that. But I also believe it is possible to have "raw visceral contact with wild nature" wherever we live, if we take the time, make the effort, and leave ourselves open to wonder and mystery. Then the challenge becomes: how do we reinforce and encourage this wild awareness in each other, in our children? I don't have any easy answers. But I do have a story to share, one that shows some of the possibilities that I've found—and relearned—while living in a far north metropolis.

THE HEART OF THIS STORY is my relationship with Anchorage and adjacent Chugach State Park. At first glance, my choice to settle here may seem a strange one for someone who claims to be so passionate about the natural world. But in living along the city's edge, I've gotten the best of both worlds, natural and man-made (though of course the two are connected). I love the amenities that come with living in an urban center, with its coffee shops and restaurants, movie theaters and performing arts center, universities and libraries and sports programs. Here I've found intersecting circles of writers and outdoors enthusiasts and earth- and peace-loving activists. Yet I also have easy access to parks, trails, greenbelts, a coastal refuge, and a nearby mountain range whose remotest valleys and peaks are seldom visited. And I share the landscape with raven and bear, chickadee and coyote and lynx.

Living in Anchorage, I've rediscovered that wildness is all around us, all the time, even in the city. It's just that most of us humans don't notice the "wild side" of our busy urban lives. (Some, it's true, are simply trying to survive their urban lifestyles, which leaves little, if any, opportunity for wild connections.) Of course, in many a metropolis you have to look hard to find even hints of the wild behind the elaborate layers of human construct that shield us from the rest of nature. Anchorage's juxtaposition of malls and moose, brewhouses and bears, libraries and loons makes it easier to notice urban wildness here than in cities like Los Angeles or Tucson or even Lewiston, Maine—all places that I've lived. This city, more than any other, has opened my eyes and enlarged my awareness in a way the wilderness couldn't.

In these pages I explore my relationship with Anchorage and reflect upon notions of urban wildness in chapters centered around the Hillside neighborhood I inhabited for thirteen years; the city's coastal refuge; a roadside pond; and several of my neighbors, from birds to bears to frogs. And I return to my Connecticut days, to bridge the distance between my childhood and adult homelands and show the links that connect them.

For all my growing appreciation of Anchorage's wildness, I still find it necessary to make trips deeper into Alaska's wilderness. There I slow down, grow in awareness, move into a reality beyond city time and normal routine. I more easily open up to wildness and *feel* my connection to the larger world. I consider my relationship with wilderness landscapes in two chapters: first, my "steady" relationship with Anchorage's next-door wilderness, Chugach State Park; second, an extended solo trip into the far-away arctic backcountry, where the trappings and sensibilities of urban life are gradually stripped away.

Taking a different, but related, path into wildness, I also reflect upon three encounters with "the Other": wild creatures whose lives rarely intersect my own. Our paths cross under extraordinary circumstances, leading to new insights about the animals and my relationship with them. In one case, the Other is a grandmother halibut, caught during a guided sport-fishing trip; in another, she's a grizzly mom, protecting her cubs (they, in turn, lead me deeper into the world of brown and grizzly bears). In the third instance, I'm serenaded by howling wolves while camped alone during a backpacking trek through the Arctic. In every encounter, my senses expand, my world opens up.

Finally, *Living with Wildness* explores myths and ideas about the "Wild Man," a mythic figure with roots in ancient times who has appeared, off and on, throughout human history. I'll reflect upon my own encounters with the Wild Man, my participation in the men's mythopoetic movement, the ideas discussed in Robert Bly's best-selling book *Iron John*, and the relevance of this mythical character in today's world, as well as the critical importance of embracing our own wild natures in addition to that of the larger world.

TWO

Anchorage's Hillside

Living with Wildness

SEATED AT THE DINING ROOM TABLE ON A LEADEN JANUARY DAY, I glimpse, from the corner of my eyes, the strangest sight: an explosion of feathers.

Still not fully awake, I've been sipping coffee and reading the local newspaper's sports section, a favorite morning ritual. Every now and then I look up from the paper and gaze outside toward a backyard forest of frost-trimmed spruce and birch. Or I'll glance at my bird feeders, which in midwinter draw a mix of northern songbirds: black-capped and boreal chickadees, red-breasted nuthatches, pine grosbeaks, pine siskins, common redpolls, downy woodpeckers. It's while raising my head, looking at nothing in particular, that I notice the strike. Or, more accurately, its immediate aftermath.

The burst of feathers is followed by an equally sudden burst of loud squawking. Drawn to the window, I see four large black-and-white birds with long, darkly iridescent tails in my yard. Screaming in their harsh, raspy way, these black-billed magpies hop among spruce branches and peer at the ground, now sprinkled with dozens of tiny, gray bits of down. Beneath them in the snow is a small fluttering ball of feathers. I reach for my binoculars and bring events into sharper focus. A sharp-shinned hawk has taken down a female grosbeak in midflight and pinned her against the snow. About the size of a robin, the mostly gray songbird quivers faintly beneath the hawk, which shifts back and forth, talons tightly gripping its dying catch. Among the smallest of Alaska's raptors, the sharp-shinned hawk is a beautiful bird, with sharply curved beak, barred reddish-brown breast, dark gray head and back, striped tail, and bright, penetrating eyes.

The hawk isn't much larger than the grosbeak and is considerably smaller than the raucous, harassing magpies. Once, twice, three times, they swoop low over the huddled hawk, hoping to scare it off and steal a meal. The hawk hunches lower, glaring eyes turned upward, prey firmly clutched. Never before have I seen so many magpies in the yard; I wonder if they have been shadowing the hawk, waiting for just this sort of opportunity.

The ruckus continues for several minutes. Then the hawk makes its move: flying low and swiftly it weaves through the forest and out of sight, magpies following in scolding pursuit. My sympathies are with the songbird; I'm saddened by its fate. But now that the grosbeak is doomed, I root for the hawk. *Don't let those bullies steal your meal,* I silently urge.

With the hawk gone, I notice several more grosbeaks and siskins gathered in nearby spruce trees and wonder if they too have been watching since the attack. What memory of it do they carry? What sense of loss, what fear, if any, do they feel? The birds, strangely, seem calmer than I feel. The attack has jarred me from my weekend routine and reminded me, again, that hawks and other predators are a brutal yet routine fact of day-to-day existence for the songbirds who visit my feeders. I'm also reminded of something more pleasing: the rich wildness to be found in my backyard and the surrounding neighborhood, here on Anchorage's fringes.

A CITY OF SOME 270,000 PEOPLE, Alaska's largest community is rarely lauded for its wild nature or frontier aesthetics. Many rural Alaskans consider Anchorage a northern incarnation of Lower 48 excesses. They derisively call the city Los Anchorage, a not-so-subtle comparison to Southern California's smog-enshrouded, freeway-infested, urban-sprawl megalopolis. Other Alaskans, including some locals, ridicule Anchorage as Anywhere USA and claim its only saving grace to be the close proximity to "the real Alaska." Outsiders—anyone living beyond the state's borders—also get in their digs. John McPhee took perhaps the most famous swipes at Anchorage in his best seller *Coming into the Country*:

> Almost all Americans would recognize Anchorage, because Anchorage is that part of any city where the city has burst its seams and extruded Colonel Sanders.... Anchorage is sometimes excused in the name of pioneering. Build now, civilize later. But Anchorage is not a frontier town. It is virtually unrelated to its environment. It has come in on the wind, an American spore. A large cookie cutter brought down on El Paso could lift something like Anchorage into the air.

The truth stings: Anchorage deserved McPhee's late-1970s jabs. It still merits them and, to some degree, those of rural critics. Poor municipal planning has led to haphazard development and ugly architecture. Much of the city is an appalling mix of malls, fast-food restaurants, boxlike discount stores, massive parking lots, and steadily enlarging service stations and quick-stops. More than ever, the city's credo seems to be develop, develop, develop. Too many of the country's mega-chains have heard our state's politicians declare that Alaska is "open for business," turning sections of Anchorage into versions of the Miracle Mile.

Yet for all of this laying down of asphalt and mushrooming of boxy buildings, pockets of wetlands, woodlands, and other wild areas remain scattered through-out the Anchorage Bowl, a roughly triangular piece of land that is bounded on two sides by the waters of Cook Inlet's Turnagain and Knik arms, and on the east by the Chugach Mountains. You just have to know where to look. Those natural areas continue to sustain a wide diversity of wildlife and native plants: the bowl is seasonal home to 230 species of birds, five types of Pacific salmon, and forty-eight different mammals.

Anchorage's patchwork of greenbelts and municipal parks is threaded together by a network of bike trails and walking paths. From Anchorage's Coastal Trail, bicyclists, joggers, and walkers can occasionally spot pods of ghostly white beluga whales, chasing fish through the inlet's murky waters. Along that trail and others, people may also meet moose, lynx, great-horned owls, black bears, and even the occasionally grizzly.

Also threading through the bowl are several creeks, which connect hills to low-lands to saltwater. Some are filled in, paved over, or polluted before they reach the inlet, but others are large and pure enough to have natural or rebuilt salmon runs. In Anchorage's most industrialized section, anglers pull forty-pound king salmon from Ship Creek. The bowl is also rich in lakes and bogs, which serve as important avian nesting grounds. Anchorage, in fact, is the largest U.S. city to support nest-ing populations of loons. And wolf packs roam the city's eastern edges, sometimes sneaking into homeowners' yards to kill domestic fowl or dogs.

I'VE RESIDED HERE SINCE 1982, yet only since the early nineties have I taken delight in Anchorage's greener, wilder side. In part that reflects changing desires and priorities: once a sports reporter tied to newsroom desks and indoor arenas, I've metamorphosed into a nature writer who chooses woodland trails and alpine meadows over noisy, sweaty gyms. I now prefer watching birds and bears to TV sports. Over time, I've relearned the value of paying close attention to my home grounds, something I did as a boy while growing up on the fringes of a New England swamp and forest, but somehow forgot in my early adulthood.

Another reason for my new perspective: a relocation to the hills on Anchorage's eastern edge in October 1993. That move, as much as anything, clarified what my friend William calls the "power of place." From 1982 through 1988, I lived the mobile life of a renter. Then I became a first-time homeowner. But like my earlier rentals, that cul-de-sac property failed to draw me into the local landscape. Needing solitude or a renewal of spirit, I would invariably go "out there," to the wildlands beyond Anchorage.

Once I moved to the Hillside, such outings became less necessary. I still love my forest and mountain walks in Chugach Park and relish my longer backcountry trips deep into Alaska's wilderness. Yet I've also found joy, surprise, connection, and, yes, even solitude on Anchorage's Hillside, an area of town that mixes modern suburban neighborhoods with older homesteads on the wooded foothills of the Chugach Mountains.

I settled here with Dulcy Boehle, my wife, on one and one-third acres of land that is mostly spruce-birch forest. At the bottom of our lot flows the South Fork of Little Campbell Creek, a tiny clearwater stream born in Chugach Park among alpine meadows and groves of stunted hemlock. We're at an elevation of about nine hundred feet, high enough to glimpse, between the trees, parts of the Anchorage Bowl flatlands and Cook Inlet. When the weather's clear, we also can gaze upon "The High One," Denali, and other Alaska Range peaks. Rising more than eighteen thousand feet above the surrounding landscape, the great ice mountain has a magnetism that can be felt even here, 120 miles away. Sometimes, when I'm having a difficult day, I'll step onto the upper deck and look to the northern horizon, and be touched by grandeur, or memories of high places, or something that resembles grace.

Everything wild seems closer on the Hillside: the clouds, the mountains, the animals, the weather. It's easier, somehow, to slip outside at night and stargaze, stand in the eerie light of a full moon, or look for northern lights. Easier to go walking and exploring. In my first month here, I took more neighborhood walks than in the four and a half years I lived in a cul-de-sac. Winter comes earlier and stays longer. There's more snow. More wildlife. More frequent and stronger gales. Born along Alaska's Gulf Coast, high winds called chinooks come roaring out of the southeast and through the Chugach Mountains, then tumble down the Hillside as warm, dry, turbulent air, in gusts of fifty to a hundred miles per hour.

I love the whooshing and swishing music the chinooks make as they rush through the needles and branches of our backyard spruce. Bending and swaying, with limbs bouncing and swirling, the spruce are such models of flexibility. Not all our trees, however, have proved flexible or strong enough to survive these chinook storms. One favorite spruce just west of our house snapped during a springtime blow, shattered where a fungus had eaten away its center.

I marvel too at how easily the birds seem to ride out the winds while roosting in trees. During one April blow, a flock of redpolls took shelter in a spruce near the house. Perched on its branches, these small members of the finch family sat calmly in fifty-mile-per-hour gusts. They didn't need to shift positions or spread wings for balance as the branches sang and danced. It was almost as if they'd become part of the tree.

ONCE I'D SETTLED INTO THE HILLSIDE NICHE, all manner of things began to grab my attention in new ways: the chinooks; the pleasing rush of spring-time creek water; the winter commutes of ravens, which fly daily between their nighttime roosts in the Chugach Mountains and the scavenging-rich environs of midtown and downtown Anchorage; the spruce bark beetle and its infestation of local forests. Nothing, however, grabbed me as deeply as the chickadees. They transformed my world, showed me some of what I had been missing. In a way, they became my teachers.

"Something strange has happened," reads my Hillside journal entry for December 1993. "Something strange and magical and delightful. I've fallen under the spell of tiny forest creatures that only rarely gained my attention in days past."

My enchantment began on a Saturday morning, shortly before solstice. Lolling in bed, I glanced outside. And there, before me, were several black-capped chickadees flitting about a backyard spruce. *Wonderful,* I thought. *Here's a chance to meet some of my new neighbors.* Inspired by their presence, I put a bird feeder on the middle deck, where it could be easily observed from the living and dining rooms. My first-ever feeder wasn't much to look at: an old, slightly bent baking pan. Still, it held plenty of seeds and sat nicely on the railing. Nothing happened that first day. But Sunday they returned. Seated at the dining room table, I watched a tiny, fluffy winged creature land on the pan. It had a black-capped head and bib, white cheeks, a whitish-beige belly, and gray-streaked wings.

The chickadee grabbed a seed and zoomed off to a nearby tree. Then in flashed another. And a third. For each, the routine was similar: dart in, look around, peck at the tray, grab a seed, look around some more, and dart back out. Nervous little creatures, full of bright energy, they somehow penetrated the toughened shell of this former sports reporter and touched my heart. I laughed at their antics and felt an all-too-rare childlike fascination.

The chickadees were soon joined by several other songbirds. What started as mere curiosity quickly bloomed into a consuming passion. I found myself roaming bookstores in search of birding guidebooks, spontaneously exchanging bird descriptions with a stranger, and purchasing fifty-pound bags of seeds. All of this seemed very strange to a forty-four-year-old who had never been intrigued by birds (except for charismatic raptors) and previously judged bird-watchers to be rather odd sorts. I didn't know what it meant, except that a door had opened. And I passed through.

Now, wherever I am—city, woods, mountains—I invariably notice songbirds and their assorted voices. They're everywhere, it seems. How did I miss them before? And I wonder what else beckons that I haven't yet noticed.

For all my newfound passion, I have not become an obsessive birder. I have neither a life list nor any burning desire to identify every species found in Alaska or even the Anchorage Bowl. I prefer to know a few birds well, learn their habits and seasonal patterns. That said, I decided last year to keep track of all the birds I've seen or heard in my Hillside yard. The list numbers forty-one species and would probably include more, if I didn't have such difficulty with sparrows. *Black-capped chickadee, common redpoll, downy woodpecker, American robin, varied thrush, ruby-crowned kinglet, orange-crowned warbler, golden-crowned sparrow, spruce grouse, Canada goose, sharp-shinned hawk, great horned owl, bald eagle* . . .

PERHAPS YOU'VE DECIDED THAT I FIBBED. I do have a life list of sorts. But this is an intimate one, specific to the place where I live. Tucked away in my growing pile of journals, the list reminds me of the diverse life to inhabit my wooded yard. It also jars my memory. Nearly every name has a story behind it. I think back to the August afternoon when a squirrel's chatter caused me to look up from house-painting chores and I watched an immature bald eagle dive into one of the back-yard spruce, talons out and wings flared back, as it unsuccessfully tried to snatch the squirrel. I recall the unusual springtime visits by a pair of mallards that landed in our pondless backyard, waddled up to the house, and nibbled on leftover sun-flower seeds. And I remember, with great delight, the spring that I first recognized the April song of a ruby-crowned kinglet.

In its coloring, the ruby-crowned kinglet is a rather plain songbird, with olive head and back and grayish undersides. Males have red crown feathers, but they're revealed only when the bird becomes excited, as by a potential mate, rival, or threat. Still, ruby-crowns have certain standout traits. One is their tiny size. Among the smallest of songbirds, they weigh less than one-third of an ounce. Another is their hyperactive nature: they seem to flit about constantly, often flicking their wings open and closed as if nervous. Above all, there's the voice, one of the forest's loudest and brightest. Once learned, the ruby-crown's long warbled tune is easily recognizable, as is the bird's tendency to get "stuck" on certain parts of the song, like a scratched record.

Until moving to Anchorage's forested foothills, I'd never noticed the kinglet's song or the way that males (like those of many species) ritually sit atop trees each spring to announce their presence and proclaim breeding territories in melodious tunes. The singing is what I love most about ruby-crowned kinglets. Here on Anchorage's Hillside, their loud, bright voices herald the arrival of spring, just as the honking of Canada geese do in the flatlands below. The songs tell me that kinglets—soon to be joined by robins, thrushes, warblers, and sparrows—have returned for another nesting season, that we're again sharing the landscape.

The point, I suppose, is this: instead of once-in-a-lifetime trophy rarities, the birds on my Hillside list are neighbors—some year-round, others seasonal—who bring joy and mystery to my life. And, sometimes, sorrow. The list reminds me, too, how much of life's richness I missed before settling here.

Plants haven't engaged me to the same degree as birds but I've begun to learn and appreciate—and occasionally harvest—the flora around my home. There are the trees, of course, which helped to lure us here in the first place: spruce, birch, cottonwood, willow, aspen. And the lawn, put in long before we arrived, with its nonnative grasses, competing weeds, and invading clover. Beyond the lawn's edges, in the forest understory, is a native community of shrubs, wildflowers, ferns, mosses, and berry plants—more than three dozen species in all. Come May I find the year's first wildflowers, ground-hugging marsh violets and short-stemmed yellow anemones, in a boggy meadow beside the creek. And at summer's end I gobble juicy watermelon berries or nibble rose hips, the soft vitamin C–rich fruits of prickly rose. Out front we have a spreading strawberry patch, which seems to be going feral. And not far from home are blueberry patches that yield fruit for pancakes and pies. Besides giving us pleasure and a sense of privacy, the forest plants provide cover, food, and nesting material for numerous birds and mammals. They also nourish an assemblage of insects, which fly and crawl in far greater diversity than most Anchorage homeowners might ever suspect. Off and on I've kept a bug collection, limited only by the requirement that any insects I gather be already dead. I swatted, squashed, and picked apart enough of them in my younger days that I need not kill more for collecting's sake.

MORE WILD NEIGHBORS: THE MAMMALS. Again I've compiled a list, but it's much shorter. *Moose, red squirrel, snowshoe hare, short-tailed weasel, common shrew, meadow vole, lynx, black bear, coyote.*

Red squirrels, along with chickadees, are the most visible of my Hillside neighbors. And delightful neighbors they are, even if they insist on raiding my bird feeders—an exasperating habit that occasionally provokes me to respond in quite irrational ways. Broom in hand, I chase the thief around the deck, cursing loudly, while the squirrel squeaks and scrambles until finally he leaps from deck to nearby spruce, landing spread-eagled in a branch. (For uncertain reasons, I've always considered the seed stealer to be a male.) Even more impressive are his jumps from tree to deck. Before leaping, the squirrel stares intently at the deck railing, as though gauging the distance. Then he begins a slight rocking motion, as if preparing for liftoff, and jumps, landing safely at almost the same spot every time.

I forgive the squirrels their raids because they, more than any other animal, make me laugh. I take great pleasure in their frenetic, scurrying tendencies, their loudly scolding chatter and shining black eyes, their soaring leaps from tree to tree, their mad dashes across the yard in pursuit of one another, and their autumn spruce cone–tossing harvest.

By nature solitary creatures, red squirrels have home ranges of one-half to one acre. At least three have staked out territories that include my yard and I see one or more daily, autumn through spring. In summer they disappear for days at a time, perhaps because living is easier—and I don't put out seeds. Though the squirrels normally stay apart, they sometimes engage in furious pursuits across the snow, through the alders, up trees and down. For much of the year, such chases result from territorial disputes; but in February and March red squirrels temporarily abandon their loner lifestyles and pair up for breeding. Armed with this knowledge I conclude that late-winter chases are more often driven by romance than aggression.

Moose frequently use the yard, coming here to feed on willows, alders, or birches and also to nap or rest while chewing their cud. I don't know for certain it's the same cow moose, but one female browses throughout the yard several times a year, usually accompanied by a calf or two. I've watched twin newborn calves in cinnamon-colored coats fold their gangly legs beneath them and sleep side by side within twenty feet of our house, while their mom forages in the forest. The cow and her calves are part of a largely unhunted moose population that inhabits the Anchorage Bowl and adjacent Chugach foothills. Local wildlife biologists estimate two to three hundred moose reside in the bowl year-round, with winter numbers rising to one thousand as they're driven out of the mountains by deepening snow.

That robust population has, not surprisingly, caused an increase in moose-human conflicts. Most residents like having moose around, but some are angered by the animals' taste for ornamental plants and garden vegetables and want their numbers thinned. Others, particularly parents with young children, worry about the danger moose present. Cows with calves can be every bit as dangerous as bears. And in extreme cold or deep-snow winters, stressed-out moose may attack with little provocation. Injuries are rare, but within the past fifteen years two Anchorage residents have been stomped to death by agitated moose.

One fatal attack was caught on video and made national news. It also added fuel to a local debate. Should moose hunting be allowed along the city's perimeter, as it once was?

An experimental Hillside archery hunt in the 1980s didn't go well: residents sighted still-living moose with arrows protruding from their bodies; some bulls were killed and butchered in people's front yards. As memories and outrage over that fiasco faded, state wildlife managers organized a much smaller and more carefully monitored hunt. Since 2005, a low-profile cow-moose hunt has been allowed in Chugach State Park above Anchorage's Hillside, with only a few animals killed each year. Local wildlife manager Rick Sinnott admits the hunt does little or nothing to resolve moose-human conflicts, but it gives residents an opportunity to locally hunt an admittedly overabundant population.

I'm among the many people who have been charged by moose. Not just once, but twice. The first time was in late winter, when moose are often testy. Skiing at Hillside Park, a few miles from home, I was stopped in my tracks by a cow moose. Thirty feet away, she stood on the trail, munching trailside willows and showing no inclination to yield the right of way. Occasionally she would glare in my direction and flatten her ears, a sign of aggression. Until she departed, there would be no easy way to ski past her and the best strategy would have been to retreat. Instead, I waited ten minutes. Then, stubborn and impatient, I shifted my skis and cleared my throat. Not a wise decision. The cow again looked my way, then abruptly charged. Head down, ears laid back, and legs kicking high, she came straight at me. Slowed by my skis, I dived and rolled into a stand of willow, certain I would be stomped. At the last moment, the cow veered off and continued down the trail another thirty feet. There she stood, head down and feeding on willows as though nothing had happened. Breathing deeply, feeling shaken and embarrassed, I slowly got to my feet and skied on, whispering a prayer of thanks that the moose let me escape uninjured.

The second attack occurred a few years later, while I hiked with friends along a familiar woodland path in South Anchorage. The hour was late, nearly 11 p.m., as we returned to the trailhead; it being early summer, there was still plenty of light. The five of us were spread out, in single file, and we walked quickly while talking back and forth, sharing stories and laughter. In other words, we weren't paying close attention to the trail ahead or the surrounding woods. Second in line, I was chatting with Brad, several steps ahead of me, when a cow moose suddenly appeared. In full charge, she was no more than thirty feet away and heading straight toward us.

Where the moose came from, I still have no idea. Maybe she'd been standing around the corner, just out of sight. Or perhaps she was hiding behind the dense alder-willow thickets that border parts of this trail. But at the time, it seemed the moose had simply materialized out of the late-evening air, coming toward us at a full gallop. Head down, ears flattened, hackles raised, and legs kicking high, the cow was huge and dangerous, a picture of maternal fury.

I had no time to think, only react, and my survival instincts took over. A spruce tree stood to my right, just off the trail. The spruce wasn't especially large, but it was the nearest possible cover and big enough that the moose couldn't easily run over it or through it. I lunged behind the tree, ducking my head. But the animal's attention was focused on Brad, not me. Turned toward me while talking, he swiveled his head forward a split second after I spotted the moose, just before she smashed into his body. Later I would wonder if I could have—should have—shouted a warning or done something else to help him. But it all happened so frightfully fast, in a blur of bodies and emotions.

The cow slammed into Brad's upper body with a full frontal attack of nose, forehead, and legs, knocking him over. Then, as quickly as she struck, the moose wheeled away and disappeared into the forest. It was all over in five or ten seconds.

We quickly gathered around Brad, who was laid out on the ground, stunned and disoriented but somehow not seriously injured. A jumble of voices marveled at the surprise and sudden severity of the attack and, almost in unison, several of us asked, "Brad, are you OK?"

"I think so," he said while glancing around, his eyes enlarged. "What the hell happened?"

"You got flattened by a moose," someone answered. "Didn't you see it coming?"

"A moose? Really? I didn't see a thing. Where'd it go?"

Brad spit. No blood, we were happy to see. Then he started to stand but we urged him to stay put, afraid he might be in shock and harmed more than he realized. He was lucky, in a way, that he didn't see the moose coming, didn't have the chance to tense up. His relaxed body gave way to the blow without resistance. He was lucky, too, that the moose only knocked him down, didn't stomp him with her deadly hooves.

Cows with newborn calves are notoriously ferocious and we suspected that this moose was protecting her young. Rick Sinnott has estimated that up to two hundred calves are born in the Anchorage Bowl from late May through early June. Knowing it to be the season of birthing, we should have been more careful, paid closer attention to our surroundings.

While the rest of us encircled Brad, James cautiously walked up the trail forty or fifty feet to see if the cow was still hanging around. Looking to the right, through thick alder, he glimpsed a cinnamon-colored shape that suggested a calf and quickly backed away. Almost certainly the mom cut her attack short to return and safeguard her calf.

After ten minutes or so, Brad assured us he was all right and insisted we leave. Checking ahead, we could find no sign of the moose so we resumed our hike, more cautious now. Brad walked to the parking lot under his own power, which both amazed and relieved the rest of us.

The next morning Brad sent out an email to update us on his condition: as the adrenaline rush and initial shock wore off, his upper body had become so achy he could hardly sleep, even with pain medication. Weeks later, bothered by back and neck pains, he would get checked by a doctor and be diagnosed with symptoms of whiplash—no surprise to those of us who saw him leveled. It still seems a small miracle that he wasn't more seriously hurt by one fiercely protective mom.

Another local dilemma is moose-car collisions. Each winter, drivers strike one hundred to two hundred moose on Anchorage roads. Only rarely are people seriously harmed. Most often the damage is to the vehicles, sometimes wrecked beyond repair, and to the moose, which usually die immediately or are so seriously injured they must be killed. Hoping that some good might come from such tragedies, the state allows local charities to use the moose meat. Yet accidents, too, have been cited as reasons to have a local hunt. Better for moose to be killed with bullets or arrows, the reasoning goes, than to suffer needlessly after being smashed by cars or trucks.

Sitting in my Hillside home, enjoying the presence of calves and cow, I find it hard to support moose hunts in these foothills. I understand the concern of wildlife managers and those who feel endangered or besieged; but I'm not convinced that controlled hunts along Anchorage's perimeters will ever solve the problems of moose-vehicle collisions and occasional attacks.

Anchorage residents face a number of such difficult wildlife-management decisions. We want to share the landscape with wild creatures, yet conflicts inevitably arise. We have "problems" with the moose that have run-ins with cars, the geese that threaten aircraft as they congregate along local airfields, the coyotes and wolves that occasionally enter yards and kill pets or livestock, and the bears that develop a taste for human garbage, dog food, and birdseed.

A FEW YEARS AFTER SETTLING on the Hillside, I head into the nearby mountains to explore a 3,500-foot hill that's visible from my yard. Sometimes I can pick out sheep grazing on its upper slopes. Unnamed on most maps, the hill is called Rusty Point by locals. It's early October and autumn's reds and yellows have mostly gone to brown, while patches from a September snowfall remain on the hill's upper reaches. There's no trail to the ridgetop, so I weave my way through head-high grasses and alder thickets, while loudly announcing my presence by clapping and talking. "Hello, bear. Hello, bear. Human coming through...." Naturally I hope there's no bear close enough to hear my salutations. When I've gained sufficient altitude, I move beyond the alder patches into alpine tundra, where blueberries wrinkled by recent frosts are soft but juicy. Scrambling higher, I reach bare rock. Climbers name these gray metamorphics "Chugach crud" because the rock is soft and crumbly.

I'm pleased to be up here, on new ground. In a sense, Rusty Point is part of my neighborhood, less than three miles from my house as the raven flies. The most direct overland route requires considerable bushwhacking, so I chose a more circuitous but easier path: by car to a Chugach parking lot and then by foot along a trail to the hill's base.

I walk to Rusty Point's southern face, which drops off sharply for a couple hundred feet, then angles more gently into Campbell Creek's Middle Fork valley. Fifty feet beneath me are two Dall sheep ewes, their snow-white coats making them easy to see against the gray rocks and brown tundra. This south-facing hillside is a favorite with Dall sheep; from the valley below I've counted as many as seventy-two, mostly ewes and lambs, as they graze on alpine plants and nap in warm sunshine.

I explore the ridgeline awhile, then settle onto a small patch of tundra and face west. With binoculars I scan the Hillside and try to pick out my home from the hundreds far below me. After much searching, I find my gray-green two-story house and forest-edged lawn. Then I note other familiar landmarks: Flattop, Blueberry Hill, and Williwaw Lakes in the Chugach Mountains; downtown Anchorage; and across Cook Inlet, Sleeping Lady and the Alaska Range. Far to the north Denali appears, through a narrow break in overcast skies.

From this height I gain a wider perspective, one that shows how my yard and Hillside neighborhood fit into the larger landscape of Anchorage, and the even greater landscape beyond it. And a recognition comes with unusual clarity. This truly is home, the place where I belong. A place of bountiful wildness.

THREE

Anchorage's Hillside

Wildness Through the Years and Seasons

WITH NATURE IN ITS INFINITE FORMS GRABBING MY ATTENTION IN new and sometimes startling ways since I moved to Anchorage's wooded foothills, it was perhaps inevitable that I would begin to keep a daily home journal to record the details and delights of Hillside life. Sometimes those journal entries evolve into something more; they take on a life of their own, becoming stories of my days and seasons here, on Anchorage's eastern fringe, where even my yard is abundantly wild.

Entering Winter: Embracing the Season (October 1997)

I have watched the snow fall all weekend, part of me enjoying its soft, white beauty, another part wishing it would go away and return in another month or two. I'm not ready to embrace winter; mid-October is too early for a major snowstorm. So I keep my distance. Except for short walks to get the newspaper and mail, I remain inside the house all of Saturday and much of Sunday. Yet my attention inevitably drifts outside, as the snow piles ever higher. At times it falls in large, fluffy flakes; at other times it's a fine, mistlike presence.

Four inches cover the ground by mid-morning Saturday, ten inches by nightfall, sixteen inches by Sunday morning. TV weatherpeople say the storm is caused by the meeting of two strong weather fronts: a mass of cold and dry arctic air moving across Southcentral Alaska has collided with wet, warmer air from the Gulf of Alaska. I wonder how long they'll be mixing it up overhead and recall that only one week earlier I'd been immersed in Indian summer.

Walking along Chugach State Park's Turnagain Arm Trail on a blue-sky after-noon, I'd entered a forest that glowed with golds and yellows. From forest-floor patches of devil's club to the highest reaches of cottonwoods and birches, the entire forest radiated warmth and brightness. The reds, oranges, and purples of fireweed, wild prickly rose, and high-bush cranberry added to the fiery mix: rich October colors on an August-like day. Carrying the sweet-sour pungency of autumn's decay, the air was warm enough for me to shed my jacket and comfortably walk in shirt-sleeves; warm enough too for swarms of gnats and other insects to engage in wild, swirling dances along the trail and among the trees. It was quiet enough to hear leaves falling to the ground, the distant call of a chickadee, the footsteps of a vole. Gradually my mind quieted as well, busy thoughts giving way to an awareness and appreciation of forest and warmth. I dawdled on my way back to the trailhead, willing to be late for dinner so that I might savor this serenity and somehow store it away for future recall.

Now, as I watch my Hillside world turn white, that walk already seems like an ancient memory.

I wait until late Sunday afternoon to clear the driveway. Bundled up, I shovel off the front porch and an area in front of the garage, then push the snowblower outside. The snow is twenty inches deep, making it nearly as high as the front of my blower. The snow that's been falling today is fluffy and dry, but at the bottom there's some heavy, wet stuff. Cutting through it is slow, strenuous work. This is not something I can rush; I'm forced to slow down, be patient.

As I settle into the job, something shifts. Just as I was connected to the forest a week earlier, I am now immersed in this winter storm. I am not fighting or deny-ing the snow or wishing it were gone, but instead I'm working with it. Being with it. There's a slight breeze and snow swirls from the blower into my face. This too is OK. In twenty-degree temperatures, engulfed by snow and the roar of my machine, I enter a sort of meditative trance. I begin to enjoy the storm and appreciate the way it has so quickly and utterly transformed the landscape. And I am thankful that today, at least, I don't have to drive anywhere.

After finishing the driveway, I shovel the steps and the back decks while look-ing and listening for signs of our neighbors. The squirrel that comes for sunflower seeds and peanuts hasn't been around all day. He too must figure it's a good day to stay home. The heavy snow hasn't stopped chickadees and nuthatches from visit-ing my feeders, and I welcome their songs, which always cheer me. Out front, deep tracks in the snow show where two moose have passed through our yard during the storm and I wonder how hard the winter will be on them.

The snowfall eases in early evening, then picks up again; by Monday morning another six inches will cover the ground. Looking out the window, knowing that

I'll have to clear the driveway again, I feel a desire, a need, for playful participation with this snow. Late Sunday night I jump into an outdoor hot tub and, with my body heated by one-hundred-degree water, I turn my face to the sky. As snowflakes fall on my head and face, I celebrate the change of seasons. Smiling, I say hello to winter.

Midwinter: Feeding Redpolls (January 1999)

On a cold and gray midwinter afternoon, I stand on the top deck of my home and invite a flock of redpolls to come and eat. Body pressed tightly against the wood railing, hands cupped and filled with seeds, I face north, toward the backyard spruce trees where dozens of these northern songbirds roost. And I wait.

Songbirds visit my feeders daily from September through April: black-capped and boreal chickadees, red-breasted nuthatches, pine grosbeaks, pine siskins, common redpolls, even an occasional downy or hairy woodpecker. The birds bring me great pleasure, but in one respect they frustrate me. I have wished, for many years, to feed them from my hands. I know this is possible because I've seen pictures, heard stories. Yet all my open-handed attempts have failed.

Dulcy urges patience. "You have to be still and quiet and wait," she gently reminds me, over and over. "Don't give up so easily."

Patience, I inwardly repeat, standing with my hands outstretched. Today I'll practice patience. And stillness. I'll slow down, set aside my eagerness and expectations, and see what happens.

I didn't begin the day pondering the mysteries of hand-feeding birds. A two-day blizzard had dropped more than twenty inches of powdery snow. So, before anything else, I resolved to clear the driveway. Dulcy volunteered to sweep the decks and put out birdseed, normally part of my routine.

I finished the driveway shortly after noon, then went inside and headed upstairs to check on Dulcy's progress. She stood on the back deck with hands extended, surrounded by redpolls, those tiny sparrowlike finches. Amazed and excited, I rushed toward the sliding-glass door—and scared the birds away.

"How'd you do that?" I asked in wonder.

"Easy," she replied. "I was patient."

Figuring the birds would still be hungry after the storm, I ran downstairs and returned with boots, jacket, hat, and a supply of seeds.

Now I stand on the deck, seed-filled hands atop the railing, body facing the backyard forest, head slightly bowed. Beside me is Dulcy, once more my teacher, who urges me in whispered tones, "Stand still, don't make any sound, and keep your head down when the birds come in. Pretend you're a statue."

To sweeten our offering, we've spread shelled and chipped sunflower seeds along the railing and on the deck floor. Five, ten, fifteen minutes pass, but no birds approach. We know the redpolls are out there. We hear their high-pitched chirping, see their movements in the yard. Some feed on the ground, others perch in spruce trees or chase each other through the air.

Just as hope is fading, a redpoll flies in. Then another. They're tentative, easily spooked, and soon fly off. It goes this way for several minutes more. One or two birds are drawn in, but they quickly leave. Recalling Dulcy's advice, I close my eyes, let go of my expectations, relax. It's their choice, not mine. More begin to arrive. One, two, three redpolls, then a dozen, then thirty or more, all eating seeds. The more the birds flock around us, the calmer they seem.

I open my eyes slightly to watch. A male redpoll gazes at me quizzically, head cocked and eyes shining. Then he turns away and resumes eating. Others engage in scolding matches and territorial skirmishes. Or they hop from seed to seed, grabbing a bite and moving on as if at a buffet.

Now a redpoll hops into Dulcy's open hand. Another redpoll, a female, moves toward my hand and touches me lightly with her delicate foot. Then she steps onto my palm and picks at the seeds there. As she feeds, I wonder what the birds make of us, how they interpret our human energy.

For a few moments, at least, they accept our presence. Redpolls sit calmly in both of my hands, land softly on my shoulder and head, brush against my skin with their feathers, mingle around my feet.

I study their black, shining eyes, their yellow beaks, red-feathered head patches, black bibs, and the pinkish-red breasts of the male birds. Perhaps, if I stayed at this long enough, I'd be able to distinguish individual birds by size or shape; some are thin, others not so. Or maybe by the color of their head patches, which range from dull orange to almost fire-engine red. Or the size of their bibs. Even the shades and patterns of their mottled white-and-brown feathered backs vary from bird to bird. And what about their personalities? Some seem rather aggressive, others seem timid or complacent.

Surrounded by this feathered energy, I sneak a glance at Dulcy. She, like me, is smiling. These are smiles of absolute delight. The birds lift my spirits, offer connection. Now at last I can begin to understand why some people feed pigeons or ducks.

Feeding songbirds is what works for me.

Late Winter, 1: Whistling a Welcome (February 1996)

The wind is blowing hard outside. Has been all day. But at least the rain has stopped, so I leave the house to clear ice off the front porch and deck. Chinook winds have brought forty-degree warmth to Anchorage's Hillside, and the softened ice is easy to chop.

It's wet and sloppy, a taste of breakup in winter. The driveway is slush, and water cascades off the roof in chilling torrents, forcing me to add rain gear—despite the blue skies—as I chop and shovel. But I don't mind. Right now I'd rather have this than more snow. There's already too much piled in our yard.

My neighbors, the birds, don't seem to mind this latest meltdown either. They're busily foraging for food in the backyard, where melting snow has revealed the black remains of what might be several hundred thousand sunflower shells, the result of my bird-feeding passion.

Each morning, before refilling my feeders (which include a baking pan and rail tops, as well as more conventional tubes, suet holders, and sheltered feeders), I sweep shell husks from our middle and upper decks onto the ground below. Since September, I've swept the remains of three fifty-pound bags' worth. Through the course of the winter, the shells have become embedded in the snow, rather like volcanic ash deposits within sedimentary rock sequences. Several distinct layers of black are visible where I've shoveled a path through the snowpack, reflecting this year's snowstorms, thaws, and dry spells.

The appearance of large and growing shell piles has attracted a large flock of common redpolls on this warm and windy Sunday. The redpolls didn't appear at my feeders until December, but their numbers have steadily increased since then. For the past month and a half, they've been the predominant species.

I didn't bother refilling my feeders this morning because of the high winds and heavy rains, but the redpolls came anyway, lured by this unusual ground feast. Shortly before noon I counted nearly one hundred of them, a season high.

Now, done with my ice chopping, I walk to the backyard, where redpolls have been joined by a handful of grosbeaks, voracious sunflower-seed eaters. Thirty birds hop around the snow, prospecting for seeds. There must be enough uncracked shells among the husks to make it worth picking through the debris.

Standing there, watching them hop and peck and eat, I chuckle at the birds. And at me. Already a few winters have passed since I set out my first feeder, an old, slightly bent baking pan, and three chickadees flashed in for seeds, forever changing my life. The chickadees—and later the nuthatches, grosbeaks, redpolls, juncos, and pine siskins—touched my heart in an unexpected way. Filled with delight, I wondered how long it would take that exhilaration to fade.

It hasn't. The birds remain a joyful part of my life. They connect me with the world outside my walls and windows, even when it seems too cold or rainy or stormy to leave the house. They sing to me, in cheerful chirps and whistles that I'd barely noticed until moving here. And their songs invariably lift my spirits.

Sometimes, while standing on my upstairs deck or shoveling the driveway—or even chopping ice in chinook winds—I whistle back to the birds. It's my way of welcoming them. And saying thanks.

Late Winter, 2: Listening to Owl (March 2001)

It's a Wednesday night in March, which in our part of Anchorage means take-out-the-garbage night. Shortly after 10 p.m. I put on bathrobe, gloves, and boots, and prepare to haul our green plastic trash can to the edge of the driveway for Thursday's early-morning pickup. First, though, I take a broom and head out the front door to clear three inches of fresh snow from the porch. I've just begun sweeping the soft, fluffy powder when a voice calls out from the darkness.

Hoo. Hooo-hoo. Hoo. Hoo.

I lift my head in surprise, my heartbeat quickening at this familiar yet uncommon call. Uncommon, at least, in my neighborhood. I've been told that dozens of great horns are scattered throughout the city, most often heard—and occasionally seen—in large, wooded areas like Kincaid and Hillside parks. Yet in seven and a half years on Anchorage's Hillside, only once before have I heard a great horned owl while standing in my yard. Not that I spend lots of winter nights outdoors. Except for occasional hot tubbing, snow clearing, or aurora gazing, my forays into the yard are brief: to and from the car for meetings, classes, basketball. To and from the road, hauling trash.

The owl hoots again. And again. It seems to be calling from the wooded lot beside our next-door neighbors, the Nelsons. I wonder if they've heard the owl. Unlikely, unless they too have by chance gone outside. Then, off in the distance, a faint response. *Hoo. Hooo-hoo. Hoo. Hoo.* It could be a competitor responding. But when told of the back-and-forth hooting, local birder Bob Dittrick thinks it more likely that two mates are "talking" to each other on this night. Great horned owls hoot year-round, he adds, but they're most vocal from late winter through early summer, during courtship, nesting, and fledging of their young.

Ears still tuned to the hooting, I finish sweeping, then grab the trash can and carry it to the road. Along the way I cross hare tracks, freshly imprinted into today's snow. I follow the tracks, hoping to glimpse their maker, but lose them where they cross the newly plowed road. Snowshoe hares, like great horned owls, are mostly nocturnal animals. They're also one of the owl's favorite foods, along with rodents and birds. Trying to imagine the hare's response when it first heard the owl tonight, I suppose it instinctively froze in place, depending on its snowy white coat to avoid detection. Perhaps now the camouflaged hare is watching me while listening for the owl, long ears rotating this way and that.

I'm feeling lucky. If not for my garbage-hauling duties, I wouldn't have noticed either owl or hare. They provide a glimpse of mostly hidden lives, a reminder of nightly dramas played right outside my door, yet so rarely noticed. A few flakes of snow drift groundward. The twenty-degree air is still, the night unusually quiet. The fresh snow that covers the ground and drapes trees helps to muffle noises. No other sound but owl until a jet briefly passes through the night sky, mechanical roar muted, on its approach to Anchorage's airport. Then, once more, marvelous silence except for the owls' periodic hoots.

Back on the porch, I simply stand and listen, relishing the owl's *hoo, hooo-hoo* . . . I consider waking Dulcy, who went to bed early, exhausted by her work with the local school district. No, she needs her sleep. I'll hope the owl returns this weekend. And, come morning, I'll ask Dulce if she would prefer to be roused when an owl is calling, as she's requested when the northern lights are especially magical.

There's no doubt the owl is working some magic on me. The hooting has an eerie, haunting quality, but that's not entirely it. The call, like the wails of loons and the howls of wolves, speaks of wildness and mystery. The lives of owls are secrets, rarely revealed. Tonight, I briefly glimpse a sliver of one owl's life through the darkness. Its repeated hoots send messages to my brain and create images: I picture the great horned owl perched in a nearby spruce, head swiveling, claws gripping branch, eyes wide open, calling into the night.

I'm reminded of another winter night, six years past. Can it already be so long ago? Camped with two friends in the Alaska Range foothills, I heard the rapid *hoo-hoo-hoo-hoo* of a boreal owl. The rapture of that night's campfire, subzero cold, forest stillness, ink-black sky, wildly flashing stars, and owl calls are forever imprinted on my brain and heart.

The hooting also reminds me how much I love my life here in Alaska, here on Anchorage's Hillside. To be part of a world that includes this owl's voice is a gift indeed. I wonder if any others in the neighborhood are standing outside their houses, temporarily pulled away from familial responsibilities or the technological distractions of TVs, CDs, videos, computers.

The calls stop. I wait a few minutes to be sure, then turn toward the door. Still under the owl's spell, I know that six years from now, even twenty, I will remember this take-out-the-garbage night. I'll remember the fresh snow, tracks of hare, and hushed stillness of the air. I'll remember standing alone on the front porch, no rush to go inside, listening, listening. I'll remember my heart beating wildly and my mind growing calm, serenaded by owl.

Breakup: The Secret Lives of Shrews (April 2003)

By winter's end, large piles of snow mixed with seed debris normally cover the ground beneath my Hillside home's back decks, the remnants of a season's worth of bird feeding, shell sweeping, and snow clearing. This year, though, the snow piles melted away by early February, leaving only the debris: a mix of opened and unopened shells, sunflower seed bits, bird poop, and mold.

It seemed a good idea to get rid of the mess, rather than wait for spring. Without the snow to complicate matters, I raked and shoveled and hauled away several bucketfuls of the slimy, putrid stuff—some thirty gallons in all. A job that usually takes me several hours (spread over a week's time) lasted only forty-five minutes.

More shells have piled up in the weeks since then, intermixed with the few inches of snow that fell in March. So I still have a bit of April raking and hauling to do. But Anchorage's peculiar winter, with its record-setting warmth and dearth of snow, has made my annual seed cleanup so much easier. And by mid-February I'd largely eliminated a possible temptation for any early-rising bears.

The melted snow piles did perhaps rob me of a late-winter spectacle, however. Last year, in winter's final days, I noticed that some new neighbors had moved into the yard. Well, not exactly new. But ones I hadn't paid much attention to before.

One bright morning, while standing on our upper deck and listening to birdsong, I happened to glance at the snow piles below. And I noticed something unusual: flashes of gray. As I kept watching, those dashing bits of fur took shape. Shrews were darting in and out of the snow. This discovery both surprised and delighted me.

Because they're such tiny creatures, and they stay under cover while rushing about the world, we humans rarely see shrews, the smallest of the world's mammals. And few people, besides researchers, tend to seek them out. Most Anchorage residents, I'd guess, don't even know—or care—that they share our local landscape with these voracious insectivores. Yet they're all around us, living secret lives.

Over the years, I've seen an occasional shrew in the yard. But no more than a handful in all. Now below me, at least a half dozen were poking their noses out of tunnels they'd dug through the snow. I watched for awhile, entranced by this discovery. Why hadn't I ever noticed them before? Surely this wasn't the first winter that a colony of shrews had moved into the seedy snow mounds beside the house. Or was it?

Wanting a closer look, I headed downstairs and sat a few feet away. Perhaps because they'd heard or otherwise sensed my approach, the shrews stayed hidden for awhile. Awaiting their reappearance, I noticed more and more holes in the snow. The piles were honeycombed with dozens of minute entranceways and passages. Clearly they'd settled in some time ago.

In my stillness, I began to hear a faint scratching. Then a miniature head popped out, its pointed, twitching pink nose bright against the gray fur. A new entryway had been completed. Soon another head appeared, in a different opening. And another and another.

It was hard keeping track of their numbers, as the shrews almost immediately pulled their heads back in, after poking them out. A few darted completely out of their burrows, trailing thin gray tails nearly as long as their tiny bodies. But none ventured more than a few inches before rushing back inside. During their brief but frequent forays into the light, they'd worn narrow runways across the snow's surface.

I knew that a handful of different shrews live in the Anchorage area; these were almost certainly common or masked shrews (*Sorex cinereus*). The most widespread of their kind, they inhabit much of North America. Though I didn't catch any (or try to), I estimated the shrews' length to be between two and four inches, from the tip of their noses to the tip of their tails. Weighing only a few ounces, their bodies constantly twitched and quivered, giving them a skittish, nervous appearance.

I tried to imagine the network of tunnels, passages, and chambers they'd built beneath the snow. And I wondered what had lured the shrews to this spot. Was it something about the piles themselves? Or the abundance of seeds? The shrews seemed to be grabbing bits of seeds when they scampered from their holes, but I couldn't be sure. Though shrews are insect feeders, maybe they were taking advantage of the seeds to survive the winter more easily, much like insect-eating songbirds turn to seeds during Alaska's coldest, harshest season.

I kept watch on the shrews until mid-April, when the piles began to melt away and the tunnels collapsed or flooded. They disappeared long before the snow did, escaped back into their hidden world.

Now it's April again, with winter all but past, and I still haven't seen a single shrew. As I do some final raking and hauling of seeds, I can't help but wonder how my tiny, secretive neighbors fared during this strangely warm and mostly snowless Alaskan winter.

Spring: Songs of Robins (May 2005)

The afterglow of a late-evening sunset filters through the upstairs windows of my home. To the northwest, a crimson band of sky hangs over a mountain known locally as the Sleeping Lady, as if ready to enfold her in soft red robes for the night. I spent much of this spring day in the yard, raking up debris from winter storms and a half year's worth of bird feeding. Now, freshly showered and relaxed, I sit in dwindling light and listen to one of the world's great singers.

Perched in a nearby spruce, a male robin serenades me with a sweetly familiar melody. His warbled song touches some deeply buried memory, from a time and place far, far away. I didn't pay much heed to birds while growing up in Connecticut during the fifties and sixties, but a few species got my attention. None more so than the robin.

I still vividly picture robins running across Dad's well-manicured lawn, then suddenly stopping, dropping their heads to the ground, and lifting up a worm or caterpillar. I remember their color and shape much more than their songs from those long-ago days. But the voices of robins must have been among the most recognizable wild sounds to echo through my Trumbull neighborhood in spring and summer, along with the chirps of crickets, the croaking of bullfrogs, and the shouts of friends playing softball in the open lot beside my family's yard.

I don't remember robins inhabiting the places I lived en route to my adopted home, Alaska: Maine, Arizona, California. Yet the map in my field guide to North American birds clearly shows we shared those landscapes. It must be that my attention was focused on other things during my twenties and thirties. First there was college and grad school, followed by a short-lived career in geology, then a shift to journalism; plus sports, romantic relationships, and my first tentative steps along the long and winding path of personal and spiritual growth.

Though I've always loved nature, it was only after I settled in Anchorage in 1982 that I seriously began to pay renewed attention to "the natural world" as I once had. Though I wouldn't fully welcome birds into my life for another decade or so, early on I noticed a remarkable thing about my new home: robins.

Like most people, I'd built images of Alaska that included polar bears, wolves, Eskimos, great mountains, and glaciers. But robins? They didn't seem to fit somehow. They seemed too . . . I don't know, too eastern, maybe. Or maybe too commonplace. I'd imagined them to be creatures of milder, tamer environs. Then again, until I came here, I never imagined myself becoming a resident of America's "last frontier."

In a curious way, robins deepened the link between my original and adopted homelands. While providing a natural connection between Connecticut and Alaska, they also stirred sharp memories of my boyhood. As some other familiar critters have done—for instance, chickadees, rainbow trout, frogs, and dragonflies—robins increased my desire to better understand my boyhood bond with nature and, at the same time, learn more about the wild community of my new home.

If seeing a robin in Anchorage seemed strange, imagine how I felt upon spotting a robin deep in the arctic wilderness, miles and miles from any well-kept lawns, or gardens, or trees. Traveling alone, without anyone to verify the sighting, I thought I might be hallucinating. Until I saw another. And another. Since then I have learned that robins seasonally occupy nearly all of Alaska, from the Panhandle's old-growth forests to the North Slope's tundra plains.

Here in Anchorage, robins are among the first migratory songbirds to arrive each spring. Come April, I anticipate their fluid, high-pitched song, along with the trill of the varied thrush and loud whistled notes of the tiny ruby-crowned kinglet.

Once arrived and settled into their springtime routines, robins seem to sing (or, when annoyed or frightened, screech) all day long and deep into the night. Often their songs are what I hear first in the morning and last before sleep. At the end of a long, dark winter—or long, busy spring day—few, if any, sounds are more delightful.

Perhaps I'm appreciating robins more these days because of another connection. After eight decades of East Coast living, my mother came north to Alaska to spend her last years with me and Dulcy. Soon to reach eighty-three, Mom can't get outdoors like she used to. And, like many older folks, she's lost the ability to hear high-frequency sounds.

Even when I open the windows and sliding glass doors, Mom usually can't hear the chirps, buzzes, warbles, and whistles of our backyard birds. For someone who welcomed songbirds to her house for many years, that's a hard, frustrating thing. Yet the robin's song is loud enough, and apparently deep enough, that it sometimes registers. On a recent outing along Anchorage's Coastal Trail, I asked if she could hear the bird's whistled notes. "I think so," she replied. Then, listening intently, she turned her head toward me when the bird whistled again. "Is that it, over there?" she asked, pointing.

"Yep, you've got it."

We both smiled at that.

Then, earlier today, a robin started singing right outside the sitting room window. Before I could say anything, Mom turned in her chair. "That's the robin, isn't it?"

Mom's in bed now and her door is closed. But the robin continues to sing, a little softer now, while the sky darkens. He'll still be singing when I head to bed, sending forth a calm, assuring sort of lullaby with its own touch of wild magic that stretches across the continent, across the years.

Early Summer, 1: Tending the Yard (June 1994)

Sometimes, as I work in my Hillside yard, I get the strange sense that my dad's spirit is hovering nearby. Surely it's only my imagination, that chuckling I hear.

Ed Sherwonit's son, the reluctant yard worker, finally—in his mid-forties—has a lawn of his own. And a lawnmower. Perhaps you believe that one implies the other. Not necessarily so. At other times, in other places, I might have chosen to let my grass grow with abandon, rather than keep it neatly trimmed. Case in point: before moving to Anchorage's eastern foothills, I lived at the end of a cul-de-sac in the city's Oceanview area. All the neighbors had nicely manicured lawns, more or less. But not once, in five summers, did a lawnmower touch a single blade of grass on my quarter-acre property—though I did swing a weed whacker more than a few times and eventually went high-tech with an electric trimmer.

The backyard was semi-wild—knee-high grasses, birch and spruce trees, fire-weed and wild prickly rose, even devil's club, plus several varieties of weeds—while the front yard was merely scruffy: mostly dirt and gravel, with scattered dandelions and one raggedy section of unkempt grass.

Such is what I inherited from the previous homeowner, and what I chose to live with. That's not to say I never worked on the yard. Each spring I raked leaves, picked up debris, pulled weeds, trimmed here and there, and tended to a small plot of strawberries. But inevitably, as the summer progressed, I took more of a laissez-faire attitude, allowing the grasses, dandelions, and other plants to go their own way.

Though not a dedicated gardener or grass cutter, at Oceanview I did finally begin to comprehend my father's love for yard work. As a boy, I never quite understood Dad's passion for lawns, shrubs, and rock gardens: the long hours he spent raking and mowing and weeding and watering, often in the evening after a hard day's work, or on the weekends. I helped, but only out of duty, much preferring to wander through the Connecticut woods, explore the nearby swamp, go fishing with my Uncle Peach, or play ball with the neighborhood gang.

Besides being hard to fathom, Dad's passion proved bothersome at times. All too often, my pals and I were barred from using his beautifully green and neatly trimmed grass for our ball field. A real shame, since he usually had the best-kept lawn for miles around.

My attitude toward yard work didn't change much over the next thirty years or so. If I thought about lawns or gardens at all, it was to consider myself lucky for not having any—or for being a renter with no yard-keeping responsibilities. But at Oceanview, as a first-time homeowner, something began to shift. Working on my own yard each spring, I would enter a calm, almost meditative state.

The earthy smells, the sweat, the dirt under fingernails—even the aching muscles, buzzing mosquitoes, and blisters—all had a grounding effect, while giving me a better sense of that word's meaning. They stirred memories of times long ago and far away and offered insights into Dad's passions.

Even bigger shifts have occurred since I moved to Anchorage's Hillside. Most of the one-and-one-third-acre property is spruce-birch forest. A place of wild beauty, the forest, more than anything, is what lured me here; it has dozens of native plant species and is a refuge for numerous woodland creatures, from siskins and squirrels to moose and black bear and lynx. But not all the lot is wooded: much of the front yard and part of the back are covered by a carpet of lawn.

It's not the most attractive lawn. In fact, Dad would probably consider major repairs a necessity. There are some bare spots, mossy areas, dandelion patches, and at least three or four different types of grass. The front yard has a growing community of clover, while the backyard's edge of grass and forest is increasingly blurred by horsetails, ferns, wild rose, berry plants, and tiny wildflowers.

But it's my lawn and I've taken on the challenge of keeping it healthy. And moderately manicured. Though, truth be told, I rather like the backyard lawn's increasing unruliness. I'm doing things I'd never before imagined. I've gotten lawn-care tips from the local Cooperative Extension Service, read newspaper columns, browsed through the home-and-garden section of a few stores, conducted independent research—and I've bought a rear-discharge, air-cooled, four-cycle rotary mower with brake assistance.

I've raked the lawn in spring and fall, watered it, mowed it, cut back encroaching alders, spent hours and hours futilely picking dandelions—because I stubbornly won't use chemical weed killers—and, on a few occasions, even fertilized the grass (though in recent years I have opted against chemical additives). And the funny thing is, none of the yard work feels like a chore the way it used to.

At the same time, I've become a gardener of sorts. In the front yard is a small but growing patch of semi-wild strawberries. Once enclosed in a boxed garden plot, the strawberries have spread beyond it and now occupy a corner of the front lawn. The past couple summers these feral plants have produced enough sweet pink fruits for me to make homemade strawberry pies, using one of Mom's recipes.

In a curious and delightful way, the unruly, dandelion-sprinkled lawn and expanding strawberry patch balance the forest's larger wildness and help define my living space. They pull me outdoors, force me to pay more attention to my surroundings, connect me in new ways to the earth and local landscape, remind me of the many contradictions I carry within. Dad, I think, would understand all this. And I'm certain he'd be pleased.

Early Summer, 2: Leaving the Nest (June 2002)

Stepping out the front door on my way to get the Sunday newspaper, I glance to my left, toward a birch tree at the edge of the lawn. Nailed to the tree is a wooden nest box, about eight feet above the ground. And within the box is a brood of seven boreal chickadees, northern songbirds that inhabit much of Southcentral and Interior Alaska. Born sometime in early June, they have grown large enough, by the end of the month, to tightly pack the artificial cavity.

There's a fluttering of wings just inside the small, round entryway and at first I guess it to be one of the parents, feeding insects to the nestlings. But as the little brownish-gray bird emerges, it drops awkwardly toward the ground. Taken by surprise, I worry that one of the youngsters has somehow fallen out of the nest while still unable to fly. I reach inside the door and grab my binoculars for a better look. Bringing the box into focus, I see a couple more heads and beaks jostling at the entrance. Then a second bird exits the box. Flapping furiously, it flies to an alder bush beside the birch. Landing awkwardly and unable to get its balance, this one too drops and flutters out of sight, into a dense thicket of alder and elderberry.

Now it's clear what is happening. The chickadee nestlings have become fledglings. Blessed by serendipity, I have been granted the rare opportunity to watch young birds leaving their nest.

After I've realized my good fortune, two questions immediately arise: How many birds are left? And, should I awaken Dulcy? If it were early morning, I might hesitate to disturb my late-rising wife, who relishes her weekend sleep-ins. But she too has been heartened by the nearby presence of nesting songbirds; just last week we excitedly peeked in the box together, to check on the nestlings. Besides, it's already 10 a.m.

I rush upstairs, nudge her gently, and lift the pillow she's draped over her head. "Dulcy," I whisper. "The chickadees are fledging. You'll have to hurry if you want to watch."

Bleary-eyed, Dulcy rolls out of bed, grabs her eyeglasses, and joins me on the porch. We stay here, at a respectful distance, so we don't disturb the birds in their ritual. A minute or so later, a third chickadee flutters out of the nest and lands nicely on an alder branch. Watching through the binoculars, Dulcy murmurs her pleasure, a soft echo of my own.

Now and then we hear faint nasal chirping, as heads and beaks and necks poke out of the hole, then pull back in. I imagine the box's interior to be a raucous place right now as the birds push and shove each other in their clamor to get out.

A fourth chickadee pops out of the hole. Beating its wings hard, it floats through the air as if in slow motion, then cleanly sets down in an alder that's more tree than bush, some fifteen feet above the ground and thirty feet from its launch point. A beautiful takeoff, first flight, and landing.

The fifth fledgling, like the earlier ones, tumbles and flutters into the bushes below. There's a lull, then, as the remaining birds seem hesitant to take the leap. First one, then the other, pokes its head and upper body outside, only to pull back in. As if to encourage the reluctant fliers, one of the adult chickadees zooms in and perches on the entrance's lip. It briefly peers inside, then leaves, and the other parent repeats the routine. They remain nearby, moving among the trees and bushes, keeping watch on their young.

Again a fledgling cautiously emerges, bit by bit. First beak, then head, then neck and shoulders. The chickadee looks this way and that, turns its head upward, looks toward the ground, stays put.

"They remind me of the first time I jumped in a swimming pool; I stood on the edge for the longest time," says Dulcy. "That would be me, the insecure one, waiting right to the end. Needing assurance."

Turning to me she adds, "I bet you'd be the first, or one of the first ones out, given your competitive nature."

"I don't think so," I smile in reply, with a shake of my head. I too can identify with the birds' apparent hesitancy. I know the push and pull of conflicting impulses: a desire for safety and comfort competing with the urge to explore and grow. With change and growth comes risk. Often, when perched on a threshold, it seems a leap of faith is required.

The fledgling is now mostly out of the nest box. At the last moment, it hooks its tiny claws onto the entryway's ledge. Hanging against the box, the bird flaps its wings hard yet refuses to let go. "I think it wants to go back in," Dulcy says.

That's not going to happen. One of the parents flies in and gives the struggling bird a soft nudge. It drops away, a falling, flapping body.

Now there's one. The last chickadee pokes out its head, pauses a couple moments, then launches itself into the air, a grand first flight to the alder tree where at least three of its siblings now perch. Where the others are, it's impossible to say.

I check my watch. Only twenty minutes have passed since the first fledgling tumbled out. "It still amazes me," I tell Dulcy, "that I happened to walk out the door just as it was starting and then looked over at just the right moment. The chances of that happening are so small; it would have been so easy to miss. We were really lucky."

Dulcy reminds me of something I've come to believe, but sometimes still forget: "There are no accidents, remember? This was a gift to you." To us both.

Dulcy stays a few more minutes, then returns inside the house. I go in too, but only briefly to grab journal and pen, then head back outdoors. For the next hour or so, in between bursts of note taking, I try to track the boreal chickadees' movements. It's not easy to do. Occasionally they chirp softly, but mostly they remain quiet and still, except for fluttering feathers.

Hidden by leaves, the chickadees are nearly impossible to spot, except when they take short flights from branch to branch, tree to tree. Soon I lose track of all but a couple of the newly fledged birds. The parents remain busy, hunting moths and flies and other foods for their offspring, and keeping tabs on their family's movements.

By midday the birds have left our yard, crossed the road, and disappeared into a neighbor's woods. I wish I could follow them, gain more glimpses into their lives. Returning to the house, I glance at the now-empty nest box and my faint longing becomes a smile. *All seven,* I think. *We got to watch all seven of them go out into the world.*

Midsummer: A Moose in the Berry Patch (July 2004)

I now more fully appreciate the angst of northern homeowners whose ornamental trees and flowering gardens have become meals for moose, for I have caught one raiding my prized strawberry patch.

The first hints that something was amiss appeared earlier in the week, when I found a couple of the plants uprooted, ripening berries still attached. I wondered what—or who—might have pulled the plants. A rambunctious dog? A marauding teen? A rogue rabbit? (Nearby neighbors "rescued" a few rabbits last year and then turned them loose; they have since become regular visitors to my yard, but from what I can tell they prefer clover and dandelion leaves to berries. Hooray for that good fortune.)

Because the plants had been pulled but not eaten, and the patch as a whole was largely undisturbed, it didn't even cross my mind that a passing ungulate might be the culprit. Besides, in the eleven summers Dulcy and I have lived on Anchorage's Hillside, no moose has ever shown a taste for our patch of feral strawberries. In fact, the only animal I've ever seen foraging in our small, unkempt berry garden was a robin, which simply took bites from several ripened fruits. Berry-burrowing bugs and occasional slugs have been bigger problems than birds or furry beasts.

To be completely honest about this, for several years our patch was hardly big enough to attract much attention from anything bigger than a beetle (or the occasional bumblebee, when the berries' flowers were blooming). But the past few years, we've let the berries run wild, and the plants have greatly expanded their range. Now covering some forty square feet, our personal—and, by most standards, still tiny—strawberry fields have annually produced one to two gallons of small, pinkish fruits that are juicy and lip-smackingly sweet. Still, they never attracted much attention, beyond the odd robin. Until this midsummer morning.

Walking along the upstairs hallway to check on my mother, I happened to glance toward the downstairs hallway and front door. Just outside the door's window, partially obscured by blinds, was a large, brown, hairy form.

What the heck is a moose doing on our front porch? I wondered to myself.

Then I rushed downstairs and looked out the window. To both my surprise and dismay, a cow moose was standing with one foot in the berry patch, head down and mouth chomping away. Just beyond her, a cinnamon-colored calf lay sprawled among the strawberry plants, seemingly at peace with the world even as my own peaceful morning was being shattered.

"Oh, no," I moaned. What was I going to do? Hoping to scare the moose off without having to confront them, I banged on the door. The cow lifted her head and looked toward the house, but that was all. Clearly, more drastic measures were needed. I began to unlock the door, but had enough presence of mind to remember the house alarm was triggered. I didn't want to set it off and perhaps frighten the beast, so I punched the keyboard combination. Then, very carefully, I opened the door several inches, stuck my head outside (ready, at a moment's notice, to retreat and slam the door shut, if necessary) and talked to the moose in a calm but stern voice.

"Hey, what do you think you're doing, eating my strawberries? Get out of there. Go on. Get out."

Her huge, oblong head no more than five feet from my face, the cow moose looked at me with an expression that seemed a mix of curiosity and bewilderment. It was the sort of look a person might have while thinking, *Who's this guy and what's his problem?*

Happily, she seemed neither flustered nor agitated. On the one hand, this was good news. I didn't want a riled-up moose on my doorstep. On the other hand, she didn't appear ready to give up her newfound snack.

Emboldened by the cow's easygoing manner, I opened the door wider and took a small step forward. Then, once more, I softly urged them to leave my small but precious strawberry patch, while both mom and calf watched intently. I too felt calm; but I was ready to bolt inside at the slightest sign of aggression.

The calf stood. And the cow, God bless her, took a tentative step backward, as if not quite sure how to respond. It was then that I noticed the second calf, lying twenty feet away on the lawn. Neither of the twins seemed anxious. Like their mom, they seemed more curious than alarmed by the unfolding encounter.

Ever so slowly, the cow backed out of the berry patch. Followed by calf No. 1, she began to cross the front deck, head still turned toward me. Every now and then she would roll her tongue across her lips. I know it's a tricky and potentially foolhardy thing, to read or interpret an animal's behavior or intentions, but I got the strongest sense that the cow was savoring those strawberry plants, with their dark-green leaves and ripening berries. She really didn't want to leave such a tasty meal, when so much remained on the dark earthy plate of my garden.

"Go'wan, go'wan," I continued to urge the moose family. "I really don't want you eating my strawberries, so leave them alone, OK?"

Strangely enough I didn't feel foolish, talking to the moose this way. And whether it was the tone of my voice, my body language, or something else I can't imagine, the mom and her calves seemed responsive to my pleas. Very slowly, almost reluctantly, they continued their retreat across the yard. The cow looked huge; her legs likely reached up to my chest and she must have weighed close to a thousand pounds. The gangly calves reminded me of young colts; now several weeks old, their heads probably came to my shoulders.

Within a few minutes, they reached the far end of my front lawn. There the cow began gulping down alder and birch leaves. The calves, too, picked at the bushes. But from time to time, one or more would look back at me.

By now I was out on the deck, arms crossed and gaze steady in their direction. Almost since I first opened the door, part of me wanted to go into the house and awaken Mom, tell her about this amazing spectacle. But I didn't want to abandon my post. I felt sure that if I went inside, the cow would return to the berry patch. And I wouldn't be able to so easily shoo her away a second time.

So I stayed and watched while the moose ate wild greens. At a casual browsing pace, they gradually moved downhill from the front yard to the back, still occasionally glancing in my direction. Not once did they seem agitated by my presence. From the lawn they slipped into the thick forest that borders the backyard, still eating as they moved. Nearly a half-hour had passed from my first sighting to their disappearance among birch and spruce trees.

I walked over to the patch to inspect the damage. Several plants had been cleanly clipped; a few had been pulled from the ground and others trampled. But overall, the losses were light.

Anticipating the moose family's eventual return, I've been wondering how I might protect my strawberries until I've harvested enough for at least one scrumptious pie. Yet any frustration over their raid and concern about possible future ones has been softened by the absolute joy of this unexpected encounter. Moose and berries: I never would have guessed. Given our shared taste for strawberries, how can I begrudge the cow her nibbling of the plants?

Only time will tell if I'll remain so generous with the fruits of my gardening labors, though really I don't have to work so hard to tend this crop. For now I can only chuckle at the memory of the cow moose licking her lips and reluctantly leaving the berry patch behind, much like a kid retreating from an unhappy neighbor's apple orchard, the taste still sweet in her mouth.

Late Summer: Thunder and Lightning (August 2004)

Lying in bed, the lights turned off, I savor the last flashes of lightning and the final peels of thunder that mark the passing of an unusually violent late-summer thunderstorm through Anchorage. It's been a full year since I last witnessed such atmospheric mayhem; then I was visiting my brother, Dave, and his soon-to-be-bride, Jane, in New York's Catskill Mountains.

Both that eastern storm and this Alaskan one stirred vivid memories from my Connecticut youth. I can still recall the heart-thumping excitement, the goose-bump flesh, and the tinge of fright when hair stood up on the back of my neck, as lightning blazed across the skies and thunder shook our Old Town Road neighborhood. Often the sky would take on an eerie glow, as if issuing a warning, before it unleashed the buckets of rain, the searing, jagged streaks of incandescent light, and the loud cracking and booming that sent us scrambling for cover.

Though they intimidated us, those Connecticut thunderstorms never harmed family or friends or wreaked destruction on the landscape, at least not that I recall. I suppose that helps to explain why I miss those fierce storms: we got a taste of unimaginable power, without suffering from it. Perhaps I wouldn't be so keen on thunder and lightning storms if I lived in Interior or Arctic Alaska, where more than five million acres have burned this year, mostly because of lightning strikes.

Here in Anchorage, thunderstorms are rare. And those that do pass through hardly ever last more than a bolt or two. In twenty-two years of local living, I've never experienced anything close to this night's power display. So I've reveled in the late-August storm, which seems to have swept through town without causing any great or lasting damage.

Besides the thunder and lightning, the storm has brought much-needed rain, heavy and pounding at times. A regular deluge. And, the weather forecasters tell us, it is marking our entry into a welcome few days of wetness, after a spectacularly unusual summer of hot, dry weather that has put local firefighters and Hillside residents like me on high alert.

Sparked by lightning strikes, thunderclaps, and vivid memories, other thoughts about storms and weather flash through my revved-up mind. For instance: in commanding our attention, the ferocity and threatening nature of storms such as this act something like a wake-up call. Unlike day after day of bright sunshine or drizzly grayness, they're striking reminders that we city dwellers remain part of wild nature.

The fact is, we modern, urbanized humans are surrounded by wildness, whether we pay attention to it or not. Both the earth and the sky remain uncontrollably and sublimely wild. (Earthquakes, like storms, remind us of this simple truth.) We may insulate ourselves behind wood, glass, metal, or concrete; we may immerse our lives in artifice and make things easier with grand modern technologies; but there's no escaping wildness. Or the fact that, ultimately, we humans aren't in charge of things, though we often behave as if we are.

I think that's a big reason, maybe the biggest, that people continue to pay such close attention to the weather, even when we're largely insulated from it. It's why we're fascinated with tornadoes, hurricanes, flash floods, blizzards, and droughts that don't directly affect us or those we know. Such weather events remind us that we're vulnerable to what we sometimes call "nature's whims." There are forces much bigger than we are, that we can't control or sometimes even predict.

Think about it. The newspaper has its daily weather page, and local TV newscast teams have their weathermen and women. In Anchorage, and I'd bet many other places, some of those television weatherpeople are among the community's most recognizable personalities. And their reports often lead off the news hour, even when there's little new to say.

I'm among those who check the weather page regularly. And I faithfully note something about each day's weather in my home journal: the temperature range as recorded by my own thermometer, whether there's been any precipitation (and what kind), whether the day is calm or windy, whether any records have been broken, that sort of thing.

When I talk over the phone with distant friends or relatives, or send them emails, the weather is often among the first things we mention. It comes up frequently with local friends, too, or even strangers. This summer everyone in town is talking about Anchorage's record-breaking heat and unusual dryness. If a conversation goes flat, there's always the weather to discuss. Surely we'll be talking about this thunderstorm for days, and perhaps years, to come.

As it moves out of town, I imagine the storm to be something like a darkly fearsome sky beast, rushing wildly through the city. The image of its flashing teeth and booming voice will remain among the sharpest and brightest memories from what has been an unforgettable Anchorage summer.

Autumn, 1: The Hidden World of Hares (September–October 2000)

With breakfast finished and the daily sports section skimmed from cover to cover, I get up from the dining room table and pile newspaper, coffee cup, crumpled napkin, and plastic yogurt container on the kitchen counter. Then, drawn more by instinct than deliberate thought, I step to the dining room's north-facing window and peer outside. The window is a favorite observation post, a looking glass through which I study the nature of my Anchorage backyard, a semi-wild mix of lawn and spruce-birch forest.

On this September morning, my attention is drawn to a smallish, rounded brown form, huddled in the grass and nibbling on clover: a snowshoe hare. A favorite food of lynx, great horned owls, northern goshawks, foxes, and coyotes—all of which prowl Anchorage's wooded areas—hares survive by stealth and camouflage. Completely white in winter, except for large brown eyes, they are nearly invisible on snow. In summer, their grayish-brown fur excellently blends with the forest's mottled, shadowed floor.

A hare's natural disguise doesn't work so well on monochromatic green, though, which is likely why I see them most frequently from May through September, come to dine on lawn grass and clover.

To be honest, I don't normally pay much attention to the neighborhood's hares. Their habits don't make for easy or interesting study: in the open, they tend to remain still, depending (for better or worse) on the effectiveness of their camouflage; in the forest, they're almost impossible to track. And though secretive in nature, they're common creatures of the woods. Seeing a hare is nothing like catching a glimpse of a bear or lynx, or even a moose or hawk. Their furtive qualities also make them less engaging than other common forest residents, for instance the delightfully excitable chickadees and squirrels that visit my backyard, looking for meals.

Today, however, my interest in the animal lingers and grows. It's the fur that immediately grabs my attention; we're still a month or more from the first heavy snows, yet the shift to winter white has already begun.

I grab my binoculars and take a closer look. Hares always retain some white on their undersides, where it's easily hidden in summer. But this one's long back feet are solidly white from toes to ankles and above, as though it has slipped on large white slippers. Small patches of white also mark the hare's face: around the mouth, under the chin, on the cheek. Atop its head, the hare's ears are already mostly white, with brown-and-black tips.

Maybe it's the sharp contrast in color between white ears and brown body, but I more easily notice how the hare is almost constantly moving its ears, often independently of one another, like thin, oval, furred mini satellite dishes.

Nose twitching steadily, the hare is busily munching clover when a magpie calls in its loud, raspy voice. The hare sits tight, motionless except for its rotating ears. One ear forward, another turned ninety degrees to the right or left. Both ears forward. Both ears to the sides, then flicked backward.

I wonder when the transformation began, when it will be complete. How long does the color shift take? Does it vary from year to year, from individual to individual? And why do I almost never see hares in winter? Is the white disguise that good?

A WEEK PASSES. WORKING AT the computer I glance up and out the sliding glass door, and notice two hares in the backyard. One I recognize by its pattern of white patches; the other remains more fully brown. As I watch, the two engage in behavior I've never before witnessed. As one hare sits still, the other jumps high into the air, again and again. Leaping, it punches the air with its back legs, quick, sharp jabs. What's going on?

There's a frolicking nature to the jumping and kicking. I imagine it to be a spirited attempt at play. But I'm also reminded how little I really know about hares, or my other wild neighbors.

Curious now about both the hare's behavior and its changing coat, I do some reading, track down a couple of wildlife researchers. This is some of what I learn: the hare's jumping and kicking is not play, but ritualized aggression; a show of dominance that apparently communicates something to the effect of "Get outta here. This is my turf."

Things get especially wild in spring and early summer, time of mating. Male hares will chase and scrap and generally lose all good sense—namely their normal instincts for secrecy—in their frenzied desire to breed with females in heat. In losing their heads, sex-crazed hares will often also lose their lives, either to predators or to cars, while madly dashing across streets. Females stay in estrus for only a few hours at a time, so the zaniness is short-lived. But it's intense enough to lead to the notion of "Mad March Hare Syndrome."

As for the color shift: that usually lasts about a month, though the duration and timing varies from hare to hare. Scientists believe the change is driven mostly by daylight, but temperature also likely plays a role. And the transition is indeed patchy, rather than smooth.

One other bit of natural history helps to explain their annual "disappearance" in winter: *Lepus americanus* is a mostly nocturnal creature. Given the length of Anchorage's winter nights—more than fifteen hours of darkness from late October through mid-February, with a peak of eighteen and a half hours on the winter solstice—hares have abundant time to feed and move about unseen. Combine that with their superior camouflage and my own greater tendency to remain indoors during the cold, dark months, and it figures I'd be less likely to notice hares in winter's white. Come spring and summer, daylight hours lengthen, I spend more time in the yard, and hares go crazy with passion. So our paths more regularly cross.

NOW IT IS OCTOBER. Several days have passed without any sign of the hares. I wonder how white their coats have become. It's already snowed once on the Hillside, but here, at 1,000 feet, the snow melted within a few hours. A fully or mostly white hare should be easy to spot on this gray and brown late-autumn landscape. Have they already gone into nocturnal hiding? Vanished for the season?

I continue to check for them daily, but usually only for moments at a time. This morning as I watched, a cow moose passed just outside the sliding glass doors. We gazed at each other a few moments, then she sauntered off into the woods. Here then gone, so quickly.

These recent episodes with hares and moose have me thinking (again) about how much goes on in my yard and neighborhood that I never see or sense. I'm given glimpses now and then. But these only hint of the "hidden" world that I too rarely notice. Even with my passion for wildlife, for nature, I easily become cocooned within the walls of my house, consumed by the busyness of work or distracted by computer, television, newspaper. I urge myself, once more, to make room in my busy schedule; to watch, listen, pay attention, get "out there" more often. And have patience. These neighbors, after all, bring immeasurable pleasure and wonder into my life. Whether bears or moose or hares, they are all worth knowing better.

Autumn, 2: Fall Harvest (September 2002)

Sitting at my office desk, I gaze absentmindedly out the window into the backyard and my wandering thoughts are pulled into sharp focus by the sight of spruce cones falling to the ground. Well, not falling exactly; being hurled. The red squirrels with whom I share my Anchorage yard are once again busily preparing for winter.

Among the most common residents of Alaska's forests (and northern cousins of the gray squirrels that inhabit most of the U.S.), red squirrels remain active year-round. And they depend heavily on spruce cones to survive winter's scarcity. In Anchorage, squirrels begin collecting cones in August and they continue to build their caches through September and even into October, assuming supplies last.

In more remote areas, the success of a squirrel's autumnal cone harvest will largely determine whether or not it survives our longest, harshest season, but starvation isn't a problem in my Hillside neighborhood. Here, squirrels can supplement their cone diet with the peanuts and sunflower seeds put outdoors by people like me. (I offer peanuts to keep the squirrels from raiding my bird feeders; it works most of the time, but now and then I catch one sneaking seeds.)

Still, the cone harvest remains an instinctive ritual. Watching the squirrels' frenzied movements in backyard spruces, I sense a life-and-death urgency, as if there were no time to waste.

The squirrel I'm watching this September morning is a study in agility and hustle. After sprinting high up a tree trunk, it scampers out to the far reaches of a flimsy, swaying branch and stretches its body as far as it will reach. Then with quick, precise bites, the squirrel snips several cones and, one after another, it flips them with mouth or paws to the ground below. The cones carve a smooth arc through the crisp autumn air and land with a soft thud on the lawn or adjacent forest floor.

Sometimes reaching far overhead, other times hanging upside down, held in place by the strong grip of back feet on branch, the squirrel is a marvelous contortionist, the envy of any gymnast.

Finished with one clump, it rushes to another. And another. I wonder if the squirrel somehow knows that this is a year of plenty. The spruce trees in my yard alone have produced tens of thousands of cones; their tops are heavy with huge clusters of bright, scaly, greenish-brown fruits. There are more cones, by far, than I've ever seen in my nine years here. Enough for several winters, it seems. With so much to choose from, I wonder, what's the rush? Perhaps the squirrel's hoarding instinct has been sent into frenzied overdrive by this unusual abundance.

Watching the squirrel, I'm reminded of my own fall harvest: picking blueberries. Though I've picked and gobbled these tiny wild fruits for as long as I can remember, only in recent years has such casual picking become a more formal, and valued, seasonal ritual. Now, I annually head into the backcountry in late summer and early fall expressly to collect wild berries.

My motivations, of course, are much different from the squirrels'. Certainly the berries feed my body; but more than that, the deliberate act of harvesting them feeds my spirit.

In Alaska, where summers seem too short and autumns are even shorter, berry picking is one way to celebrate the changing seasons, instead of fighting the downhill slide into winter's cold and darkness. It's also a way of becoming better acquainted—and more physically connected—with my home landscape. By collecting and consuming the berries that grow in my wild "backyard," I more fully participate in the seasonal cycles; I digest and absorb the fruits of my homeland.

This season I've picked about two and a half gallons of blueberries, on a handful of trips into the mountains. That's a tiny haul by most harvesting standards and hardly worth mentioning when compared to the bulk of foods that I'll purchase at the grocery store this year. Yet it's enough to make a few meals of blueberry pancakes and several pies, which I'll share with family and friends—another valued part of the ritual.

While the squirrel's harvest is directly tied to its survival, mine becomes a symbolic act, a personal reminder that *all* my food comes from the earth, not from supermarkets and food-packaging producers.

Later in the day, I walk through the yard, checking on the squirrel's work. Beneath one tree, I count nearly five hundred cones, scattered on the lawn. Beneath another spruce, I count several hundred more. I also find a midden, the place where a squirrel has begun storing the cones it has dropped to the ground.

While my harvest has already ended, the squirrels will continue theirs for several more weeks. Snipping, tossing, and caching cones, rushing up and down one spruce and then another, they are daily reminders that winter is fast approaching, once again. They also remind me to celebrate, and give thanks for, the abundance in my own life.

Return to Winter: Watching Birds with Mom (January 2003)

"Where are those redpolls?" I wonder aloud while gazing out the sliding glass doors toward our bird feeders.

"Yeah, where are those birds?" Mom echoes. "I thought you said the redpolls would be here by now. I'm gonna give up on them if they don't show up soon."

By late January, the redpolls that normally swarm my feeders in winter remain a no-show. Sunflower seeds placed on upper-deck railings and an old, banged-up cookie tray have pulled in pine siskins and pine grosbeaks, boreal and black-capped chickadees. But so far, not a single redpoll. That's highly unusual.

Since I began keeping track in 1993, redpolls have usually arrived in December and stayed around 'til April, when they disperse for breeding. Some days—especially when it's bitterly cold or there's been a huge snowfall—one hundred or more have swarmed my feeders. When they've gathered in such large numbers, the redpolls zoom back and forth from nearby spruce trees, as though at some avian fast-food diner. Squeezed wing to wing in the food line, they chirp and screech and flutter about in frenzied pandemonium. For such little creatures, they make a mighty racket.

Though she's heard many of my redpoll stories, Mom has never seen the birds themselves. So now and then she'll say, "Remind me again what they look like."

I tell her they're among the smallest of Alaska's birds. And though they look a little like sparrows, they're actually finches, with distinctive red splotches or caps on their heads, small black bibs, and heavily streaked brown-and-white wings and back. Adult males also sport pinkish to bright red breasts. From a distance, I add, redpolls are hard to distinguish from the siskins that are crowding our feeders in unusually high numbers.

Tiny brown-and-white streaked birds, siskins rarely hang around our neighborhood this late in winter. But this year their numbers have continued to grow. Several times I've counted more than eighty siskins, a record at our feeders. I wonder if there's a connection between the siskins' abundance and the redpolls' disappearance; maybe the strange weather we've been having.

THIS FEEDING AND WATCHING and recording of Anchorage songbirds, and pondering of patterns, has become a favorite winter ritual since I first put out that baking tray with sunflower seeds, in December 1993. This year, though, it's taken on a new and delightful twist, since my mother has joined in the seasonal rite.

A lifelong easterner who spent her first eighty years in Connecticut and then Virginia, Torie Sherwonit moved across the continent last summer to live with me on Anchorage's Hillside. As you might expect, this late-in-life cross-country move has been a challenge. But it's only part of a larger and even tougher transition.

Until last year, Mom was an active, self-sufficient woman, albeit slowed by eight decades of life. Widowed and living alone for more than a decade, she went on daily walks with friends, ran errands in her car, helped at church, and visited shut-ins, bringing food, conversation, and a warm smile.

Now largely housebound, Mom has difficulty getting around even with her walker. Though we take her out occasionally, she spends most of her waking hours in a former bedroom that's been converted into a dining-and-sitting room. There she watches TV and videos, chats and plays games with Dulcy and me, writes letters to friends and family, keeps a daily journal, and reads. A voracious reader, she goes through a book every day or two, it seems. Still, after awhile even reading loses its appeal. Sometimes Mom will simply sit in her chair and gaze longingly outdoors.

When the weather was warmer, we sometimes went out on the backyard deck. Bathed in sunlight, we listened to birdsong and squirrel chatter, watched the clouds, traded stories. Sometimes I would read to Mom. Now, though, it's far too cold to sit outdoors. So, with the help of songbirds, we've brought a taste of the outdoors inside. Sitting in her favorite chair, a mauve, cushioned rocker, Mom has a perfect spot to watch the birds come in to feed.

Bird watching is nothing new; in fact it's a pleasing tie to her life back east. In Virginia, Mom put seeds in tubes and trays and a roofed feeder built by Dave, my younger brother. (A skilled carpenter and longtime birder, Dave is the one who got Mom interested in bird watching after Dad's death.) Over time, she came to recognize many of the local residents that visited her feeders: tufted titmice, Carolina chickadees, white-breasted nuthatches, blue jays, purple finches, gold-finches, and others.

Here in Alaska, most of the regulars are different, so Mom is starting over. But only a few species show up at our feeders, which simplifies things, and one of those is easily recognizable to her: the black-capped chickadee, which she knows from her Connecticut days (and which are very similar to the Carolina variety).

Instead of white-breasted nuthatches, there are red-breasted ones, with rusty-brown underparts. But again, they're close enough in form and behavior for Mom to make the connection. Unfortunately, the local nuthatch pair disappeared in late November and none have so far returned. Then there are the boreal chickadees, northern members of the chickadee clan, which can be distinguished from black-caps by their gray-brown heads and brown flanks. The largest of our regular visitors are pine grosbeaks, another type of finch. Mom is taken by these robin-sized birds, especially the rose-colored males. "They're just so pretty," she enthuses.

Whenever possible, Mom and I watch the birds together. It's become one of the pleasant activities that have eased the transition into her new home. I point out the differences between boreals and black-caps and explain how the chickadees instinctively cache the seeds in preparation for winter's food shortages. Mom describes an unfamiliar bird she saw in the yard, and piecing together the clues, we decide it must have been a junco. Both of us wince when a bird thumps lightly against the sliding glass door—it flies off, apparently OK—and together we wait for the redpolls.

As winter gives way to spring, other species will join the neighborhood mix, as migrants arrive. But for now, a handful of species is plenty. In fact, though Mom anticipates the overdue redpolls, I think she would be satisfied if only the black-caps showed up. They're her favorite, for reasons that seem to delight so many people: they are peppy, high-spirited creatures that seem to take great joy in being alive. Zooming in and out, pecking at seeds, and singing with gusto, they add brightness to Mom's days. "I get such a kick out of watching the chickadees," she confides. "They boost my spirits. I feel happier just having them around; they're good company."

This is important, because these days Mom needs good company, especially that of family. And Dulcy and I aren't always able to be with her. The chickadees, being familiar, longtime acquaintances, are almost like part of Mom's extended family. Bringing cheer with their hunger, they come around every day, several times a day, welcome guests at our outside table.

FOUR

Connecticut Roots

IT'S THE MOST NATURAL THING, TO WANT TO CONNECT WITH nature. For as much as we humans ignore or deny the fact, we are of nature. It's our original home, the ultimate source of our being, the "environment" in which our ancestors evolved over millions of years. Like many who have studied the origins and evolution of our species, I've come to believe that we carry primal memories of our wild roots, whether it's in our genes or what might be called the human spirit. Human ecologist Paul Shepard argues forcibly (and, I think, convincingly) that we modern, high-tech folks are "genetically wild." Despite any highfalutin notions we may have about our evolved condition, genetically we remain Pleistocene hominids adapted to life in the wilderness. "The savage mind is ours!" he writes in *The Tender Carnivore and the Sacred Game*. "We may be deformed by our circumstances, like obese raccoons or crowded, demented rats, but as a species we have in us the call of the wild." Look in the mirror and what do you see? Wild thing. It's an idea I can live with, joyfully.

For all of the ways that the "natural world" has been diminished and degraded in the past few hundred years, our planet remains a miraculous place, marvelously rich with wild life, from algae and lichens to spiders and frogs, chickadees and grizzlies and, yes, people. No matter where we've chosen to settle—Mexico City, Paris, Calcutta, or Barrow, Alaska—wild nature is manifested all around us, if we only take the time to notice. Even our nation's greatest metropolis, New York City, has its pockets of wildness, Central Park chief among them. As Anne Matthews has documented in *Wild Nights: Nature Returns to the City*, an amazing assortment of critters has penetrated this most intimidating of American urban-culture strongholds: coyotes, deer, herons, even the peregrine falcon. But whether or not you share your neighborhood with falcons or foxes, there is always the sky and the weather. And even the insects that bug us so.

When we're new to the world, I think we sense, we intuit, the wonder and mystery all around us, including others of our own kind. We've all seen the wide-eyed wonder and in-the-moment glee that shines brightly in the eyes of an infant. But as we grow older, we seem to lose that understanding, and, as Loren Eiseley writes in *The Immense Journey*, "tend to take it [the world] for granted." This is especially true in modern high-tech cultures like ours, where, says Eiseley, "We rush to and fro like Mad Hatters upon our peculiar errands, all the time imagining our surroundings to be dull and ourselves quite ordinary creatures."

In our society, and around the world, there's a large and growing disconnect between humans and wild nature. This is old news, of course. Visionary Americans have been telling us so since at least the latter half of the nineteenth century. Yet it continues to happen, at what seems to be an accelerating pace. We grow more and more separate from the "natural world" as our attention increasingly turns toward the technological wonders and distractions of our time: TVs and cell phones, movies and videos, computer games and the Internet, snowmobiles and jet skis, cars and trucks and SUVs. We go from home to car to office or shopping center or health club or movie theater, barely noticing the wider, more-than-human world around us, unless the weather has inconvenienced our busy schedule or a moose steps into traffic.

It's not just in the cities. The residents of Anaktuvuk Pass, a small Nunamiut Eskimo village nestled deep in Alaska's Arctic wilderness, have satellite dishes, televisions, and computers with Internet links. People get around on ATVs and snowmobiles and jets. Native elders in Anaktuvuk Pass and most other Alaskan villages mourn the fact that youngsters are forgetting "the old ways" as they are drawn into the new, that tribes are losing the centuries-old traditions that bonded their people with each other and with the larger community of life.

Kids spend less and less time outdoors. And when they do go outside, it's often to participate in organized sports where the attention is given to the competition, not the surroundings. For children, as for adults, life seems faster paced and more structured than what I recall of my own childhood. In one vivid memory from my early teens, I am playing baseball with several buddies. Only four of us have come to the ball field on this splendid June afternoon, not nearly enough for a game, so we're playing "hit it out": we take turns hitting the ball and fielding. At one point I take a break while the others continue playing. Flopping to the ground, I lie on the field's soft green grass and gaze up into the sky, which is an incredibly rich, soothing blue. A slight breeze tickles my face and bright sunlight warms my skin. Held by both the earth and sky, with my friends' laughter and chatter echoing faintly in the distance, I am as relaxed as I can ever remember. How often does that kind of play happen today? Not often enough, I'd wager.

Kept indoors (by circumstance or choice), youngsters learn less and less about the nature of the places in which they live, even in Alaska, with its wilderness and wildlife riches. When Dulcy taught in the Anchorage School District, she was amazed to learn how few of her students had been to the hills and coastal areas along the city's fringes, or even the parks inside the city. Given the abundant evidence that early experiences greatly influence our later beliefs, passions, and behavior, people's relationship with the greater world—and consequently their empathy with it—has to suffer from this insulation. I suspect that our ability to recognize the miracle of life, and its grand diversity, would suffer as well, along with our ability to love the world.

Over the years I've come across an idea, or belief, that's expressed in various ways by different people who care deeply about the earth and wildness in its many forms, among them Gary Snyder, Jack Turner, Terry Tempest Williams, Richard Nelson—the list goes on and on. What they say and write rings ever more true. And it requires our attention: only in getting to know a place (or person, animal, plant, etc.) can we really learn to love it. And only when we truly love a place are we likely to care for it, protect it, nourish it. We can learn about "the wild" in many ways: from books, TV documentaries, talks, the Internet. But the best way, as Jack Turner puts it, is from knowledge gained "from direct, intimate personal experience." It seems intuitively obvious. Yet how many kids have a firsthand, hands-on relationship with wild nature today?

The "natural world" was an essential part of my boyhood in Trumbull, a place of refuge, play, and healing. Except my buddies and I didn't call it that. To us it was the outdoors. Or even the outside. "I'm going outside, Ma" had all sorts of meanings. It usually meant that homework or house chores had been done, which in turn meant play. Adventure. Freedom. Escape from the rules and demands of adults. Escape from the tyranny of judgments.

THIS, THEN, WAS THE WORLD of my youth, as best as I can reconstruct it more than four decades later. My family and I lived on Old Town Road, a roughly east-west street that was a dividing line of sorts. On the south side of the road was Bridgeport, Connecticut, a large industrial city. To the north—my side of the street—was Trumbull, a still largely rural-suburban community of about thirty-five thousand people in the 1950s. When I was younger, I liked to tell people that Old Town Road marked the edge of rural New England; it wasn't exactly true then, and it's not true at all now. But our neighborhood did have a rural feel to it, especially in the fifties. Ours was among the first houses put up along Old Town Road, or at least the mile-long stretch that I came to consider my home turf. Dad and Uncle Peach built it with their father, just as they built Peach's and Grandpa's houses, a row of three Sherwonit homes separated by large empty lots.

A stern, wiry, white-haired man, William Frederick Sherwonit had settled in Connecticut in the early 1900s after immigrating to the U.S. from Germany. A carpenter by trade, he taught both his sons to be talented builders too. Grandpa's and Dad's skills were then passed on to my brother, who has made a career of carpentry, but I somehow missed out. As an adolescent, I enjoyed my occasional visits to Dad's construction sites, but I didn't care much for the work itself. Nor was I especially talented. Though an excellent student overall, I received only a "fair" in shop class. My parents didn't seem bothered by the middling grade, but I felt embarrassed, being the son of a well-respected carpenter. And naturally, I got razzed by my schoolmates.

Looking back now, two aspects of that neighborhood stand out. First, all of its families were white and middle class, and nearly all were second- and third-generation Christian Americans of Irish or German descent. Second, the neighborhood had lots of open space in which to play. For starters, there were the two empty lots on either side of our own spacious property. Even better, our backyard abutted acres and acres of New England forest. "The Woods," we called it. Our woods. In fact, much of it *was* "ours." My dad inherited nearly two dozen acres of forested land when his father died from a heart attack in 1954, though he'd eventually lose most of it in business dealings that went bad. By my teens, much of those woodlands beyond our house were gone, cut down and replaced by new roads and neighborhoods.

The Woods was open forest, with stands of oak, maple, and pines intermixed with grassy meadows and thick patches of briars and brush. It was hardly pristine; parts of the forest, if not all of it, were second growth, crosshatched by stone walls and trails that marked past human uses. Bounded by neighborhoods and the Merritt Parkway, our patch of New England woods didn't harbor many large animals. My mom tells me that a white-tailed deer or two snuck into our yard to browse in the family garden, but in the two decades or so that I lived in Trumbull, I never had the good luck to see a deer or coyote, let alone a bear or bobcat. Still it was wild and unruly, a place beyond the ordinary, with snakes and skunks, great impenetrable thickets and rocky ledges with hollowed-out spaces that we imagined to be caves; a place filled with the possibility of adventure and discovery. There, hidden from the oversight of parents, we built forts, played war games, staged battles between cowboys and Indians; we climbed trees, hunted for snakes and salamanders, searched for crystals in the gray, lichen-covered rocks. And on the rare occasions when adults were present, it usually meant fun, like target-shooting sessions with Dad and Peach.

We Sherwonit boys would gleefully join our two dads on hikes through the woods to a grassy field bounded by stone walls. There we would set up targets and shoot tin cans, paper plates, and other targets with our .22s. That target shooting was especially pleasing, I think, because it marked one of the few times that Dad would join his kids on outings into the wild. Unlike Peach's family, ours never went on campouts, though my brother, Dave, and I occasionally set up a tent in the backyard. Mom, in fact, never once spent a night inside a tent until she joined Dulcy and me on a trip to Alaska's Katmai National Park in 1992 and camped among Katmai's giant brown bears—at age seventy. It was probably something she would have tried when younger, if things had been different. But as a child growing up in Connecticut, she was plagued by allergies and asthma so bad that camping was out of the question. And later, when married, her occasional suggestions of a family campout were inevitably vetoed by my father.

"Dad liked his comforts," Mom once recalled. "He said he'd done enough camping during World War II. His idea of a campout was to go to a motel."

FOR ME, THE WOODS WAS SOMETHING of a scary place, too, at least in its depths. Whether my anxiety was instilled by my overly protective parents or something of my own creation, I worried I might get lost in the woods if I strayed too far from the paths and glades we knew. I never admitted my fear to anyone, particularly my friends. That would have set me up for unmerciful teasing, the label of scaredy cat. But my lack of confidence limited my explorations. For all my love of the forest, I never ventured far into it alone. I stayed on familiar paths, played at well-known haunts. And when I went with friends, I rarely took the lead if we ventured into unknown territory. The Wallace twins, Barry and Brian, especially seemed to have a knack for going off trail, taking a shortcut through unfamiliar ground, and finding their way back home. I envied that and hoped to God they wouldn't ask me to take a turn up front.

By its simple, nearby presence, the Woods added drama and adventure to our lives, often in the form of snakes. The flicking, forked tongue, the piercing eyes, the sleek, scaled, and limbless body—all of these gave snakes a sort of ominous beauty. Although serpents were a metaphor for temptation and evil in the Bible—or perhaps partly because of that—I found them fantastically alluring. It must have helped, too, that my mother and sister and most girls I knew were afraid of snakes, or considered them disgusting. That gave the creatures a special power, which could in turn be transferred to me, a snake hunter. Other, deeper energies may also have been at play. In his book *Iron John*, Robert Bly describes the snake as "the Lord of the Waters." Mythologically, it is connected to the Wild Man "and other beings who lie in the water at the bottom of our psyches." Snakes have stirred the Wild Man in me for as long as I can remember. I still get excited to find even a common garden snake in the wild and I'm saddened to see any snake held captive.

Besides hunting snakes, I cut their pictures from magazines, collected books filled with their images, and built plastic models of poisonous types that I could safely hold and admire. I wasn't the only one entranced by snakes. It seemed many of my buddies were intrigued by these secretive, slithering reptiles. All of us had snake stories to tell.

Once, Mom was in the backyard hanging clothes and chatting with Aunt Evie, when the two sisters heard a high-pitched squealing from the high grass that bordered the lawn. Approaching the cries, my mother saw a small rabbit fidgeting in the grass. Moving in for a closer look, she then noticed the bunny was being swallowed by a large black snake. As Mom tells the story, she shrieked at the sight. Her yell startled the snake, which let go of the rabbit. "All four of us took off at the same time," she told us later. "I ran one way, Evie ran another way, the rabbit hopped off in a third direction, and the snake slithered off into the grass." It was a grand story, with a happy ending (for the rabbit and sisters, anyway) and we all laughed hysterically at Mom's telling. It became something of a family legend, a story that took on its own life, with the two moms unlikely outdoor heroes.

I wished I'd been there, to see something so unimaginable. At the same time I was glad that Uncle Peach hadn't been around; he'd probably have clobbered the snake.

Another time, we found a black snake poking its head from one of Dad's stone walls. Inside the snake's bulging mouth was a large frog. Only the front of the frog's belly, its front legs, and its head still showed; both its eyes and mouth were wide open, as if the amphibian were shocked by its fate. Though it looked gruesome and we felt badly for the frog, we didn't interfere. I sort of wished to see it end, but the snake pulled back inside the rocks before completely swallowing its meal.

One of the main reasons I went into the Woods was to hunt snakes—not to kill them, but for the fun of the chase and to keep awhile and admire. And maybe I hoped to gain a better sense of something the snakes represented, something forbidden. Or at least something to tread carefully around. We rarely found serpents and even less often caught any. Our parents warned us to be careful, because poisonous copperheads and even an occasional rattler inhabited the forest, but happily for them and us, we never found any.

WE YOUNG ADVENTURERS WERE BLESSED with another nearby wild place to explore. Not much farther than a long stone's throw from our driveway was a small channel that dissected the large empty lot separating our yard from Uncle Peach's. It also drained the Swamp, a boggy place of mud, trees, reeds, frogs, snakes, catfish, crawfish, ducks, and snapping turtles.

The Swamp wasn't very large, just a few hundred feet long and maybe a hundred wide. I suspect that much of it had already been filled in by the road construction and land clearing that opened up our neighborhood. But it was so different from anything else in my small world, it held a special allure. It held mystery. That was especially so in summer, when the bog's waters and muck were rich in strange critters and the stench of gases released by rotting organic matter.

The Swamp also presented some danger, I suspect. Mom certainly believed so. Time and again she warned her two boys to "Stay away!" (Our older sister, Karen, was not a swamp fancier like us; in fact she sometimes acted as something of a guard, ordered by Mom to keep us away from the water.) But the call was too great and we prowled the Swamp's edges, hunting for animals. Now and then we would push inside its boundaries, but never very far. The small islands of dry ground were too few and too far apart to use as stepping-stones; and even where the water was shallow, the black, squishy mud was too deep and clingy for easy walking, even in rubber boots. Our parents warned us there were places where the mud could suck us right in, like quicksand. I wasn't entirely sure about that, but even along the edge, the mud sometimes pulled at my feet, hinting of greater dangers. And I knew I'd get in big trouble if I fell in or got stuck in the mire. Plus, the Swamp held snapping turtles. Uncle Peach caught a huge one in his net and hauled it onto his lawn while a crowd gathered round. He held a broom handle in front of the turtle, which was bigger than a watermelon, to show us its strength. The snapper didn't break the handle, but once he grasped it, he wouldn't let go, even when shot with a .22. Peach had to shoot the snapper several times before it would die.

In winter, of course, the Swamp froze over, so its inner parts were easy to explore. We skated there, among the trees and tiny islands, stood around bonfires that our parents sometimes built, played games like steal the flag. But the Swamp itself was dormant then; it didn't really come alive until spring and summer. That's when it was most fun to visit.

Mostly I just wanted to catch things, and plenty of life-forms inhabited the Swamp's edges, so I really didn't mind staying on the fringes. The cider-colored water was a marvel in itself, with its assemblage of strange aquatic insects. Long-legged pond skaters—which we knew as water striders—streaked lightly and swiftly across the surface as they hunted other insects or escaped my approach. Shiny black whirligig beetles danced in wildly gyrating groups, their circular paths turning the sun's reflection into dozens of swirling and sparkling explosions of light.

In any scoop of water I might find all sorts of beetles and other aquatic bugs, including one type named water boatmen for their long, oarlike back legs. As a boy, I simply knew them as diving bugs. When not actively swimming, they would sink to the bottom, to feed on marsh plants. Another, similar-looking group of divers were the backswimmers; as their name suggests, they swim on their backs. And these buoyant insects float, rather than sink, when stationary. I wouldn't learn until much later that backswimmers, unlike their vegetarian relatives, are voracious predators that feed on everything from moths to fish and tadpoles. If I'd had an insect book, I might have learned that curious kids risk a painful sting when handling backswimmers. Instead I learned that lesson the hard way: playing in our swamp one day, I reached down and grabbed a diving bug—and felt the sharp prick of a sting or bite. I always wondered if I'd imagined the sting, but that was the last diver I handled so carelessly.

Besides the myriad bugs, the Swamp was summer home to legions of tadpoles, or pollywogs as we usually called them. They hugged the mucky bottom or attached themselves to the submerged stalks of aquatic plants and moved, in tail-wiggling fashion, through the dark water. The coolest tadpoles were the ones becoming frogs, their bodies being transformed as tiny appendages became legs, the tail was lost, and gills gave way to lungs. If that amphibian metamorphosis couldn't evoke surprise and wonder, nothing could. Holding one of those pollywogs was like grabbing a bit of magic.

Several types of frogs inhabited the Swamp, from tiny peepers to leopard frogs, pickerel frogs, green frogs, and huge bullfrogs. I grew to love the songs of frogs; they're among the summer sounds I've missed the most since moving north, along with the chirps of crickets and buzz of cicadas.

Curiously, Mom tells me now that when my family moved to Old Town Road in 1953, I was initially terrified by the eerie noises coming from the Swamp. Only three years old, I would awake and cry in fright; my parents had to assure me over and over that "it's only frogs, nothing that will hurt you" before I let go my fear and welcomed the strange sounds.

Some of my most vivid early memories echo with frog songs. In one, I'm sitting on the back porch with my dad after an extended-family barbecue. There is a cacophony of laughter and loud conversation inside the brightly lit house, but my attention goes to the frogs and their sweet summer serenade.

Another time I'm standing at my sister's window; the glass pane is raised and I push my head against the screen, toward the Swamp. Peering into the darkness, I feel the warm, humid breath of a midsummer night, and I listen to a two-part orchestra. The deep bass croaking of bullfrogs mixes with high-pitched peeps of spring peepers. The calls draw me out of ordinary time, deep into the night, and I feel a soothing calmness.

One of my strongest and most delicious childhood memories is this: the echoing of frog songs, the brilliant flashes of fireflies in the darkening night, and the feel of grass against head and back as I study a star-studded sky, searching for meteors. Frogs, lightning bugs, and shooting stars are night mysteries, and I have no desire to understand, but only to marvel as I'm pulled toward something infinitely grander.

I regularly hunted frogs for years, sometimes with friends but more often alone. They were more abundant than snakes or turtles, easier to find and catch—and they didn't bite or snap. Sometimes we used nets, but more often we used our hands. Nets seemed like cheating, somehow. Occasionally we'd find frogs on shore, but usually we hunted them as they floated in the Swamp, only their heads above water, with front legs pushed forward and long back legs stretched out below, as if suspended in a jump. Moving slowly, we'd sneak up behind a frog, until within grabbing range. If it hadn't spooked, we'd lunge for its hindquarters and try to snatch the long back legs. More often than not, we missed. If the frog dived, we'd try to follow its shadowy, streamlined form through the murky water to its hiding place behind a sunken branch or under dark, decaying plants. Then we'd feel around in the muck, waiting for the touch of that smooth, slippery skin. If successful in the hunt, we'd hold the frog by the hind legs, its squirming arched-forward body quieting in the grasp.

Sometimes we'd let the frogs go right away; other times we'd put them in a bucket of water, haul them to the house, and keep them a few hours or even overnight. We'd catch grasshoppers and crickets to feed the frogs, but usually they'd ignore our offerings. The chase and catch were the main things when hunting. And making that brief connection with the mysterious Other.

Sadly the Swamp, like the Woods, was diminished during my teens. In a sense, it was tamed, by being "cleaned out" and made into a pond. Most of my neighbors liked the change, including many of my friends, who began calling it "Sherwonit's Pond." Many, if not all, of the same critters occupied its waters and margins. And after Uncle Peach stocked the pond, it became a neighborhood fishing hole for bass, pickerel, and bluegills. It was also the place we'd net "shiners," tiny minnows we used for bait on fishing excursions to other waters. The pond was better for skating in winter and you could row a boat around it in summer. But something was lost in the process. Much of the place's natural allure, its sense of otherness, had been removed with the trees and muck and other swamp life. Now it was more people-friendly. But to me that wasn't necessarily a good thing.

AS OUR FORAYS INTO THE WOODS made clear, I wasn't especially adventurous when measured against my friends. I was content to stay in the known, nearby wild, never venturing far from the familiar. Even there, were mysteries aplenty.

Though a rather timid outdoorsman, I craved the outdoors. The Woods and Swamp and even the yard were my refuge, places where I could escape family feuds and tensions and the roles I'd learned to play: the good and obedient son, the good student, the choir boy. Expectations and judgments dropped away. I could be more myself. Curiously, given my fears of getting physically lost in the Woods, I could easily lose my self in nature, at least the judgmental self. In the community of humans, it seemed that people were always judging each other. And of course God was omnipresent, watching, watching. Being good Christians, my family, friends, and I had to set a good example to the rest of the world. Of course the standard was impossibly high: perfection.

Complicating things was this fact: using the Bible as their evidence, my parents, pastor, and teachers hammered home the fact that, by nature, humans were sinful. Bad. We had to guard against our sinful tendencies and the influence of Satan. Being a sensitive sort, I took these lessons seriously. For all my talents and good behavior, I came to believe I wasn't good enough. I sure tried, though.

Outdoors, especially by myself, I didn't have to try. I could simply be me, while doing what I loved. As if by a miracle, the judgments vanished—if only for awhile—as I hunted frogs and snakes, fished for rainbow trout with Uncle Peach, explored the Woods, or skated across the frozen swamp. Nature drew me out of myself, into something bigger. I still can't define that something bigger, but it had nothing to do with religion; and unlike my Lutheran God, it wasn't judgmental, though sometimes it could be brutal or scary. Nor did it seem indifferent. It's often said that wilderness—or, more generally, wild nature—is indifferent to the fate of humans: the wilderness doesn't care if a person drowns while crossing a stream or is killed by an avalanche or hypothermia or a bear. Yet I sensed something else. I don't know if it was nature itself or something even bigger than nature, some creative force or energy. But I felt accepted by the natural world. As a young boy I sensed a beneficence that was out there but somehow included me. Sometimes I sense it even now. I suppose it may simply be my projection, but I don't think so.

Another memory, perhaps distilled from many childhood nights. Again I'm standing at a window, this time in my own bedroom, facing west. It's late at night and Dave is breathing softly just a few feet away. His face, turned toward me, looks so peaceful. I'm restless, unable to sleep. Maybe I've been having nightmares or I've heard my parents quarreling. I place my hands against the knotty pine wall, lean my head against the glass, and look out into the night. Deep inside, a longing wells up. I need hope. I need to know I fit in, somehow, somewhere.

I gaze toward a familiar form, an old oak tree that's perched upon a knob above the house next door. It used to be Grandpa's place, but the Seperack family lives there now. The season must be fall or winter, because the great tree's limbs are bare. Standing black against the sky and dominating the horizon, the oak is at first a huge skeleton, then something more. Maybe some combination of the darkness, my own mood, and night's way of shifting perception initiates the transformation, as the tree takes on an undefinable presence, beyond its usual grandness. It's the strangest thing, as if the tree is a wise old being who's somehow aware of me. Yet that recognition is somehow more calming than frightening. I wonder what secrets such a grandfather tree might hold.

After awhile, my attention is drawn from oak to sky. It's a clear night, a starry night, and as my thoughts move among the stars, I try to imagine infinity, endless space. That leads me to thoughts of eternity, time without end, everlasting life. Of course such ideas are impossible to grasp, so I settle for something else: wonder. I shrink in size, humbled by the immense grandeur of the universe, the untold numbers of suns, many of them dwarfing our own. My life, in this context, is so tiny, so insignificant. Yet, paradoxically, my life takes on greater meaning: to be part of such a mystery is a blessing. Life truly is a miracle and I am part of that miracle, along with oak and snake and swamp bug. In my own boyish way, I come to sense a sort of holiness—and wholeness—that I don't get from religion. And a voice, or something like it, whispers out of the night: You are safe. You are cared for.

FIVE

Hunting Anchorage's Frogs

IT IS THE LAST NIGHT OF APRIL, 1998. RETURNING TO MY HILLSIDE home after a show at Anchorage's Performing Arts Center, I detour to Westchester Lagoon. Shortly before 10 p.m., I step out of the car and walk to the water's edge. In fading daylight, I listen for frogs.

Though arguably peculiar, my behavior isn't as silly—or hopeless—as it might first appear, given that I live in Alaska. Or so I tell Dulcy when explaining why we must take both my Toyota and her Subaru to the dance performance (she having no desire to either join my vigil or wait in the car). Here's a polished version of my spiel: Anchorage, like much of Alaska, is home to *Rana sylvatica*, the wood frog, a remarkable creature whose range spans North America from east to west—and the only amphibian known to inhabit Arctic Alaska. Overlooked or ignored by most of the city's human residents, wood frogs occupy wetlands and forests throughout the Anchorage Bowl. On the smallish side as frogs go, adults are one to three inches long and bronze to dark brown in color, with a distinctive dark eye mask. Their mating—and calling—season begins in late April and extends into May. Thus the timing of my trip to Westchester Lagoon.

I regurgitate these facts now with full confidence, but must confess to being among the ignorant masses until joining two dozen other amphibophiles at a March '98 meeting to organize Anchorage's first-ever frog-monitoring program. Put simply, the plan is this: volunteer monitors choose survey sites throughout the bowl. Then, using established standards we will determine the approximate abundance of frogs, as well as the start, peak, and cessation of calling periods. Surveyors are also asked to describe the habitat at each census locale and note weather conditions when listening. If frogs are seen—which they're most often not—participants are also asked to look for deformities. As anyone interested in frogs already knows, over the past decade researchers have documented a startling, widespread occurrence of frogs and other amphibians with missing or extra limbs, missing eyes, or other disfigurements.

Anchorage "frogwatch" organizers Kristin Simac and Ann Garibaldi are the first to admit this local citizen effort does not entail a scientifically rigorous approach. But it's a start, and some sort of database is better than none.

My three monitoring sites are on the Hillside, where breakup—and therefore frog mating—occurs later in spring than most of Anchorage. Wood frogs spend their winters on land, buried among leaf litter, moss, grasses, and soil. Before breeding can begin, both ground and frogs must thaw—more on that later—and ice-covered ponds and lakes must open up. For most of Anchorage, the necessary meltdown usually occurs in mid- to late April; on the Hillside, it doesn't happen until May.

Hoping to study up on frog calls, I've asked Garibaldi where to practice my listening skills. She suggests Westchester Lagoon, where froggers have already heard *sylvatica* love songs. Among wood frogs (and most other frog species), only the males sound off. Biologists sometimes refer to their vocalizations as "advertisement calls," because they are intended both to attract females and to announce a fella's territory to rival suitors. There's only one problem: I've never heard wood frogs call. All I know is that they're supposed to have a staccato ducklike quack.

So here I am at the lagoon's edge, standing quietly and listening, occasionally swiveling my head to and fro to maximize my auditory range. But all I hear are screeching mew gulls, rushing wind, distant humming traffic, and quacking ducks. There's no confusion about the source of these recognizable quacks, as I watch mallards and pintails jabbering among themselves.

Frustrated by the cacophonous racket, I stay only five or ten minutes, then proceed to a second frog-calling spot identified by Garibaldi, this one a small pond in western Anchorage, near the city's international airport. I'd surely have missed it, if not on this mission, but I will later find this roadside puddle and its surrounding meadow to be a life-filled wonder. I'll even give it a name: Airport Pond.

The time is now 10:12, a few minutes past sunset. Not that the sky has changed perceptibly; it has been thickly overcast and steel gray all day and evening. What's important about the time is that wood frogs (like others of their kind) call most aggressively after twilight. Given this behavior, standard North American protocol requires frogwatch participants to monitor calls one half hour after sunset. That's no big deal in most places, but here in Alaska it means late nights by lakeside, given the April–May mating season. So the half-hour-after-sunset rule is more suggestion than dictate.

Any hopes of a quieter setting are dashed long before I roll to a stop. Even at this hour, the airport and surrounding landscape are immersed in the metallic whines and thunderous rumbling of jet engines. To make things worse, late-night road warriors speed by in pickups and SUVs. Such obnoxious noise is enough to drive a frog monitor nuts. Between wind and motorized mayhem I don't know what else I'll hear, but one circumstance favors my attempt: no ducks. Any quacking will come from frogs, not fowl.

I linger and listen in the gusty, damp night air. Minutes pass. I'm frustrated, angry at the jarring screeches and roars of jets coming and going. *AAARGH.* About to concede defeat, I hear it: a faint call. It does sound a little bit like a duck. But I would describe it as almost a gulp. Or a hiccup. That's it, a quacklike hiccup. Or hiccupy quack? The frog speaks once, twice, three times. Then once more the pond falls silent, while the rest of my surrounding world remains a mechanized roar. Several more minutes pass. I walk along the pond's edge, hoping for a better vantage point. Over there: more hiccuping. It's been less than ideal, but I've heard my first Anchorage frogs. Weary but pleased, I head home to share my small triumph with Dulcy, who kindly indulges this newest fancy of mine.

I BEGIN MONITORING MY HILLSIDE neighborhood for frogs in early May, but for more than a week I hear nothing that resembles the hiccupy quacks of Airport Pond. The three sites include my property, which has some small boggy pools (a long shot at best, but I'd hate to miss frogs in my own backyard); a man-made pond along Hillside Drive; and Hideaway Lake, a boot-shaped body of water bounded by more than a dozen homes with large grassy yards. Interspersed with the manicured lawns are small natural stretches of spruce-birch forest and thick alder-willow patches.

Hideaway Lake is by far my best bet, but access is limited by the surrounding private property. Fortunately there's one small sliver of shoreline that I can reach from O'Malley Road, near a natural-gas pipeline station. The station gives off a loud *hissssssss*, but when I crouch beside the water's edge, it's muffled.

Among its other lessons, this frog-monitoring program has forced me to notice the abundant noise that we urban residents live with daily—and largely ignore. Even late at night, along Anchorage's wild edge, there's a steady rush of traffic along Hillside streets, the overhead rumble of jets, the loud barking of dogs, the motorized throbbing of lawn mowers, the pounding of hammers. Almost lost in the auditory chaos are the sweetly warbled tunes of songbirds, the winnowing of snipe, the rush of wind through leaves, the hiccupy songs of frogs. Quiet is a fragile, elusive state.

The suspense ends May 10, beneath overcast skies that threaten rain—or perhaps sleet. The air temperature is thirty-five degrees Fahrenheit when I arrive at Hideaway Lake, a light breeze rippling the lake. Squatting beside alders and birches still days away from green-up, I hear the calls of lovesick frogs, their hiccupy gulps faint but distinct. My mood uplifted by the assurance that frogs inhabit the neighborhood, I begin my three-minute survey at 10:47. There's some overlapping of calls, but I can easily distinguish individuals. That makes it a 2, on a scale of 0 (no calls) to 3 (full chorus of constant, overlapping calls).

I monitor my sites eight more times over the next three weeks. Only Hideaway Lake yields frog calls and even there I never hear a full-blown chorus. My highest count is six males, but that's a guesstimate at best. It's no easy thing to distinguish one frog from another when they're hiccuping two hundred to three hundred yards away. Hideaway's calling period lasts from May 10 to May 29, with a peak on May 14—nearly three weeks behind Airport Pond.

Every night's singing has the feel of a small miracle; frogs simply don't fit my image of far north critter. The surprise is mixed with pleasure and perhaps a touch of longing, because I so closely associate frogs with my first homeland, Connecticut.

I wonder too if frogs will expand my awareness as Alaska's songbirds have. For most of my life I barely noticed passerines or their songs. But once they got my attention in 1993, chickadees and other songbirds added a whole new dimension to the world. Now I notice them every day, with great delight. They enrich my walks through woods and tundra, heighten my attention to seasonal cycles and different habitats. In spring and early summer, with the arrival of migrant species, birds are everywhere it seems, filling yard, neighborhood, and surrounding lands with all manner of melodies. Birds—and now northern frogs—remind me to pay attention, be open to possibilities. Again I wonder what else is out there, waiting to be discovered?

TWENTY PEOPLE—SCHOOLKIDS, PROFESSIONALS, retirees—participate in Anchorage's first frog survey. Together we monitor some sixty lakes, ponds, and puddles, finding vocal evidence of frogs at two-thirds of those sites. If plotted on a map, the initial data would show Anchorage's frog-inhabited waters to be concentrated on the city's west side; but that likely reflects a survey bias: most participants chose the Campbell–Jewel Lakes area.

When coordinator Kristin Simac later compiles and analyzes the 1998 data, this is some of what she finds: Anchorage frogs were heard in air temperatures ranging from twenty-nine to fifty-seven degrees, for periods of five to thirty-eight days. The large majority of calling began April 20–23 and, in keeping with wood frogs' reputation as "explosive breeders," activity peaked during the first week, then fell off rapidly. Call counts were highest on clear-sky nights and lowest during rains. And wind had no noticeable effect.

Besides compiling Anchorage's citizen surveys, Simac is studying wood frogs for her thesis at Alaska Pacific University. She's looked at where females lay eggs, to determine preferred breeding habitats (it appears they favor near-shore sedges and shallow-sloped pond bottoms), and followed the timetable of their metamorphosis from eggs to frogs. Locally, as in the Lower 48, eggs hatch after about five days and tadpoles then gradually transform into frogs over a two-month period. "Once they get froggy," she says, "they disappear [onto land] within ten days."

One other thing about wood frogs: they are much, much easier to hear than see. In 133 calling-site visits between April 22 and May 28, Simac finds only eight frogs. I see none at Hideaway Lake, but I'm limited to just a few feet of shoreline. Studies done elsewhere suggest that adult wood frogs abandon their watery breeding grounds soon after mating and spend most of their lives in moist grasslands, tundra, or open forest (hence the name). But little is known about the specifics of their terrestrial travels. Or how they disappear so quickly and completely.

"Where do Anchorage's frogs go after mating?" Simac wonders. "What do they do?" She'd love to try catching frogs in pitfall traps, but for now other demands—school, kids, other wildlife studies—take precedence. Up in Fairbanks, University of Alaska Fairbanks researcher Brian Barnes and some graduate students have followed the movements of wood frogs, using tiny radio transmitters. There, frogs have hopped more than a quarter mile from breeding waters.

Barnes and his students are also responsible for the little that's known about wintering adaptations of far north frogs. All six of his radio-tagged subjects survived a Fairbanks winter while huddled beneath snow and soil. "All of them dug into the soil, but not deeply," he says. "They were about one inch deep in leaf litter, three to four inches deep in sphagnum moss, or just barely buried in sand." The insulating abilities of snow keep ground temperatures at twenty to twenty-three degrees even as air temperatures sink to minus forty or below.

In an experiment he didn't intend, Barnes left several other frogs in an uninsulated crate outside his home and then forgot about his subjects. Temperatures fell to minus ten degrees, freezing them solid. Barnes naturally figured the frogs were dead meat. But when moved inside his heated garage, the frozen bodies gradually thawed. As they defrosted, the frogs began to twitch, then hop around. Scientists don't fully understand the mechanisms at work, but they believe the animals survive such frogcicle states through a biochemical process that converts body starches to glucose. In flooding a wood frog's cells, the glucose somehow prevents frozen body tissue from being lethal. This physiological marvel, combined with snow's insulating abilities, enables wood frogs to survive the extreme cold of Interior Alaska's winters.

I AM DETERMINED TO CATCH some Anchorage wood frogs, inspect them for deformities, so Ann Garibaldi suggests I try the black spruce wetlands behind the

YWCA. "I worked there a couple summers ago," she says, "and kids were catching so many I had to ask them to stop."

I visit the spot on a warm and bright July afternoon. Crossing through a meadow I come to the edge of the bog, then follow a path that wanders among spindly spruce trees, tall grasses, dwarf birches, cotton grass, and several types of berry plants. The ground is damp and spongy, muddy in places. But there are no large pools of water in this part of the wetlands and I get around easily in knee-high rubber boots. Almost immediately I'm swarmed by flies and mosquitoes; they give me space after a few squirts of bug juice.

I find my first frog in less than ten minutes. One of this year's brood, it could almost fit on my thumbnail. Dark brown in color, the frog has tiny black spots and squigglings on its back, and a thicker dark band on its face—the so-called "eye mask." A whitish "lip line" runs along the mouth, beneath the mask. The frog appears normal. It has the right number of limbs and eyes, no apparent deformities. Returning it to the ground I resume my quest and find nine more frogs during the next hour. They are surprisingly elusive and I feel my chase instincts being resurrected as they attempt to escape. Once in high grass they're almost impossible to find. Of the ten, I catch six—not bad for someone who's been out of the frog-catching business for decades. Some are brown, others bronze. All seem healthy, I'm happy to report, no matter that my sample size is small.

I hunt frogs again in August. After catching six—all young and seemingly healthy—behind the YWCA, I revisit Airport Pond. I circle it once, twice, without a sighting. After nearly a half hour of fruitless searching, I stumble across an adult frog in tall grass, fifteen feet from water. The frog becomes a brown blur; darting rapidly, changing directions, it disappears before I can even lunge. Several minutes later I find a second adult, about a hundred feet from my first sighting. Determined to catch this one, I corner it among a clump of grasses. Cupping my hands around it, I bring the frog in for a closer look—and find it has escaped. Continuing to comb the area, I rediscover my quarry. Grabbing quickly, I snatch it up. With its legs folded, the frog isn't much larger than a silver dollar, fitting comfortably in the palm of my hand. The frog is bronze, with irregular black splotches on its back and sides, a creamy underside, and black eye mask. Like the others, it seems healthy: limbs are in working order with no extra or missing parts. Eyes seem normal. No obvious deformities.

The frog sits stoically until I try stretching out its legs. Then it squirms, tries to get away. OK, no reason to continue harassing the animal. I put it back among the grasses, where it blends perfectly with the ground. In one hour here I see three frogs, catching two. Heading to my car, I wonder how many cross the road—or try. I do a quick check, see no evidence of squashed frogs, but imagine at least a few get mashed each summer.

I periodically go on other hunts. By summer's end I've caught and examined about twenty frogs, none malformed that I can tell. Elsewhere, a one-eyed frog is reported from Eklutna and Simac hears about two deformed frogs in the Mat-Su Valleys, one found in Knik, another in Talkeetna. Information is sketchy and the database is tiny, but it appears Alaska has escaped mass deformities like those found elsewhere in North America. (That will change in 2000, when researchers find twenty-six deformed frogs during a survey of sixteen ponds on Alaska's Kenai National Wildlife Refuge, or six percent of all frogs captured. But there's still nothing to suggest Anchorage's frogs have yet been harmed by disease, pollutants, or other environmental shifts.)

JUMP NOW TO JUNE 1999. I'm back at Airport Pond, searching for egg clusters. But it's already too late. Eggs have hatched into tadpoles, or pollywogs as I sometimes called them as a boy. Dark, squiggly spermlike forms, they are a quarter- to half-inch long, with large, oval "heads" and thin tails. Some of the tadpoles seem to float, hanging suspended near the water's surface. Others hide upon the pond-bottom muck or attach themselves to the stalks of rushes.

Roaming around the pond margins I see hundreds of tadpoles, which share the tea-colored water with water bugs of all kinds—including some that prey on frog larvae. Among their chief predators are diving beetles, giant water bugs, and dragonfly nymphs, all present here in considerable abundance.

I discover one tadpole in the grasp of an insect larvae with outsized jaws. With the dip net I've brought, I scoop the pair out of the pond and separate them. It seems to be part of our human nature, this penchant for meddling in the natural order. The tadpole is already mortally wounded, so I return it to its killer—and the insect larvae quickly latches back on with its pincers.

Only a small fraction of these many tadpoles—perhaps as few as one or two percent—will survive to become reproducing adults. Around the pond's perimeter are some of their parents. I count ten frogs along water's edge among sedges and rushes. All quickly dive for cover.

MORE LEAPS FORWARD: one year, two years, three, and more. Ann Garibaldi left Anchorage's frogwatch program after the first summer, leaving Kristin Simac alone to coordinate volunteers. Given other responsibilities, Simac too eventually stopped promoting the citizen surveys. Without leadership, the number of participants dwindled rapidly, from twenty volunteers in 1998 to a handful in 1999. Nowadays, only a few local diehards continue to check on Anchorage's frogs each spring, me among them.

While the citywide monitoring has ended, my own fascination with wood frogs remains high. One May afternoon I visit Airport Pond determined to find frog-egg masses, and discover more than I ever expected: twenty-three in all. Many are loosely attached to the stalks of pond sedges, within a few feet of shore. I briefly pull a couple egg clumps from the water, gingerly hold them in my hand. Soft and squishy, they roll around in my palm like incompletely hardened Jell-O, ooze between my fingers. They are crudely round in shape, in sizes that approximate tennis balls to softballs. Some of the translucent gelatin masses are colorless, others are stained green to brown by algae and pond muck.

Already, some eggs have begun to hatch. Some are tightly curled into animate commas. Others are clearly recognizable as tadpoles, with large rounded heads and narrow wriggling tails. The tadpoles cling to the egg masses or nearby sedges, a grouping behavior that may be a defensive response to predators. Later they'll disperse throughout the pond. Simac took apart four egg masses for her thesis project and counted six hundred to one thousand eggs per cluster. This one small pond will produce tens of thousands of tadpoles, a remarkable number.

Curious about the distribution of local frogs, I listen for them whenever I'm near lakes or ponds, or even ditches filled with water. I hear them at Connors Bog in late afternoon, at Potter Marsh and roadside ponds behind the marsh when driving home from evening hikes, in puddled wetlands near Earthquake Park.

I also keep my eyes open for their bronzed jumping forms, because you never know where or when they'll appear. I once spotted a wood frog as it scrambled along the forest floor beside the Turnagain Arm Trail, far from any pool of water that I know of. I crossed paths with another while hiking the Kesugi Ridge Trail, in Denali State Park. Another time a friend nearly stepped on a frog as we crossed wet, swampy tundra in the Arctic. Scarcely believing his eyes, he called out, "You're not gonna believe this . . ." I did, of course, and three of us searched for ten or fifteen minutes, but the frog had found a hiding spot from which it refused to budge.

Every spring for as long as I live on the Hillside, I return to Hideaway Lake and watch as small channels of water gradually widen, until by mid-May (and sometimes earlier) the lake is ice free. Night after night I settle into my usual spot and listen to the honking of geese, the hiss of the natural-gas station, the buzz of traffic. Soon, I know, I'll hear the now-familiar call of wood frogs. Their hiccupy voices have become as much a part of my annual spring celebration as birdsong, walks through greening forests, and yard cleanup, a prelude to Alaska's short but remarkably rich spring and summer seasons. Thousands of miles and dozens of years from my boyhood neighborhood, I have rediscovered the pleasures of hunting frogs and listening to their love songs.

SIX

Airport Pond

An Urban Tale of Discovery and Loss

THE DAY IS A BEAUTY, ONE OF THE FINEST AN ALASKAN COULD ever imagine or desire: spacious blue skies, a few scattered cottonball clouds floating across the heavens, temperatures in the mid-sixties—but much warmer to the skin in direct sunlight—with a gentle, cooling breeze and air that's been cleaned and freshened by recent rains.

It's the sort of summer day that tugs a person outdoors and inspires one to go exploring, even demands it. Normally I might spend such a day hiking forested trails along Anchorage's edges or scrambling up ridges in the neighboring Chugach Mountains. Today, however, I have chosen to muck around in a roadside pond, along the western edge of the Anchorage International Airport.

Instead of solitude and quiet, I am immersed in the noisy mechanized whine and roar of jets, float planes, cars, and trucks. Today, this does not matter, for I am a man on a mission: I've come looking for frogs and their eggs.

This airport pond was not one of my assigned Anchorage survey sites, but it was here that I first heard the hiccupy late-night mating songs of male wood frogs. More than a year later, I've come not for mating music but to find and observe the jellylike egg masses deposited by female frogs and fertilized by males. Instead, I get two surprises: first, the eggs have already hatched to produce hundreds, if not thousands, of wriggling dark-brown tadpoles; second, the pond is teeming with strange, minuscule life-forms.

The pond itself is not much to look at and most people who drive Point Woronzof Road pay it little attention, if they notice it at all. Sixty paces long and fifteen across at its widest point, the pool is hardly more than an oversized puddle that's nestled between the road and a barbed-wire–topped chain-link fence with airport No Trespassing signs.

It's likely a man-made wetland, formed during road construction. Yet since its birth, and despite its location, the pond and its surrounding meadow have become a place of unexpected vitality and diversity. A pair of ducks nests among shoreline grasses and sedges and moose leave tracks in mud along the pond's edges. Songbirds—robins, juncos, sparrows, and swallows—perch on the airport fence; forage along the ground among dandelions, fireweed, and wild rose bushes; or swoop through the air while feasting on insects. Some, I suspect, have built nests in the area's thick grasses and its willow and alder bushes, or perhaps across the road in birch-cottonwood forest.

Yellow-brown dragonflies and loudly buzzing bumblebees dart along the pond's edge, while iridescent blue damselflies—as kids, my friends and I called them "sewing needles"—hover delicately and prettily on gossamer wings. And orb-weaving spiders build complex webs and hide in alder leaves they've wrapped into tunnel-like lairs with their silk.

I scribble descriptions of the many pond-side creatures I encounter on this bright Sunday afternoon. But the water is what most grabs my attention. There are the frogs, of course, and their pollywog offspring. Circling the pond I spot ten adults. I hope to catch some, to check for deformities, but most dive for cover before I get close. The one frog I do capture appears healthy; after a quick inspection of its brownish-bronze body I release it back into the water. Pollywogs, meanwhile, hug the pond's mucky bottom, attach themselves to the submerged stalks of water horsetails, and swim, in tail-wiggling fashion, through the pond's darkly tea-colored water. Using a plastic sifter I borrowed from the kitchen, I scoop several half-inch-long tadpoles from the pond and see that some already appear to be growing tiny appendages that will become legs.

Frogs and tadpoles share the water with a remarkably strange, yet familiar, assemblage of aquatic insects. I first encountered many of these same (or similar) species while exploring a neighborhood swamp so many miles away and years ago.

The more I look the more I am drawn into the underwater world of tadpoles, boatmen, diving beetles, and even more alien larval forms. Stepping into the shallows with my hip boots, I sink several inches into the mud, squat down, and enter something that approaches a hypnotic trance. I'm reminded of the documentary film *Microcosmos: The Invisible World of Insects*, which so marvelously takes viewers into the overlooked yet wondrous "little universe" to be found within a grassy meadow. It is a revelation to see the magnified shapes, colors, behaviors—and beauty—of tiny creatures rarely noticed or appreciated.

I can't imagine that even the most bug-loathing person could see *Microcosmos* and come away from it still believing insects to be nothing more than pests. Running my hand through the pond's muddy bottom and studying the odd shapes and remarkable adaptations of its inhabitants, I wish for a similarly enlarged bug's-eye view of this watery little universe.

I'm also reminded of the many hours I spent as a young and curious boy, exploring the Swamp near my Old Town Road home. More than four decades later, I find myself marveling at this small, ordinary, and urban Airport Pond. And for a couple hours, I'm pulled back into that vaguely familiar place of enchantment and playfulness I knew so well as a boy. Netting bugs and sifting through pond muck, I'm again reminded that wildness and delight are sometimes to be found in the most unlikely ways and unexpected places.

LEAP FORWARD SEVERAL YEARS, to the month of April.

Nearing the end of an evening walk along Anchorage's Coastal Trail, I hear a familiar, pleasing voice. Somewhere across Northern Lights Boulevard, wood frogs are singing. It's the first time I've heard them this year, so I ask Dulcy if she would accompany me across the road and listen a few minutes.

In between the passing of cars and the landing of jets at the nearby international airport, we hear the frogs' curious quacklike, hiccupy calls, another sure sign that spring has arrived in Southcentral Alaska. The amphibian love songs that jump out from these small wetland puddles remind me of nearby Airport Pond, a spot I've been meaning to visit. It's late and we're both tired. But Dulcy graciously agrees to make a detour and head to the pond, which has become one of my local favorites.

We're driving down the road, getting close, when I sense something is different. Something is wrong. When we get to the spot, my gut clenches and my spirit sinks. "Oh, no," I loudly moan. "I can't believe they did this."

The pond is gone, plowed over by sand and gravel, part of the airport's expansion.

I do a U-turn and park the car. Everything is gone: the water, the sedges and reeds, the mud, the frogs, the nesting ducks, the surrounding meadow. If I didn't know a pond had once been here, I would never guess it now. Understanding my sadness, Dulcy says she's sorry for the loss. Then we sit in silence a few moments before leaving.

On the drive home I keep thinking about the pond's destruction, which in turn stirs thoughts of other local losses. In recent years, as I've made it my mission to learn more about Anchorage's urban wildness, I've discovered places that I never before noticed, or even imagined—ordinary places with their own bit of magic.

Airport Pond was one. Anchorage's coastal flats and the city's wooded Bicentennial Park are others. Yet a number of discoveries have all too soon been followed by upsetting losses.

Near a trail that I now walk regularly, twenty-five forested acres of Bicentennial Park are going to be cleared and converted into Little League fields. And two of the already-few access points to Anchorage's Coastal Wildlife Refuge are being eliminated, as builders put up new houses. A small open space atop a bluff, one of those lots has been an outstanding place to get sweeping views of the coastal flats and its annual springtime gathering of cranes, geese, shorebirds, and raptors. I only began going there last year; now it's about to become someone's yard, closed off to the public.

Anchorage remains blessed with abundant parks and greenbelts and wetlands and creeks where salmon still spawn, but the losses keep adding up. It's only natural, I suppose, that the more I get to know the city's landscape, the more I notice what's disappearing.

With each new loss, I've felt sadness and disappointment, sometimes mixed with anger at the choices our community has made. But the pond's destruction hits me especially—surprisingly—hard.

By most standards, it's a small loss, easy to overlook. I'd guess that many people who drive Point Woronzof Road haven't noticed, or at least don't care, that the pond is gone. Yet since I first visited it five years ago, I've found this urban roadside pond and surrounding meadow to be a place of unexpected vitality and diversity. And, yes, magic.

Over the years, it's become one of the spots I faithfully visit to celebrate the arrival of spring and the passage of summer. In other words, Airport Pond has become a special place, filled with memories and small delights. I know that many such places remain scattered throughout my adopted hometown; and I'm confident that I'll discover others that will grab hold of me and become special in their own enchanting ways. But for now I can only mourn the passing of this pond, this loss of habitat and life, however small. And my loss, too.

SEVEN

Living with Bears

ON A SUNNY MORNING IN EARLY JULY, RICK SINNOTT LEAVES HIS Fish and Game office and, with sidekick Chris Kleckner, drives north from Anchorage to Eagle River Valley on yet another house call. Already this summer, Rick has received hundreds of phone messages from local residents, some calm and others frantic, alerting him, "There's a bear in my neighborhood. Do something!" As wildlife manager for the Anchorage area, he must decide which situations warrant immediate attention. The one in Eagle River qualifies.

Just before reaching road's end and an entrance into Anchorage's "backyard wilderness," half-million-acre Chugach State Park, Rick pulls his truck into a yard surrounded by spruce-birch forest. On the front lawn is a large culvert pipe, several feet across, that's been made into a trap. And within the trap is an adult black bear, lured into the metal cage by dog food and stale Christmas cookies.

As he approaches the contraption, Rick smiles and waves. "Good morning, Bill. Nice day, isn't it?"

Passionate about bears and greatly interested in local bear-human relations, I've been bugging Rick for weeks to include me on one of his bear calls. Middle-aged, with curly brown hair and a gray-flecked moustache, Rick is a good-natured and soft-spoken guy who tapes Gary Larsen's "The Far Side" cartoons to his office door, writes poetry, and is fascinated by all sorts of critters, from bears to ravens to humans. In other words, he's just about perfect for his job, which requires people skills as much as wildlife expertise. Patient and courteous, he avoids confrontations whenever possible; but he can be hard-nosed when he has to and is willing to make tough decisions, whether that means shooting a nuisance bear or someone's dog that is harassing a moose.

Rick is usually the first person I contact when I have questions about local wild-life. We've spent time in the field together, tracking Anchorage moose and look-ing for goose and crane nests. But I've been waiting a long time to see him handle one of Anchorage's bears. Today, finally, he invited me to come along. Wasting no time, I drove straight here and arrived a half hour before the biologists, who were delayed by yet another plea for help: a woman in downtown Anchorage had a black bear rummaging through her garbage. After vainly trying to chase it off with a BB gun, she called Fish and Game. But by the time Rick and Chris showed up, the bear, as so often happens, had departed.

While waiting, I had walked quietly to the cage and peeked in. The dozing bear was silent then and has remained quiet, except for heavy breathing and an occa-sional snort. Last night, though, it made a racket. "About 12:30, I heard a door slam. Then there was all this banging and beating and growling," says a renter staying in the nearby house. "Sure got my two dogs' attention."

The renter, named Tom, had never given much thought to bears being in the neigh-borhood, even though some large animal had recently broken a porch railing while raiding his dogs' food dish. But now that two bears have been caught in his yard—today's is the second within a week—Tom plans to be more careful. He's already taken down his bird feeders and he's begun keeping the dogs and their food inside while at work. After all, he says, "No sense taking chances." As for the trap's presence, Tom fig-ures, "If it teaches the bears to stay away, sure, let 'em keep it here." That's unlikely to happen, though, because a bunch of other residents have been screaming for traps and Rick plans to move this one to another locale within the next couple days.

Talking with me earlier, Tom had guessed the bear might be a female, since a neighbor had reported seeing two cubs in the neighborhood. But Rick points out that the cubs would have stayed around if this were indeed their mom. Besides, this bear seems awfully big to be a female. Sure enough, "she" turns out to be a he.

Awakened by truck doors slamming and our conversation, the bear lifts his head, moans loudly, and then pops his jaws as we approach. But his actions seem more resigned than aggressive. "Oh, he's a big boy," Rick says as he points a gun into the trap, aims at the bear's left back thigh, and darts him with Telazol, a com-bination muscle relaxant-tranquilizer-anesthetic drug that field researchers have used on bears for more than a decade, apparently with good success. Pricked by the dart, the bear recoils, rattling the cage. Then he moans some more. This is rou-tine stuff for the biologists, but I'm feeling badly for the caged, harassed bear, even while knowing that the trapping and the insults to follow are for a good cause: to help wildlife managers better understand Anchorage's ursine population and, through that knowledge, increase the odds that bears and people can peacefully coexist in Alaska's urban center.

After waiting ten minutes for the Telazol to kick in, the two men drag the drugged animal onto the lawn. Rick is a lean, fit guy and Chris, a former wrestler, is a young, burly grad student who goes 240 pounds or so. But they struggle getting the bear out of the culvert. "This guy's a monster," grunts Chris. "He's about as big as we've gotten." A mature male, the bear has scarring on his head and neck (from fighting other bears), several missing teeth, and fur that's become matted and soiled from lying in his own piss and shit. Heavily sedated, he reflexively flicks his pink tongue in and out while his dark eyes take on a vacant, glazed appearance. Then the flicking stops, the eyes close.

For the next forty-five minutes, the bear is measured, poked, prodded, and stuck. Reading from his ruled tape, Chris calls out a series of numbers while Rick records them in a book. The bear is just less than six feet long, with a twenty-eight-and-a-half-inch neck, forty-three-inch girth, and nineteen-inch skull. Skulls measuring twenty inches (length plus width) are trophy sized for black bears, so he is indeed a big fella, nearly as large as the brown bears Rick has seen around Anchorage, in fact.

After determining the bear's dimensions, the biologists take belly hairs for DNA fingerprinting, pull a pre-molar tooth for aging, and jab a needle into the inside of a thigh to take blood for chemical analysis. The first blood sample goes smoothly, but Chris struggles with the second. "Damn, I just can't find that artery," he mutters. Then, after several unsuccessful jabs, he tells the bear, "OK, I give up. I'm not going to stick you anymore." Rick just watches, an amused look on his face.

Besides giving, the bear also receives: the men stamp a tattoo—No. 751—into his gum, attach colored tags to his ears, and place a large, white collar with a radio-transmitting device around his neck. The collar will gradually rot and drop off within a year or two, after the radio has stopped sending the signals that reveal the bear's whereabouts and movements.

While the biologists do their work, I study their captive. Moving close enough to smell the dank odor of his dirtied black coat and feel his warm breath, I softly trace the arc of the bear's sharply curved claws, feel the roughness of his footpads, run my hand through his fur, gently rub his head. For all of his soiled and smelly hair, the gobs of feces, the staining and scarring, this is a beautiful animal. I admire his heavily muscled body, the licking tongue and yellow teeth, the hardened paws, the humanlike form. And I feel a complex blend of emotions: though saddened by the bear's capture, I am curious to know what the biologists are learning. There's even some pleasure, a sense that I'm lucky to be watching this.

While I appreciate the investigators and their research and I'm confident their motives are good, I still have misgivings about the collaring and probing, and especially the drugging. Bottom line: this is harassment in the name of science and management. Is it necessary? Researchers say of course. But I'm not convinced.

The longer I watch, the more my sympathies are with the stupefied bear. The drug that put him in this state is primarily a muscle relaxant and anesthetic, but it is reported to have some hallucinogenic properties. And though the bear is "out of it," he never completely loses consciousness during the sometimes rough handling. "They can hear, see, and feel the whole time," Rick says, "so they must have some awareness of what's going on."

"Yeah," adds Chris, "I guess in a way you could consider this whole thing a massive dose of aversive conditioning."

Trying to picture the human equivalent, I imagine what it would be like to have root canal work, give blood, get stitches, have your ears pierced, be fitted with a neck brace, and be given a thorough physical exam that includes a prostate check, all while breathing nitrous oxide (and having your gums shot up with novocaine). You know some nasty stuff is being done to your body, but through the gas-induced haze you can't really feel the trauma. Even at that, the comparison falls short. At least nitrous oxide puts you in something of a giddy, feel-good state—and doesn't leave you with a hangover.

The indignities of data collection finished, the bear is subjected to one final humiliation, as he is half-carried, half-dragged across the lawn and driveway toward the woods, where he will soon recover and resume his life along the edge of city and wilderness. The biologists stick around until the bear shows clear signs he's recovering from the Telazol. The animal opens his eyes, which are less glazed now, and he lifts his head, swinging it slowly from side to side. Soon he'll lift himself from the ground and walk away, more slowly and wobbly than usual, until the drug's full effects wear off.

Before leaving, I say a short, silent prayer for the bear, asking for his safe and full recovery and safe passage as he moves through the valley, with its many homes and roads. I pray too that some good comes from his trauma. The prayer doesn't help. At least not for long. Before year's end, Bear No. 751 will be killed by a hunter. So it goes.

A LONGTIME BIOLOGIST and the Anchorage area's wildlife manager since 1994, Rick is used to dealing with large and potentially dangerous mammals, including the "urban" bears that roam the perimeters of Alaska's largest city and sometimes penetrate to its downtown core. Chris is less experienced, but he's learning rapidly. A biology graduate student at the University of Alaska Anchorage, this red-haired and goateed scientist-in-training is following radio-collared black bears around the city and adjacent wildlands.

By the end of his two-year field study, Chris—with Rick's help—will collar and track twenty bears, from two to seven years old. Nearly half will be either wounded or killed within months of being tagged and collared. Two bears are poached, two are killed legally by hunters, two others are wounded but survive, one is killed by Rick after becoming a garbage-conditioned nuisance, and two simply disappear. The statistics are troubling; they suggest that many bears shot by locals are never reported.

Another surprise, this one not so alarming: Chris's radio and GPS tracking will show that local bears cover more ground than wildlife managers had suspected. A bear roaming South Anchorage in the morning may be ten or fifteen miles to the north by evening. By moving so far so quickly, a single bear passing through heavily populated neighborhoods may prompt many calls to Fish and Game. Thus a small number of bears may be causing most of the problems. Though not conclusive, the data also suggests that some bears may learn the city's garbage pick-up patterns, moving from one neighborhood to another on trash-collection day, when garbage is most accessible. That's in line with what Craig Gales has observed. An employee with Waste Management of Alaska, Gales says a bear has begun hanging out in his neighborhood every Friday, looking for easy pickings in trash cans put out by residents.

As would be expected, Chris has found that the number of radio-signaled bear-location data points diminishes as housing density increases (suggesting fewer bears) while the number of reported sightings often rises. Again, the perception of bear abundance may be greater than the reality.

Chris is also studying local bears' dependence on native plants and how it affects their garbage-seeking behaviors. What he'll discover is this: the number of bear calls to Fish and Game can be linked to the seasonal abundance of certain wild foods, particularly berries. Residents' complaints about bears peak in June and July, then drop precipitously in August and remain low through late summer and into fall, when local wild-berry crops have ripened. The evidence suggests that bears roaming Anchorage's more developed areas in search of food move out of town in late summer to feed on blueberries, crowberries, and high-bush cranberries, and they remain in the forested and tundra foothills east of town as long as berry supplies last. In a good berry year, they might not come back before denning; in a bad year, bears can be expected to return, looking for calorie-rich urban foods.

Rick hopes that Chris's study of bear movement patterns and the seasonal availability of natural foods will help to lessen human-bear conflicts. As he succinctly puts it, "The more we know about bears, the better we can live with them." Even before its completion, Chris's work has had a positive spin-off. Thanks to media coverage and his own presentations at schools and community events, the study has increased residents' awareness of bears. "Chris's work has been a great educational tool," Rick says. "It has definitely heightened bear awareness around town and reminded people what they can do to minimize conflicts."

CERTAINLY THERE ARE INDIVIDUALS who still believe "the only good bear is a dead bear." But surveys show that most Alaskans prefer live bears to dead ones. And therein lies the challenge, because nearly the entire state—including parts of Anchorage—is bear country, inhabited by one or two of Alaska's three species: grizzlies (the Interior-dwelling relatives of brown bears), black bears, or polar bears. Communities from the Panhandle to the Arctic face the identical question: If we want bears around, how can we peacefully coexist with our ursine neighbors? Relations between the two species are far more complicated in cities and villages than in wilderness landscapes. Bears, like humans, are innately curious creatures and opportunistic omnivores whose diets run the gamut from greens and berries to fish and scavenged carcasses. Where the homelands of our two species overlap, bears are inevitably attracted to human foods and leftovers that become garbage. They've also shown a taste for dog food and seeds used in bird feeders. There's lots of evidence that bears are inherently shy of *Homo sapiens*. But they're fast learners, too. When they discover humans aren't a threat and come to associate us with food, bears often lose their innate wariness of people. They grow bolder, more aggressive. Humans, understandably, then feel threatened. Only rarely, however, are people harmed when encounters turn violent; the usual result is a dead bear, killed "in defense of life or property"—or DLP. Hundreds of Alaska's bears become DLP statistics every year, several of them in and around Anchorage. In other words, cities and villages around the state may become death traps for bears.

All too often, conflicts aren't addressed until things have reached a crisis stage. In 1991, large numbers of black bears roamed Juneau neighborhoods, lured in by garbage when wild food sources were in short supply. By summer's end, fourteen so-called "problem bears" had been killed in Alaska's capital city. "That was a low point," says Bruce Dinneford, state wildlife management coordinator for the Juneau area. "But it was also a galvanizing year, because people knew we shouldn't be killing so many bears."

Concerned Juneau citizens formed a Save Our Bears group to raise public awareness, while the Department of Fish and Game began working more closely with the city to improve Juneau's garbage storage. The city-borough assembly passed an ordinance that requires homeowners and businesses to store trash in clean, odor-free containers with tight-fitting lids. But it defeated another proposal requiring residents to put out their garbage on the day of collection, not before. "What we've got isn't perfect, but it's better than it was," says Dinneford, who believes cooperation between wildlife managers and city officials is essential when dealing with urban bears.

As evidence of Juneau's recent success, fewer than three bears, on average, have been killed there annually since 1992 . Still, says Juneau-area biologist Neil Barten, "People get careless or they think it's someone else's problem. We have to keep working to get the message out. It's a never-ending process."

Towns and villages may also face increased conflicts when they fence or replace community dumps that bears have adopted as feeding grounds. Case in point: Kodiak, a town of about seven thousand people in Southwest Alaska. During the late eighties and into the nineties, increasing numbers of brown bears began using the dump as an easy source of food to supplement berries and salmon. In 1999, an electrified fence was installed around the dump, eliminating it as a food source. That same year, Kodiak Island's berry crop was poor, and pink salmon runs were down. Hungry bears came into Kodiak and the nearby Coast Guard base looking for food and sometimes finding it in open dumpsters. As bears became bolder, encounters with humans increased and tensions rose accordingly. Between June 6 and August 3, eight bears were killed, including five cubs, matching the DLP total for the entire preceding decade.

State wildlife biologist Larry Van Daele described the August killing of a female and two spring cubs on the Coast Guard base as "ugly" and unnecessary. But because of it, he said, "The Coast Guard has completely changed the way it does business. They have a new protocol for dealing with bears and they've made their dumpsters more bear resistant. So at least the incident turned out to have positive consequences."

With the nearby Coast Guard base and a population dependent on commercial fishing, Kodiak's community is both transient and culturally diverse. About half its residents are Asian or Latin American, forty percent are white, and ten percent are Native Alaskan. To keep the ever-changing population "bear aware," Fish and Game biologists meet with cultural groups, do radio call-in shows, visit local schools, and sponsor bear-safety clinics. Given Kodiak Island's high density of bears—one brown bear for every one and a half square miles—"bears are a daily fact of life here," says Van Daele. "It's essential that people know how to behave around bears."

FROM MAY THROUGH OCTOBER, bears are also a fact of life in Anchorage, a bustling metropolis of 270,000 people with more than its share of malls, congested multi-lane streets, big-box stores, and densely packed housing subdivisions. Biologists estimate that two hundred to three hundred black bears and fifty-five to sixty-five brown bears (the coastal cousins of Interior-dwelling grizzlies) inhabit the lowland forests, wooded foothills, and high tundra meadows in and around the city. By late April or early May, most have awakened from winter's sleep and abandoned their dens. After several months of hibernation, they're hungrily moving about, looking to fill that aching emptiness. Especially in this lean season, they'll eagerly consume all kinds of food, from winter-killed moose to last autumn's shriveled berries to people's leftovers. Human garbage isn't necessarily what draws the bears into town; in May and June, bears will prowl the city's wooded areas, hunting for newborn moose calves. And from midsummer through early October, they'll fish local creeks for spawning salmon. For all of that, many residents seem remarkably unaware of their presence, until a bear gets into the trash, pet food, livestock pens, or birdseed.

Local biologists estimate that a third of the area's black bears pass through Anchorage's residential zones. Even more surprising, as many as six brown bears have been reported in town within a single day. I haven't been among the lucky ones to see a brown, but at least a couple times they've been spotted chasing and killing moose calves within a mile of my house.

The occasional incursions of brown bears into Anchorage's more developed areas are always big news, particularly so when children are present, as at a school or playground. Being larger and fiercer than their cousin the black bear, they are more likely to attack—and do serious harm—when they feel threatened. (Even brown and grizzly bear attacks are a rarity in Alaska and throughout North America, the species' aggressive reputation notwithstanding.) To date, however, no one has been killed or severely injured by a bear that's entered the city. And since neighboring Chugach State Park was established in 1970, only two people have been killed in Anchorage's 495,000-acre backyard wilderness. Those maulings occurred in 1995, when three runners had the bad luck to pass near a dead moose that a brown bear had recently killed, or discovered, just off a popular woodland trail.

Brown bears are renowned for their fierce protection of food caches and this one behaved predictably. Though the runners had started off as a group, they were spread out and most likely moving silently through the thick forest understory by the time they reached the moose carcass. In other words, they were traveling swiftly and alone in an area with low visibility, without announcing their approach, toward a bear guarding its food supply, thus setting up the worst possible sort of encounter. For some reason—perhaps because the bear had been napping or eating or its guard was otherwise down—the lead runner slipped past unharmed. But alerted and likely agitated, it attacked and killed the two who followed. The tragedy was compounded by the fact that the victims were a senior citizen and her middle-aged son. Besides being a mother and grandmother, Marcie Trent was a highly respected member of Anchorage's running community, while Larry Waldron was well known in both running and music circles.

The bear had departed by the time rescuers arrived and though rangers and biologists searched the area, they couldn't find it. In the end, they decided not to hunt down and destroy the animal, which all the experts agreed had acted as you'd expect a brown bear to behave, given the circumstances. This infuriated some relatives of the victims and others in the community. But at least as many people—including me—argued against any revenge killing. And a good number of us pleaded for more tolerance toward bears, both in Anchorage and around the state.

As I wrote at the time (in a newspaper opinion piece titled "It's time to end our war on bears") and still agree with years later:

Much media attention has been focused on bear attacks this summer. So what else is new? Whether it's been too much coverage, or too sensationalized, is open to debate. But I wince whenever someone is even scratched by a bear because it's almost certain to be front-page news in the local paper, often with banner headlines. And what that does is strengthen stereotypes of bears as marauding, unpredictable killers lurking in the shadows.

Certainly the deaths of Anchorage residents Marcie Trent and her son Larry Waldron were shocking, tragic, and unprecedented, the first deaths by bear mauling in Chugach State Park's history. And both were high-profile people . . . [so] extensive press coverage was inevitable. But I wonder how the local print and broadcast media would have responded if they'd died in an avalanche, fallen off a cliff, been attacked by a dog, or even stomped by a moose. What is it that makes a bear mauling so sensational?

More disturbing to me than the attack stories, however, is the Waldron and Trent families' attitude toward the bear that killed Marcie and Larry. They clearly believe that a bear that has killed a human should in turn be tracked and killed, no questions asked, even if that bear were acting in a predictable, normal, nonpredatory manner. My guess is that many other Alaskans feel similarly, which is unfortunate. It's common knowledge that grizzly [or brown] bears will aggressively defend their kills; Marcie and Larry happened to be in the wrong place at the wrong time. No more, no less. I am sorry for their deaths and their families' loss. But the bear was not to "blame." And there's no evidence that it now presents a greater public danger than any other brown bear. In similar circumstances, I would hope that relatives and friends would mourn my death and not seek revenge on a bear that behaves like the wild animal it is.

Even as we "bear lovers" made our pleas, local bears were being gunned down at an unprecedented rate. By the end of July 1995, ten bears—all blacks—had been killed in the Anchorage area. Four were chronic "garbage bears," shot by biologists or law-enforcement officers who had no other realistic choice. Six others were citizen kills. Rick believed all six to be dubious DLPs, at best. Only by a wild flight of the imagination were people or property threatened. One bear was shot simply because he stood up while checking out a homeowner's yard. (Another myth—one that's been perpetuated by ridiculous magazine and book covers—and has proved deadly to bears—is that a standing bear is a dangerous bear. Bears stand for many reasons: to pull food from bushes and trees, to play, to mark trees, occasionally to fight each other, but mostly because they're curious and they're checking out something they've heard or smelled. But standing does *not* signal an imminent attack.) The bears were killed out of ignorance and fear. Or spite. Some people just don't like bears.

In one sense, all ten deaths were senseless, because each bear had been lured into yards by human garbage or pet food. Rick, who's checked out more than his share of DLP kills, guessed that all of them had probably tasted garbage at one time or another.

NOW AND THEN, A BROWN BEAR will somehow stumble into the heart of downtown. Almost inevitably, the wanderer is an adolescent—an ursine teenager—perhaps escaping harassment by older and bigger bears that have established their own "turf," or maybe simply one seeking to find its place in the world. Most of these misplaced bears manage to find their way back to the wilds, sometimes shadowed by biologists or police. But an unlucky few are killed, because of the threat they pose, whether real or imagined.

In one particularly saddening case, a radio DJ alerted his listeners to a young brown bear's presence in downtown Anchorage, and began broadcasting updates of its location. Before long, a large crowd of gawking spectators hoping to see the bear had swarmed the residential neighborhood where the bear had taken refuge.

Perhaps emboldened by the dozens of people present, a few fools approached the bear, trying for pictures or a better look. The bewildered animal retreated, but that only encouraged more people to take up the chase. Local biologists who'd hoped to safely escort the bear out of the area were faced with an unhappy dilemma. Though people, not the bear, were the ones behaving badly, the biologists worried that, if pushed too hard, it might finally attack its tormentors and seriously hurt or even kill someone. Reluctantly, they shot the young, hapless bear. The killing, of course, caused an uproar, though the DJ and crowd's behavior deserved the blame—and to some degree, I'm happy to say, they received it.

If nothing else good came out of it, the tragic slaying at least prompted serious (and sometimes heated) discussion about the responsibilities of radio jocks and other media types when reporting "live" on potentially dangerous circumstances—whether bears or fires or armed criminals on the run—as well as what's proper and appropriate behavior around bears and other dangerous animals, whether in the city or the backcountry. The public's outrage at the killing also reflected a surprising community tolerance of brown bears whose wanderings bring them into town.

"No other large city in the world is inhabited by grizzlies or brown bears," says Rick. "Most cities wouldn't stand for it, but here they're accepted. We brag about our bears." As evidence, he points to a late-1990s survey in which seventy percent of local respondents answered that Anchorage has either "just the right amount" or "too few" brown bears.

Among those to applaud the community's tolerance is Canadian bear authority Stephen Herrero, author of the acclaimed book *Bear Attacks: Their Causes and Avoidance*: "I see the situation in Anchorage as world class and certainly unique. It's something to be proud of."

Yet even in Anchorage, with its progressive attitudes toward wildlife, people frequently invite conflicts with bears, despite numerous reminders and warnings. Residents leave pet food in the yard, put garbage in open trash bins, or keep bird feeders filled with seed throughout the summer, when birds don't need handouts.

Bird feeding has only become a problem in the last decade or so. Rick says people never reported bears getting into their feeders back in 1994, the year he began handling Anchorage residents' "nuisance bear" complaints. But by 2000, birdseed was running neck-and-neck with garbage as a bear attractant.

"Most people are dumbfounded to see bears in their bird feeders, but it makes sense," Rick says. "Think about it: bears are looking for foods that are high in fat and protein. And what do people put out for birds? Sunflower seeds, peanut butter, suet."

Sunflower seeds, it turns out, have a very high fat content. No one can easily explain how a bear (or chickadee) "knows" a particular food is rich in the calories it needs to fatten up, but perhaps the critter instinctively learns through its body's response. Or maybe the seeds and suet are simply tasty. We humans tend to love the taste of high-fat foods; maybe the same is true for bears. We know that bears are both curious and fast learners, so once they discover a food that's easy to get, reliable, and good-tasting, you can bet they'll be looking for it.

Given local bears' hankering for birdseed and other avian delicacies, Rick and others do their best each spring to spread the word citywide: stop feeding birds before May 1 (and don't start up again until the end of October); and clean up your mess. Either a lot of people aren't getting the message, or they're ignoring it. Or maybe, they're just being lazy. Almost every year, black bears get into dozens of Anchorage bird feeders.

Like many folks who live here, I like the fact that black and brown bears wander through Anchorage, occasionally even through my yard. Their presence, even if unseen, changes my relationship with a place: it makes me more attentive, more aware of my surroundings. It's also a reminder that, for all of our city's sophistication and development, we've preserved much of the landscape's wild nature. Think about it: Anchorage is wild enough for brown bears. That's not a small thing. It says something positive about our community—and our tolerance for wildlife— that a population of bears still inhabits our town, without threat of extermination. I want to do what I can to help keep it that way and usually consider myself part of the solution, not the problem. Still, I get careless sometimes. I make mistakes. A few years ago I messed up big time.

SINCE I FIRST SUCCESSFULLY EXPERIMENTED with bird feeding in 1993, I've become an avid participant in that spectator sport. Every year from autumn 'til spring, I put out daily meals of sunflower seeds for chickadees and nuthatches, grosbeaks and redpolls, then enjoy their company as they visit my house. Most years I shell out five hundred pounds or more. Over the months, bunches of shells, bits of seed, and some unknown quantity of bird poop are tossed, dropped, knocked, and swept from my decks and railings to the ground below, then buried by successive snowfalls. As March gives way to April and May, the melting snowpack reveals a thickening and messy debris pile of shells, seed fragments, fecal matter, and mold.

One recent spring had cooler-than-normal temperatures and a slowly vanishing snowpack. As the snow melted, the seedy morass atop it piled up. I kept holding off, figuring I could wait until all the snow was gone, simplifying the cleanup. Still, as April turned to May, I worried. Already there'd been several bear sightings in town.

On May 7, I decided to wait no longer. Carrying a rake and shovel, I went out the front door, across the deck, turned to go down the steps to the backyard—and then stopped in my tracks. Thirty feet away, a large black bear lay sprawled in the seeds. He looked big enough to be an adult male, which is what I guessed him to be. Caught up in his feasting, with his head turned away from me, the bear hadn't noticed my approach and he continued to dine as I watched. Every few seconds he would dip his head and grab a mouthful of seeds. It must have seemed like bruin heaven.

At first I wasn't sure what to do. Then, because he was a black bear (a species known to be generally timid of humans), and I stood close enough to the front door if retreat proved necessary, I loudly clapped my hands and shouted: "HEY, GET OUTTA HERE!"

The startled bear lifted off the ground several inches, landed on his feet and turned toward me, all in one motion. After a moment's hesitation, he bolted for the woods behind the house, stopping only once, briefly, to look back. As this was happening, I noticed a couple other things about the bear. First, he wore an ear tag; that meant he was one of the Anchorage bears being studied by biologists. Second, he looked fat, not skinny as you might expect a bear to be after several months of fasting. Maybe my yard was just one stop on his bird-feeder rounds.

I spent the next few hours cleaning up my seed dump, raking and hauling the debris away. The bear returned once more that evening. He approached slowly through the forest, drawn back to what must have seemed like a good deal. Again I shouted. Again he retreated, but this time more reluctantly, it seemed. I don't know that I got the bear started on sunflower seeds, but I certainly contributed to his habit. I still feel badly about that.

It's a worrisome thing, this hankering that Anchorage bears have for sunflower seeds. It draws bears onto porches and decks, brings them closer to pets and kids. And it's only going to get worse, as moms pass their feeding habits along to cubs. We can't blame the bears for craving an easy-to-get, high-calorie meal. But we humans can become a little more disciplined ourselves. We can take down our bird feeders earlier, clean up our messes more promptly.

There's no way I can get to all the seeds, as long as large piles of snow remain. But now when spring comes late to the Hillside, I no longer wait for the snow to melt at its own slow pace. Instead I'm out there regularly, raking and skimming seeds from the dirty snowpiles beside my house, then bagging and hauling the mess away. I keep pace with the gradual meltdown and associated seed-pile buildup, removing temptation from beside my house.

FOR ALL THE TOLERANCE THAT locals express in surveys, interviews, and letters to the editor, human-bear conflicts have increased greatly in Anchorage since the mid-1990s. One indicator: "bear calls" made to the local Fish and Game office. Numbering a few hundred in the early to mid-1990s, calls skyrocketed to more than a thousand by the end of the decade. They've since dropped in the early 2000s, but remain about twice as high as they were ten to fifteen years earlier. Another measure is bear DLPs. Between 1981 and 1995, an average of one brown bear was annually killed in Anchorage; but over the next decade, the annual toll doubled. For black bears, the 1981–1995 average was less than three DLPs per year; from 1996 to 2004, it jumped to nearly ten; in 2005–2006, the toll jumped again, to an average of fourteen. I wonder what it will take to convince us there's a more sensible, less harmful way to coexist with bears—twenty bear deaths? Fifty? A mauling? A human death? (A new—and disturbing—trend in the early 2000s is increased ursine "road kill." Between 2000 and 2006, seventeen black bears and six browns died when hit by Anchorage-area drivers.)

Three circumstances have contributed to this worrisome trend: urban expansion, limited hunting, and sloppy human behavior. New subdivisions and businesses reach deeper and deeper into bear habitat, increasing human-bear encounters. At the same time, hunting restrictions in the greater Anchorage area have enabled local bear numbers to increase (not that hunts are entirely forbidden; black bear hunting has been allowed in parts of Chugach State Park for years, and in 2007 the state's Board of Game unanimously voted to allow a limited brown bear hunt in Chugach Park, after many years of closure).

As a consequence, says Rick, "you get more bears being rewarded with garbage, while learning humans aren't much of a threat." And people remain a continuing source of food, despite the annual barrage of warnings and pleas. That's proved to be a deadly combination, especially for curious "teenage" bears. At the bottom of the ursine pecking order, recently weaned adolescent bears are most likely to roam long distances and take food wherever it's available. Rick, like his Juneau counterparts, has tried working with local government to reduce bear-human conflicts. In the late 1990s, he and a member of the Anchorage Assembly, Pat Abney, proposed an ordinance requiring property owners in defined high-use "bear areas" to use bear-resistant garbage cans. Though most of Anchorage would have been excluded, Rick considered the ordinance "a significant step to deal with bears getting into garbage on the edge of town."

The idea seemed reasonable, yet it proved too radical for Anchorage. Some community councils opposed it, but what really doomed the proposal was Mayor Rick Mystrom's opposition. Evidence to the contrary, Mystrom maintained that existing rules were sufficient to address the "garbage bear" problem. His staff also argued that the ordinance would require the municipality to replace more than a thousand garbage cans with bear-proof containers, at a cost of more than $300,000. Economics and public apathy lost the day for improved bear-human relations.

Even more troubling, local government was, until recently, among Anchorage's worst garbage offenders. While tracking bears through several municipal parks in the late 1990s—at the height of ursine-human tensions—Rick noticed that few, if any, city trash cans had lids. That, of course, meant free and easy pickings for the bears. But as he lamented, "People in the city's parks program don't see it as a problem."

Things have improved with a new city administration. Rick applauds a new spirit of cooperation between city officials and wildlife managers and he gives Mayor Mark Begich passing grades, rather than an F, for the city's garbage-handling efforts. Still, Rick sometimes wonders what it will take to convince local residents and politicians that more safeguards are needed if we are serious about addressing this problem with "garbage bears." Even with more enlightened leaders, there still isn't enough political support or will to pass the bear-resistant garbage-container ordinance that Rick has repeatedly proposed. And he worries that someday, a person—perhaps a child—will be killed by a garbage-conditioned bear.

Perhaps citizen activists need to become more involved, as they have in Juneau and Girdwood, a small resort community south of Anchorage that's within the municipality's borders. In 1999, a group of Girdwood residents began a Bear Aware program, intended to reduce food-conditioned bears and DLPs. Emphasizing public education, the group made posters, distributed fliers, and produced public-service announcements to raise people's consciousness of bears. Members have also worked with the local trash-collection company to design bear-resistant garbage containers. They're available to Anchorage residents, too, but they're not required even in well-defined bear "hot spots" and there's been no organized political push to get people to use them.

SHORTLY AFTER 9 ON A WEDNESDAY evening in late spring of 2003, I get into my car and go for a neighborhood drive, looking for bear bait. Tomorrow is trash day in my part of town and I've been wondering how many people put out their garbage the night before, leaving temptations for hungry bears.

By now, all of the bears that live in and around Anchorage have left their dens. After fasting for several months, they are eager to fill empty bellies. At this time of year, with green-up still under way and the prospect of newborn moose calves, salmon runs, and ripened berries still days, weeks, or months away, the pickings are lean. So they're inevitably attracted to foods left lying around by people.

Despite bear-aware stories in the local media and public-service announcements, many residents remain lazy about cleaning up after themselves. Or they're forgetful. Or apathetic. Or they believe it's unlikely a bear will roam through their own neighborhood. It's also an inconvenience to take out the garbage in the morning, when you know the trash collectors may come by at 6 or 6:30.

For years I took out my garbage late Wednesday night because of such early-morning pickups; after all, I'd never seen a bear pass through our neighborhood. And the odds seemed in my favor. What were the chances of a bear stumbling into my trash cans between midnight and 7 a.m., that one night a week?

A couple of things prompted me to change my habits. First, my neighbors the Nelsons told me that on three different occasions they'd watched a black bear climb the stairs to their back deck and raid their bird feeders. As evidence, they pulled out several pictures of their ursine visitors. One shows a black bear gazing into the Nelsons' house, ears pointed out and eyes brightly alert. Not long after that, I met a black bear in my own yard. (Yes, the one in the seeds.)

I'd been lucky. None of my trash cans were ever raided. But it seemed only a matter of time. So I went to a "morning shift." Nowadays I rise early every Thursday from April until sometime in October, when most bears have returned to their dens. Yet neighbors on either side of me still put out their trash the night before, so I've grown curious about the neighborhood as a whole.

In a notebook that I've brought along on my evening drive, I make two columns. In one I mark the number of houses I pass; in the other are the number of homeowners who've already put out their garbage. I end my survey at fifty houses and count my slashes: twenty-three people have put out their trash early. To be honest, I'm surprised. I expected more. But the night is still young. In winter, when I too take out the trash at night, I often don't haul it to the roadside until 10 or 11 p.m., and sometimes later. I suspect others keep similar routines into spring and summer.

The garbage is stored in black and white plastic bags, in boxes and in plastic cans, most with tops but some without. None are even remotely bear resistant, though one property owner has at least secured his trash cans with bungee cords. I don't leave the car, but I'm sure that some of these trash containers are sending rich aromas into the night air.

I don't see any of the bear-resistant "cages" that Waste Management of Alaska is offering for rent this year. For an extra $20 a month on your trash bill, you can rent a bear-tested cage that holds up to three thirty-two-gallon containers. WMA's Craig Gales says his company has supplied a number of the cages to locals, but none of the renters appear to be in my neighborhood.

WMA will also soon be offering another, cheaper solution: ninety-six-gallon garbage cans that, like the cages, have earned a bear-resistant rating after being tested by Zayk and Mavis, two black bears residing at the Alaska Zoo. The containers aren't perfect; they wouldn't stand up to a grizzly's assault and even a persistent black bear would likely eventually break in. Yet as Rick has commented, "They may not be totally bear proof, but they're a heck of a lot better than a Rubbermaid with bungees."

They're also more affordable than the cages. According to Gales, my monthly garbage-collection fee would increase just a few bucks. And residents would only have to rent them during bear season, say from April through October. I'm no economist, but it seems a cost-benefit analysis would greatly favor such a strategy.

Such bear-resistant containers would help address another problem: erratic trash pickup schedules. Some weeks the garbage truck comes rumbling down my gravel road before 7 a.m., but other weeks it doesn't arrive until late morning. A couple times this spring the trash collectors didn't show up until afternoon. Even at homes where the residents are doing their best to be good citizens by putting out the trash in the morning, the smelly stuff may sit beside the road for several hours.

So it doesn't surprise me that bears get into garbage here in Anchorage. What's more amazing is that so few of them get hooked on human leftovers. Every night of the week, in some part of town, hundreds of tiny, easy-to-rip-into garbage piles sit outside people's houses. The worst spots—the "hot spots"—are neighborhoods like mine, on Anchorage's Hillside, along the city's wild fringes.

Driving around at dusk, seeing the piles of garbage, I'm reminded again that bears aren't the real problem. Temptation is everywhere. Who can blame them for seeking an easy meal, especially at a time of year when food is scarce? If we Anchorage residents really like having bears as neighbors, and if we want to continue bragging among ourselves and to "outsiders" about our bears, then we're the ones who have to become more disciplined, more responsible. I know it's possible to change old habits. Thursday morning I'll get up an hour early, take out the trash, then go for a morning bird walk before work. Instead of another burdensome chore, it's become a great way to start the day.

WHILE APPLAUDING GIRDWOOD'S ACTIVISTS, Rick continues to seek other ways to improve bear-human relations. And he sees some hopeful signs. Chris Kleckner's study has certainly helped. Another big step in the right direction is the Anchorage Bear Committee, whose fifteen or so members represent more than a half-dozen local, state, and federal agencies that manage land or wildlife within the Anchorage municipality, which encompasses nearly two thousand square miles and extends from the Cook Inlet coastline to the jagged peaks of the Chugach Mountains. Formed in 2002, the committee's primary goal is simply stated, but hardly easy: to minimize the problems and maximize the benefits of living with bears in Anchorage. To that end, the ABC has launched several programs to increase residents' awareness of the actions we humans must take if we truly want to have bears as neighbors.

The group can point to many accomplishments, some small, others quite substantial. Among its chief successes, the ABC is bringing consistency to the messages that land managers, biologists, park rangers, and city leaders give the public about bears—and proper behavior in bear country. "We really want people to understand that they can take positive steps that will affect their interactions with bears," says Colleen Matt, who acted as the group's facilitator during its initial eighteen-month charter. "People don't have to be victims."

Another big deal: led by Rick and wildlife biologists, the committee has compiled a series of Anchorage-area bear-habitat maps and written an accompanying report, to guide city planners who are developing new land-use codes and an updated municipal parks plan.

Members have also produced (or are still developing) interpretive signs, "Living in Bear Country" brochures and posters, a bear-deterrent website, and a "Bear Aware" coloring book for kids. They've produced bumper stickers, distributed door hangers, and met with community councils, the mayor's office, assembly members, and school-district administrators.

Through stories in the local paper and TV news programs, the ABC has served notice that residents who attract bears with garbage or other foods, even if unintentionally, may be cited and fined $100. By 2004, trash collectors were "red-tagging" residences where garbage cans have been raided by bears. The public was warned that citations would eventually follow, but during this initial push, Rick emphasized education over enforcement: "With me it's a black-and-white thing. If I start giving out citations, I'm going to treat everyone the same. I could spend my entire summer just handing out citations and I'm not quite ready to be a garbage cop." Still, he understands the need to punish people who behave badly or ignore repeated warnings. Highly publicized programs in places like Juneau and Whistler, British Columbia, have shown that active enforcement diminishes bear-human conflicts.

"It's just human nature," Rick says, shrugging. "If you want people to change their behaviors, you need both the carrot and the stick. There's always going to be some small percentage of people who won't follow the rules unless you force them to."

Already there are signs that the ABC has made a difference. Bear calls to Fish and Game have decreased, though they're still higher than a decade ago. And, in one telling statistic, the number of documented bears-in-bird-feeder calls dropped by half between 2001 and 2003, from forty to less than twenty. At the same time, DLPs have dropped substantially: five black bears and one grizzly were killed in 2002; four black bears and two grizzlies in 2003. Still, it's way too early to say if those declines are temporary, or whether they reflect a real, long-term shift in people's behavior. (Sadly, as noted below, it will prove to be only a temporary lull in the killing.)

Rick and other members of the ABC also know the education never stops. Though the essence of their message is both familiar and simple, they must repeat it again and again: if residents of Anchorage—and other Alaskan communities— truly wish to share the landscape with "urban" bears, we will do what is necessary to eliminate food temptations. Where problems exist, they almost always begin with humans, not bears.

LEAP FORWARD TO SPRING 2007. When asked about local efforts to reduce human-bear conflicts, Rick can point to some hopeful signs. Mayor Begich, he notes, "helped convince Alaska Waste to begin collecting residential garbage a little later in the morning and not on Saturdays, which has probably helped." While 8 a.m. starting pickups were the rule throughout Anchorage in 2006, only those parts of the city that qualify as "garbage-bear" problem areas will get the later pickup in 2007. Rick continues, "He recently reassigned enforcement of the garbage ordinance from the Health Department to the code-enforcement office, which vastly improved compliance and the number of warnings and citations the city issues for leaving garbage out all night or in unsuitable containers. The APD [Anchorage Police Department] has started to write a few bear-feeding citations, helping us to enforce the state law. Parks and Recreation continues to replace old fifty-five-gallon drums with bear-proof trash containers in parks.

"If Juneau is a good example of an A, I'd give Anchorage a B-minus but I have high hopes that will become a B-plus or higher this summer."

On the other hand, many local residents continue in their state of denial. There are still pockets of town where residents leave out garbage or continue to feed birds, despite regular visits by bears. Over the past three years, Rick and his assistant Jesse Coltrane have issued ten to twenty citations (which come with a $100 fine) and, he says, "we could issue twenty a day if I could figure out how to be everywhere at once."

Rick hasn't cited any bird feeders yet, because "it was a big change in the [wildlife-feeding] regulation and we chose to inform and educate people first. This year Jessy and I will cite people for intentionally or negligently feeding bears from bird feeders." That should create quite a stir.

As for the fines themselves, Rick is seeking to have them raised to $250. "Snagging a salmon can cost that much," he notes, "and the city can charge $50 to $600 for just leaving trash outside all night, even if a bear doesn't get into it."

On the waste-management front, residents can again rent bear-resistant containers for just a few dollars extra a month. Or they can buy steel-drum garbage cans with locking lids for as little as $60 to $70. Every year, I notice more of them around town, another hopeful sign.

Less encouraging is the DLP count: fifteen black bears and four browns in 2005, thirteen black bears in 2006. The numbers reflect a combination of continued bear-human conflicts sparked by people's unwillingness to clean up their acts, and an intolerance for bears on the part of some residents. Even with an enlightened, progressive administration and increased enforcement efforts, it's ultimately up to the public to do what's necessary—and right—to lessen our "problems" with bears. Here's hoping that Rick is right and Anchorage continues to move closer to the standards established by Juneau, Girdwood, and other bear-aware communities around Alaska.

On a more personal note, I now live in another part of town, one rarely frequented by bears. I love my new neighborhood, but I miss the bears and often think of them. Seated in my new home, writing these words, I'm reminded of an ursine encounter from my years on the Hillside.

EARLY EVENING, MONTH OF AUGUST. I'm sitting beside the front deck, picking sweet pink fruits from our small patch of wild strawberry plants, when for no particular reason—maybe movement caught my eye—I lift my head and look off to the left. By the corner of the house, a black bear is walking across the lawn. He's big and fat, with a beautiful, glossy coat. It's likely he'd been following the South Fork of Little Campbell Creek, which flows near the bottom of our property and is bordered by thick woods of birch, spruce, and alder; then, perhaps following some ursine whim, he left the forest and cut through our yard. The bear and I seem to spot each other at the same instant. He stops, hesitates a moment, then wheels around and leaves. It happens so fast, I don't have time to say a word or move a muscle before he's gone.

Still startled, heart beating fast, I cross the deck and cautiously peek around the corner. The bear is headed for the woods; not running exactly, but moving fast. Rushing inside the house, I yell to Dulcy and to Mom that there's a bear in the yard, then climb the stairs and go out on our upper deck, but it's already too late. The bear has disappeared. In a decade of living on the Hillside, it's only the third time that either Dulcy or I have seen a bear in the yard. Each "encounter" lasted only a minute or two, if that. But weeks, months, and even years after the bears' brief visits, the memories—and in some curious way, the spirit of their presence—remain strong. So the bears have become part of our local family lore and they've deepened our appreciation of this place we call home. All three of us consider it a gift to share our neighborhood and yard with bears.

Returning to the front yard I listen awhile, figuring that barking dogs or yelling neighbors might betray the bear's movements. Hearing nothing, I wish him well as he maneuvers through the Hillside's maze of houses and manicured lawns, streets and trails. *Stay in the woods*, I silently urge him. *Steer clear of people and the temptations they may offer.* Then I go back inside, where Dulcy and Mom are waiting to hear more details of this latest brief, and marvelous, encounter with bear.

EIGHT

Anchorage's Wild Coastal Fringes

ON A BLUSTERY, GRAY MID-MAY MORNING, I TOSS JOURNAL, binoculars, and rain gear into my daypack, grab my knee-high rubber boots, and hop into my '86 Toyota Tercel. A seven-and-a-half-mile drive takes me down the Hillside to South Anchorage's Discovery Hill area, one of the city's more upscale neighborhoods. I park my aging, banged-up car at the end of a cul-de-sac bordered by shiny SUVs, well-manicured yards, and half-a-million-dollar homes. Then I cut across a muddied, weedy lot, where yet another airy, big-windowed behemoth of a house with four-car garage is nearly completed. This house stands apart from the rest, however. Its rapid growth from the ground marks the final pinching off of a long-used access point to the Anchorage Coastal Wildlife Refuge. Once the new homeowners move in, they're not likely to let strangers cross their yard to reach the wetlands behind and below their property. And this neighborhood, like the others around it, will become another dead end for someone like me, who lives miles away but would like to explore the city's wild coast.

People have lived along South Anchorage's coastal bluffs for decades, but only in the 1990s did a serious house-building boom begin here. Now, in the first years of the twenty-first century, this construction is rapidly eliminating several of the prime spots that locals have traditionally used to enter the coastal refuge. It seems that neither the city nor the state had sufficient foresight to set aside public easements; so as development proceeds, the few unofficial gateways—privately owned open spaces—are disappearing.

Most Anchorage residents don't realize, or care, that this loss is occurring, because they remain ignorant of the wild treasure along our community's western fringes. It's not a place they value, or visit, or pay attention to.

Until recently, I was among the many who know little, if anything, about the coastal refuge, except that it includes Potter Marsh. Because it has a paved parking lot, boardwalk, natural history displays, and viewing area to watch salmon, and because it stretches two miles beside the heavily traveled Seward Highway, Potter Marsh is a popular stop for both locals and visitors. It's an easy, accessible way to get a glimpse of wild nature without investing much time or energy. Still, a glimpse is better than nothing. And sometimes that peek may reveal moose, bald eagles, king salmon, a coyote, or even trumpeter swans (not to mention the many ducks, geese, gulls, terns, songbirds, and shorebirds that seasonally inhabit the marsh). In summer, the parking lot is sometimes jammed with tour buses, RVs, vans, and pickups, bearing license plates from the far reaches of the U.S. This, I must emphasize, is a good thing. I applaud almost anything that gets people out of their houses and cars, or lures them away from malls and big-box stores, and puts them in closer touch with nature.

But Potter Marsh is just a tiny, developed slice of the larger coastal refuge (which despite its name is managed by the state's Department of Fish and Game, not the city). In fact it's really a man-made habitat, formed when a berm was constructed across South Anchorage's coastal flats, so that the railroad and highway could cross. That berm blocked the area's natural drainage, forming a ponded wetland. Though the resulting marsh is used by a wide range of wildlife, it's not exactly "natural." That's not to say the rest of the refuge is entirely pristine. There's a shooting range within it, as well as sewage pipes, man-made ponds, junked cars, and various other sorts of human debris. Still, the refuge as a whole remains a largely wild and unspoiled place of mudflats and sedgeflats, of ponds and tidal guts, inhabited by all sorts of birds and mammals and myriad smaller creatures that fly, swim, and crawl.

I barely paid attention to the refuge my first two decades in Anchorage. For five years in the late eighties and early nineties I lived within a mile of its boundaries, but not once did I descend the bluffs and walk upon the coastal flats. Heck, I didn't even spend five minutes taking in the view. I knew that local waterfowl hunters went after the refuge's ducks and geese in fall, yet I still imagined it to be a mostly lifeless place of dangerous mudflats, where you could get trapped in the quicksandlike muck and then drown in incoming tides if not careful. Back then I wasn't much interested in birds. And when I wanted to explore local wildlands, I turned toward the Chugach Mountains.

So, here's the irony: just when Anchorage's coastal wildlands have finally gained my attention, the best places to enter the refuge are disappearing fast. Since April 2002, I've been introduced to four excellent access points. But in less than two years, two have sprouted homes; No Trespassing signs mark a third. This sad state of affairs naturally frustrates and upsets me. What's the sudden rush with building up these places? But it upsets Dave DeLap even more. A retired teacher who worked twenty-five years in the Anchorage School District, Dave settled here in 1965. And he's been visiting the city's coastal flats every spring and summer since 1966, mainly to watch birds. Over the years he's identified more than a hundred species, including a local rarity called the terek sandpiper. As far as Dave knows— and if anyone knows such things, it's likely to be him—the terek sandpiper has been positively identified three times in Anchorage. He and a birding buddy were the first to ID one; they spotted it June 15, 1979, from what Dave calls the Klatt Spit. Besides being a top-notch birder, he's an obsessive record keeper.

The spit is where I'm headed this overcast May morning. Now a broad, grassy, peninsular knoll that juts into and overlooks the coastal flats, it's actually a buried landfill. Originally used as a disposal area for builders replacing the area's peat deposits with more stable foundation material, it eventually became a dumping ground for all sorts of garbage. Dave introduced me to it along with a few other favorite entry points. And now they're being gobbled up by builders.

Passing by the house, I remember our visit here in spring 2002. There was no house then, not even a foundation. But bulldozers had cleared the lot and we both knew what lay ahead. "It's a shame," Dave lamented. "I've been coming here thirty-six years; now I wonder how much longer I have. It's definitely coming to an end." Then, with a brief, wry smile, he added, "I guess I'm gonna have to make some new friends."

Beyond the house, I come to a weathered wooden fence and skirt around its end. On the other side is a broad, flat, grassy meadow. Larger than a football field, the meadow would seem to make an ideal neighborhood park. Such a park, in turn, could provide access to the coastal refuge. But like Dave's spit, this grassy open space overlies the former dump. The owners don't want kids playing or families picnicking here, so they've fenced most of the meadow and posted the property with No Trespassing signs. A distinct foot trail shows that people still regularly cut through here, but from the owners' perspective, they do so at their own risk.

An assortment of songbirds fills the meadow and adjacent alder-willow thickets and birch-spruce forest with warbles, trills, buzzes, and chirps. I pick out the morning melodies of one year-round resident, a black-capped chickadee, and several seasonal inhabitants: robin, junco, ruby-crowned kinglet, orange-crowned warbler, Lincoln's sparrow. By walk's end, I will hear or see at least a half-dozen other passerine species, making it a good day. That may not seem like many to a bird-watcher living in more moderate climes; but after a long northern winter, even twelve to fifteen different songbirds is an abundance.

With new migrants arriving almost daily, May is arguably the best month for those of us Anchoragites who love birdsong. As always, I'm cheered by their sweet voices and challenged to distinguish one warbler or sparrow from another. And I'm still amazed that I failed to notice, or appreciate, the songs of birds for so long.

There are strong links among my middle-aged "discoveries" of songbirds and Anchorage's coastal refuge and several other things that have become important to me—and to my understanding of the world—over the past decade or so. Two examples that come immediately to mind are nature writing and a yearly Alaskan event called the Sitka Symposium, which for two decades has brought together many of our nation's finest writers, scientists, naturalists, philosophers, theologians, and earth-loving activists to explore the often complex interrelationships of nature, culture, and story.

Looking back, it seems I had a dim awareness of all these things—songbirds, coastal refuge, nature writing, symposium, and more—for years, as they moved in and out of my life. Yet I didn't, or maybe couldn't, sense their power, their ability to expand, deepen, enrich, even transform a life, until some triggering event opened my eyes, my capacity to understand. The trigger itself might be perfectly ordinary: putting out birdseed, attending a reading, becoming curious about the local debate over whether to extend Anchorage's prized Coastal Trail. But each somehow lifted a veil, opened a door, revealed a previously hidden path. And suddenly my world opened up. I learned new ways of experiencing the world that I had never before imagined. Of course such opening up isn't limited to middle age; it can and does happen throughout our lives, if we're lucky. Or paying attention.

I think about these things in my own life, because I want to know more about the ways that we humans broaden our perspectives, the circumstances through which we willingly change or reshape our core beliefs and behaviors, the triggers that open us to new possibilities. How do we become more engaged with the wider, other-than-human world—and each other? How do we learn to embrace and cherish, or at least accept, the wild Other? How do we come to treasure the ordinary in our own backyards and neighborhoods? How do we bring a greater appreciation of wildness into our day-to-day lives, while more fully embracing our own wild nature? As Gary Snyder says in *The Practice of the Wild*,

> wildness is not limited to the [nation's] 2 percent of formal wilderness areas. Shifting scales, it is everywhere: ineradicable populations of fungi, moss, mold, yeasts, and such that surround and inhabit us. Deer mice on the back porch, deer bounding across the freeway, pigeons in the park, spiders in the corners.... Exquisite complex beings in their energy webs inhabiting the fertile corners of the urban world in accord with the rules of wild systems, the visible hardy stalks and stems and vacant lots and railroads, the persistent raccoon squads, bacte-

ria in the loam and in our yogurt.... Wilderness may temporarily dwindle, but wildness won't go away.

And yet we fail to notice. Or we try to keep our distance. Or subdue it. Or, if some form of wildness has value as a "resource," we may try to exploit it.

Consider trees, fish, gold, oil, "game" animals, or the land itself. Alaska has been prized for the abundance of its natural resources since the Russians first colonized its southern coastal areas in the 1700s. Even now, many of Alaska's residents—as well as government agencies and international corporations—continue to treat the state's natural riches as commodities. Attitudes seem to be changing, but the change, for some of us, seems excruciatingly slow. And there's much backsliding. Too many people still see wild nature's value only in terms of its utility to humans. Why is it so hard to see that life-forms have their own inherent value, irrespective of any usefulness to our species?

So, how *do* we modern, urbanized humans become more welcoming, embracing, and celebratory in our relationship with the wild earth? How do we open ourselves to the possibility of a triggering event that will both enlarge us and deepen our engagement with the world, whatever our age or experience? It seems one way we might do this is by consciously paying more attention to the places in which we live, the other beings who share our homelands, and the lessons (or teachers) who pass our way. This gets back to the notion that we only truly love and value—and protect—that which we know. Anchorage's coastal refuge provides me an opportunity to reflect upon the learning process even as I explore a part of my homeland that until recently I ignored.

BEFORE HEADING OUT TO THE SPIT, I take a few minutes to wander through the meadow. On my first visit here, Dave told me that he has sometimes found flocks of horned larks, pipits, and lapland longspurs hunkered down in these grasses during the spring migration. Small birds, not much larger than a song sparrow, all three are "open country" species that breed in Alaska's tundra or coastal areas. I'd never seen, or at least recognized, them in Anchorage before, so I've checked for the birds every time I've returned here. Today, as before, I come up empty. Still, the possibility that they might be present adds pleasure to my walk.

Following a narrow dirt footpath through dense alder thickets, I stroll out onto a grassy peninsula that juts several hundred feet beyond the natural bluffs, whose once-forested tops are now packed with houses. The slopes that drop from blufftop to coastal flat are still largely wooded. And this narrow strip of birch, spruce, aspen, and cottonwood forms an important wildlife corridor, inhabited by numerous songbirds and also traveled by many mammals, ranging from squirrels and voles to moose, coyotes, and even an occasional lynx or bear.

Because it extends so far past the neighboring bluff and stands thirty to forty feet above the coastal flats, the spit's outer, pastured edge is an excellent place to capture a broad sweep of Cook Inlet and surrounding mountains, from the Chugach Range east of Anchorage to the Alaska Range across the inlet. It's also an ideal spot to observe the wildlife refuge's lowlands, which consist of two main zones: sedge marsh and mudflats. The sedgeflats vary greatly in width, from almost nothing to a half mile or more across, and some parts are rich in ponds and channels, while the more monotonous, dark-gray mudflats stretch for miles at the lowest tides. Patches and streaks of green have appeared among the browns, grays, and russets that dominate the sedge marsh for most of the year, but another two to three weeks will have to pass before they're fully greened up. I know little about this intertidal community and one of my goals for the summer is to learn at least a few of the major plant types.

I'm greeted by the now-familiar springtime cacophony of coastal bird chatter: the screeches of gulls, honks of geese, roarking bugles of cranes, whistles of yellowlegs, caws of ravens. And from out of the sky above me comes a distinctive *hoohoohooing*: the winnowing of a common snipe. The first time I noticed this sound a few years back, I thought an owl must be hooting. So I was doubly surprised to learn that the "call" is made by a shorebird, and it's produced when a snipe, circling high in the sky, dives at high speed. Air rushing past the bird's spread outer tail feathers then produces the low, pulsing, whistled sound. I sometimes hear snipe from my Hillside yard, but they are much more abundant and easier to follow along the open coast. Since I've been coming here regularly, I've been treated several times to the spectacle of dueling snipe as they circle and dive, then reascend with rapid wingbeats and circle and dive again, over and over. Maybe because of its unusual origin, the winnowed *hoohoohoohoohoo* has become a favorite sound of spring, along with the songs of the first-arriving migratory passerines—ruby-crowned kinglet, varied thrush, and robin—the loud honks of returning geese, the rush of meltwater down our backyard creek, and the hiccupy love songs of wood frogs.

Dale Gardner, a good friend and occasional coastal companion, stubbornly resists the idea that winnowing snipe are using their tail feathers and not their vocal chords to whistle. Or maybe he's just giving me a hard time. "How can you tell for sure?" he asks with a grin. On one leisurely walk through the sedgeflats, we watched and heard several snipe dive through the still morning air. But even with the benefit of binoculars and my coaching (for whatever that's worth), by the end of our hike Dale would only shake his head, chuckle, and say, "I'm just not convinced it's their flying and not their voices." He, like me, can be an obstinate cuss, so I let it go. It might have helped if one of the snipe had perched and shared with us its *wheet-wheet-wheet* display song, but none did that day. They were too busy circling and diving and generally showing off.

While listening to snipe and gulls, I scan the flats, to see if there's anything unusual out there. And there is. A lone person is crossing the mudflats north of the spit, a tripod slung across his shoulder. This is a rarity. Though I've found foot and boot prints, I've never met or seen anyone along that stretch of beach in the dozen or so times I've walked it. *Photographer or birder (or both)?* I ask myself. Curious to know, I drop down onto the flats. A few minutes later, we're close enough to wave and shout hellos. But only when he's a few feet away do I recognize the figure as Dave DeLap. I should have guessed, but his field outfit fooled me. Blue jeans, knee-high boots, and a bulky camouflage jacket cover his lanky frame, while a baseball cap tops his thinning, silvery-white hair and dark sunglasses hide pale blue eyes.

Dave is even more surprised than I am to have company out here. "Well, I'll be . . . Good to see you, Bill. I was wondering who that could be. Usually there's nobody else out here. You're the first person I've seen in a long, long time. Have you seen much?"

"Not really, beyond the usual stuff: gulls, geese, ducks, cranes, songbirds. What about you?"

"To be honest, it's been kind of slow overall. There should be a lot more shorebirds here by now," he replies in his deliberate, thoughtful way. "But a little while ago, I had a flock of two hundred or three hundred sandpipers land all around me. I saw them from a distance, skimming the flats, and stood absolutely still. And wouldn't you know it, they landed within twenty feet of me. They were too close, really, for me to use my new spotting scope."

A Zeiss twenty-to-sixty-power model, the scope is the first that Dave has bought since he got his first one, back in 1965. He confides, "It's a birthday present to myself and it's way overdue. Now that I've got it, I'm sorry I resisted upgrading for so long; I know what I've been missing all these years. It's expensive, but it's the best."

Like a starstruck kid who's just been given a long-desired telescope, Dave enthusiastically shows off his new gear and offers me a look at some ducks in a nearby pond. I agree: the clarity and magnification are superb, way better than what my binoculars can do. And I'm usually quite content with their performance. There's no question a spotting scope is a useful tool on these expansive flats, particularly when trying to distinguish one sandpiper from another, a greater from a lesser scaup, or a long-billed dowitcher from a short-billed. But for now, at least, my budget makes it clear that binocs will have to do. (Besides, I'm not sure even a scope would help me with the subtleties that so often distinguish one shorebird from another.) I suppose that's one measure of difference between a bird-watcher like me and a serious birder like Dave: how much we're willing to invest in specialized equipment.

In a similar manner, seriously dedicated birders are likely to chase around the countryside—or even travel on short notice to remote locales—for the chance to ID a rare bird. I have more of a naturalist approach: I'd rather devote my time and energies (and resources) to learning more about local residents, even if common. In many ways the "ordinary" critter, the one so often taken for granted, is just as fascinating as the extraordinary. Every being has its own unique story. Venturing a bit further along our distinct but interweaving paths, I'd suggest another difference: Dave's a specialist, I'm a generalist. Now that I've decided to learn about Anchorage's coastal refuge, I want to know about its plant communities, its human use, its many forms of wildlife, its changes through the seasons. Dave, meanwhile, is keyed into the birds. They are what lured him here and they keep bringing him back. This can work to my advantage; Dave is one of the experts who'll teach me about this place and its inhabitants. He'll show me things I wouldn't notice on my own.

The gear talk done, we return our attention to birds. Dave tells me this stretch of the coastal refuge is one of the best places he's found to watch the shorebirds that annually migrate through Anchorage. In fact, it's where he learned to tell them apart. From memory, he quickly runs down the list: sandpipers, dunlins, dowitchers, godwits, whimbrels, sanderlings, plovers, yellowlegs, snipe, and others. But shorebirds aren't the only draw. The ponds here attract lots of ducks and geese. And then add in the cranes, swans, pipits, horned larks, terns, gulls, and numerous songbirds—the list goes on and on.

It's no surprise that Dave, an obsessive statistician, is a serious lister. That's another difference between a bird-watcher like me and a dedicated birder like him. I've never been driven to keep track of all the species I've identified, or the where and when of first sightings. I have no life list. Yet I am something of a compulsive journal keeper and, as noted elsewhere, I've kept track of the various birds, mammals, and wildflowers I've identified in and around my yard. And I do take great pleasure in learning the names of local animals and plants and landscape features like creeks and mountains. Dulcy is at the other end of the spectrum. She's content to enjoy the beauty of a flower or birdsong or mountain without necessarily knowing its "identity"—or, to be more accurate, the identity we humans have placed upon it. And she sometimes wonders about my need to know, to name, to identify. I don't have a good answer for her, except to say that I get a certain satisfaction and enjoyment in learning—and remembering—the names (and, in the case of birds, the voices) of my wild neighbors. Maybe sometimes I take a little too much satisfaction in my knowing until being reminded, again and again, just how little I really do know. Then humility returns. In any case, for me the ritual of naming seems an important, maybe even critical, step in getting to know my neighbors better. Or recognizing them at all.

For all the differences in our approaches to watching birds, Dave, like me, is a guy who appreciates solitude. (I'd guess that's true of most bird enthusiasts.) So while other parts of the refuge may draw bigger crowds of birds, he enjoys coming to an area where he's likely to see lots of avian variety and few, if any, people. Though he visits this spot twenty or more times a year, some years pass without his meeting another human soul.

There's another thing that lures him back: a mix of the familiar and the unexpected. Over the years, this has become Dave's stomping grounds, the place he has taken the time and energy to know. And in getting to know what's usual, he's developed an eye for spotting the extraordinary.

This spring, as usual, Dave started coming here in early to mid-April, with the arrival of the first migrants. On his first several visits, he was content to stay atop the spit, or visit another point along the bluffs, about a mile to the north, and scan the flats with his brand-new scope. Only today did he finally see enough shorebirds to walk the beach. And along the way, he found himself surrounded by sandpipers.

Now ready to call it a day, Dave invites me to come along on his return hike. He'll show me yet another entry point; though it's marked by No Trespassing signs, he's gotten permission from the owners to cross their property and figures no one would mind if I passed through. Before starting, he asks me about the Klatt Spit entrance; he's stayed away this year because of the construction. I say I've entered there twice and nobody has bothered me so far.

Dave shakes his head, frowns, and repeats his now-familiar lament. "That's really a shame, the way we're losing places [to enter the refuge]. There used to be all kinds of access, but we're hanging by a thread now. I'm afraid we're going to lose it all. It just doesn't seem right."

As we cross the flats, Dave notes that the best time to come here is at high tide, because it pushes the shorebirds closer to the bluffs, making them easier to see. At extreme low tides, like the one this morning, the birds can be spread across thousands of yards of mudflats. "But you have to be careful at the extreme highs," he cautions. "There are places you don't want to be caught when the tide comes in." He then points out an "island" where he's gone a couple times at high tide, "just to do it." It's really not much more than a small grassy hillock of sand and clay that rises ten feet or so above the surrounding mudflats, a few hundred yards from the bluffs. Surrounded by Cook Inlet's frigid, muddied waters, he would nap, recon the area through his scope, and watch the savannah sparrows that nest on the island each spring.

We're nearing "Dave's Island" (as I would later name it) when a flock of two dozen sandpipers swoops across the tidal flats in tight, synchronized formation and then lands en masse nearby. Taking full advantage of serendipity, Dave quickly sets up his scope and aims it at the birds. Through my binoculars, they all look pretty much the same: tiny, short-billed, brown-and-gray shorebirds that pace quickly across the mud and through the shallows of a pond, dipping their heads frequently to probe for food. But where my eyes see one type of bird, Dave identifies three species. Most are least sandpipers, but he also picks out a few western and semi-palmated "peeps"—birder shorthand for the smallest sandpipers, which make high-pitched peeping calls. The mixing of species doesn't surprise him, because they often hang out together.

Beckoning me to his scope, the retired teacher serves up a lesson.

"OK, what I've got in there now are least sandpipers," he coaches. "It's the smallest of the peeps and it has yellow legs and a thin, pointed bill."

After I've studied them awhile, Dave maneuvers the scope until it's focused on a small group that happens to include all three types. "Look quick," he urges, "before they move off. See the two with rusty feathers on their heads and wings? Those are westerns."

The semi-palmated peeps also have black legs, which distinguish them from least sandpipers, but they don't have the westerns' bright rufous coloring. And their white sides, below the wings, aren't as heavily spotted.

I've looked at mixed flocks of sandpipers before while in the company of experienced birders, incuding a couple times at shorebird festivals. But this is the first time I've really seen and understood the differences. My private tutorial is already paying dividends. Now, if I can only remember the lesson.

We've mostly been walking on mud. But as we turn toward the forested shore, we splash through marshy fields of sedge, then come to a channel too wide to hop across. "You need to be careful here," Dave advises. "Some of these channels are deeper than they look. And when the tide's coming in, if it's an extreme high, crossing these could be a problem. There are places you want to avoid." He then points out some examples.

Between the sedge marsh channels and dry ground is a series of ponds, separated by mounds. Many of the ponds are angular, as if they've been carved out of the flats. That proves to be the case: they were excavated years ago by the Alaska Department of Fish and Game to "improve" the coastline's waterfowl nesting habitat. By all appearances, the ponds have done their job: dozens of ducks and geese now nest among these artificial ponds each summer, along with gulls and terns.

With Dave in the lead, we stay dry while weaving our way past the open bodies of water. I feel privileged to be learning features of this unfamiliar and potentially hazardous landscape, guided by someone who's been coming here for nearly forty years and clearly knows its nature.

Once back atop the bluffs, we follow a trail through open birch-spruce forest. Among the few stretches still not developed, this large wooded area appears to be both a neighborhood playground and longtime unofficial dumping ground. Scattered through the woods are kids' forts made from tree limbs, empty paint-ball packages, and all sorts of junk, from worn-out tires to rusting car parts, discarded appliances, broken glass, and plastic bags. There's even one old railroad car, its sides now charred and collapsed and a five-foot-high spruce tree growing from its rotted-out middle. How that got here, I can't begin to imagine.

Dave leads us to a puddle-sized water hole, where we wash the inlet's mud from our boots. Then we cross a tall-grass meadow, also a place where he has found pipits and larks, and enter another of South Anchorage's fashionable neighborhoods, this one named Resolution Point and located at the western end of Campbell Lake. Like several other local lakes, Campbell is surrounded by houses, with no public access.

On our way back to my car over by the spit, after I've thanked him for the tour, Dave says, "You know what? Friday morning is going to be one of the year's highest tides. Should be a good one for spotting shorebirds. Do you want to meet and see what we find?"

How can I turn down such an invitation? "Yeah, that would be great. Let's do it."

WE RENDEZVOUS SHORTLY AFTER 7 A.M. at Resolution Point, then carpool over to the Klatt Spit. By 7:30 we've passed the vacant house, rounded the fence, and peeked into the landfill meadow. Still no pipits, larks, or longspurs. "By golly, they're making a liar out of me," Dave grumbles. Serenaded by sparrows and warblers, we walk to the end of the spit. High tide is just a few minutes away. And because this is an extreme tide, the flats are flooded right to the forest's fringes. It will be awhile before we can descend to the mudflats, so we pull out binoculars and scope and look up and down the coast.

"For a bird-watcher, you just can't beat the spit," Dave exudes. "I mean, look at this view. We can literally see for miles. I sure hope there's a way someone like me can still keep coming out here. Maybe what I'll have to do is get a bunch of my friends to go in with me and buy a house along the bluff, then turn it into a B&B that caters to birders. That's about the only way I could afford to live along here."

The newly submerged coast at first appears empty of birds, but gradually they reveal themselves to us. In the distance, a juvenile bald eagle perches patiently atop a snag that pokes above the inlet's mocha waters. Violet-green swallows swoop and dive, while in the bushes below us, white-crowned and Lincoln's sparrows buzz and whistle. Two dozen white-fronted geese fly past, their pink bills, bright-orange legs, white rump, and white face stripe contrasting with mostly dark, brownish-gray bodies. Though they're not our main target, this is a noteworthy sighting, because white-fronts aren't very abundant locally. And of course there are the screeching gulls, a steady, raucous presence from mid-April through September. But no shorebirds.

"Well, this is surprising," says Dave, who gives a steady commentary on what we're seeing and hearing. Or, in some cases, not. "This should be a great time to see shorebirds. So where are they? Maybe we just need to be patient. Sometimes, when the tide starts going out, swarms of them just seem to come out of nowhere.

"You know," he adds, "big tides like this one revitalize everything. It brings in all sorts of good food. The birds must know that."

Finally, a small gang of peeps flies by, but they are far offshore and gone before we can get a good look. "OK, that's a start. They were probably least sandpipers. But that's really just a guess. There are a few people who could tell for sure, even at that distance, but I'm not one of them. I don't know how they do it. Maybe they're just guessing too."

The peeps are followed several minutes later by a group of five dowitchers: medium-sized shorebirds with long, straight bills and rusty-brown bodies. When feeding, they move their bills up and down rapidly while probing the mud in what's known as a stitching or sewing-machine motion. Dave is both pleased and disappointed by the sighting. On first spotting the birds at a distance, he'd hoped they might be whimbrels (which are larger, more brown than rusty, and have down-curved bills), which he hasn't yet seen this year.

The tide has receded enough by 8:45 for us to begin our walk. Down on the mud, Dave marvels again that "there's just nobody ever out here. Your common, ordinary birder is just not going to come out here and walk across the mud."

To avoid trampling the fragile vegetation we stay mostly on the squishy but firm mud, carefully working our way past tidal guts still running thick with the inlet's silt-rich water while skirting the outer edges of the sedge communities and ponds that border the bluffs. At first, things are quiet. Too quiet for Dave. Where are the sandpipers, the dunlins, the whimbrels, the plovers? Heck, we haven't even seen a yellowlegs. And Dave always sees yellowlegs here.

While waiting for the shorebirds to show, we turn our attention to the waterfowl swimming and feeding in the pond to our right. We see the usual suspects: mallards and pintails, shovelers and American wigeon, and of course Canada geese. By day's end we'll also add green-winged teal and greater and lesser scaup to our "bag." But the biggest prize of the day is a Eurasian wigeon.

"All right, now here's something special," Dave announces in his calm, understated way, his eyes still riveted to his scope. "Take a look at this."

Within the field of view is a duck with a pale gray body, pale rusty breast, darkly rufous head, and buff crown.

"That makes my day, right there," Dave says. "I first saw a Eurasian wigeon in Anchorage in May 1975 and I've seen at least one every year since; but there's only a couple pair that breed around here and you have to know where to look. For a lot of people, this would be a life bird"—a new addition to their life list.

When I tell Dave it is indeed a life bird for me, that makes the sighting all the more precious. "Oh, I didn't realize that. That's great."

The birding continues to improve. First we see a semipalmated plover, a handsome shorebird about the size of a sandpiper, with dark brown back and wings, white undersides, a dark brown to black breast band, short, black-tipped yellow beak, and bright yellow legs. The plover walks rapidly across the mud, then flies off with rapid wingbeats and high-pitched whistled call. "That's another good one," says Dave. "I was pretty sure we'd see some, but the way things were going, I was beginning to wonder."

Next, he spots a pectoral sandpiper. It's another first for me, and uncommon enough locally that Dave says he'll call it in to the Anchorage Audubon Society's bird hotline. In color and form, the pectoral resembles the least sandpiper, but it's considerably larger (though still on the small end of the sandpiper spectrum) and has an abrupt edge between its heavily brown-streaked breast and white belly, forming what some guidebooks describe as a bib. For all their differences, I'm not sure I could easily tell this sandpiper from the others we've seen without Dave's tips; unless, perhaps, they were standing still, side by side. Not a likely thing to happen.

"I've never seen just a single pectoral before," Dave notes. "What does that tell us?" Then, answering his own question, "I really don't know. Maybe the rest are hunkered down in the grasses."

We're approaching Dave's Island and nearing the end of our two-hour walk when, as if on cue, a group of eighty or more sandpipers wing into view. Swooping and turning in remarkably synchronized fashion, they move as one grand creature that flashes brown, then white, then brown again as the tiny birds expose their backs and bottomsides while twisting and turning at high speeds above the flats. It's a breathtaking show that the Blue Angels' precision-flying pilots would likely both admire and envy.

This is among the largest shorebird flocks I've seen locally, but Dave is unimpressed: "It gives you a taste, but it gets lots better than this. I've seen flocks with hundreds, even thousands."

We stand still, hopeful the birds will move closer, and they kindly oblige. Landing within a hundred feet, they gradually come our way, constantly jabbing the mud with their sharp beaks and murmuring in soft, peeping voices. Like the flock we watched earlier in the week, this one includes three species. Even looking closely, it's impossible to tell what the sandpipers are picking from the mud's surface or just below it, but their favorite foods include the polycheate worms, tiny clams, and other invertebrates that live in these dark sediments. Eventually we're surrounded by peeps, some within fifteen feet, maybe less. They go about their business as if we're not present and show no alarm even when we finally move on. Even as the Eurasian wigeon made Dave's day, these sandpipers make mine.

Soon after leaving the peeps, we're joined by several churring, clicking, dive-bombing arctic terns. Upset parents, no doubt. We must have invaded the nesting territory of these fiercely protective birds, but we keep walking and soon they fall behind.

The tide has now fallen enough that we can easily cross the channels and negotiate the ponds between the mudflats and shore. After following a footpath to an open, grassy bench atop the bluffs (complete with green plastic lawn chair), we stop for one last look. A morning that began overcast and calm is still gray but now windy and I slip a windbreaker over my head. Swarms of swallows slice through the air, hunting insects, while dozens of ducks and geese inhabit the ponds below. And a handful of dowitchers—maybe the ones we saw from the spit—are poking around one of the pond's margins.

"Don't ask if they're long- or short-billed," says Dave, who then does his best to determine which, in fact, they are. "Trying to tell them apart by the bill length is ridiculous. There just isn't much of a difference. To be honest, I think there's a lot of guesswork among the amateurs, even the good ones. Maybe the professionals"—meaning research biologists—"can tell, I don't know."

In the end, using the dowitchers' rusty color as his primary guide, Dave decides these are long-billed birds. "But your guess is as good as mine," he snorts.

Going down our list, we agree it's been a good day, though perhaps a tad disappointing from a shorebird perspective. "I just don't know why we haven't been seeing more," Dave says. "I wonder if they moved through early. Or could there have been some sort of die-off? Who knows. But these are unusually small numbers."

Sweeping his arms from left to right, he shares one final, wistful thought before we head into the woods. "Sometimes you can stand here, turn completely around, and see shorebirds in every direction. You'll just be surrounded."

GIVEN OUR SHARED INTEREST in the city's wild western fringes, my conversations with Dave have inevitably included some discussion of the controversy that finally got me interested in the coastal refuge: the proposed extension of Anchorage's much-beloved Tony Knowles Coastal Trail, named after the former mayor (later to become a two-term governor) who helped make it a reality.

Anchorage is blessed with one of the nation's finest trail systems. It is, most residents agree, one of the chief attributes that make our city a desirable place to live. The community's 128 miles of maintained trails are used year-round, by all sorts of recreationists. Joggers (and more serious runners), roller bladers, walkers, bicyclists, stroller-pushing moms and dads, wheelchair-pushing sons or daughters, horseback riders, ambling bird-watchers, anglers, wildflower collectors, berry pickers, and wildlife photographers frequent the trails from the end of breakup until snow covers the ground; and skate skiers, diagonal striders, walkers, snowshoers, and, yes, even wildlife watchers take over during the winter months.

Stretching some eleven miles along the city's northwestern edge, from downtown Anchorage to wooded Kincaid Park, the Coastal Trail is arguably the jewel of the system, given its easy access, variable terrain, scenic delights, and opportunities to see wildlife. Parts of the route are within an easy stone's throw of the mudflats, while long stretches follow bluff tops that rise a hundred feet or more above Cook Inlet beaches. The trail also winds along Westchester Lagoon, a popular gathering spot for boaters, bird-watchers, kite flyers, and picnickers in summer, and ice skaters in winter; and it crosses the mouth of Fish Creek, Anchorage's only remaining wild estuary.

From various points along the trail, it's possible to view 20,320-foot Denali and other snow-covered Alaska Range peaks, the Sleeping Lady (Mount Susitna, across Cook Inlet), moose, all sorts of birds, and even the occasional black bear, lynx, or, out in the inlet, beluga whales. There are also bluff-top parking lots from which people ogle the city's downtown skyline and neighboring Chugach Mountains, or watch sunsets, passing ships, and the jets flying in and out of Anchorage International Airport. In short, there's something for just about everyone. Not coincidentally, the Coastal Trail is one of the few places you can meet people of virtually every race, creed, nationality, and age group to inhabit the community. On a midsummer weekend, thousands of people wander the trail for all sorts of reasons: exercise, romance, family outings, solitude, relaxation, and engagement with nature.

Almost since the downtown-to-Kincaid segment was finished in the early 1980s, some residents have pushed to "finish" the trail; that is, extend it another thirteen miles across town, to the southernmost tip of the Anchorage Bowl. That push got a boost in the 1990s, when the state government funded a study of the potential routes. But the possibility that this trail might really be extended has also stirred up considerable opposition.

While trail boosters desire a "true" coastal route—that is, one that closely parallels the bluff-flats interface—opponents argue that any new trail should go inland, or not go at all. The reasons vary. Many of those opposed to the Coastal Trail extension are homeowning NIMBYs who live along the bluffs. They worry that a popular trail just beyond or below their backyards (and in some cases, perhaps, through their yards) will disrupt their views, their peace, their privacy, their property values. Others fear that a heavily used trail through the Anchorage Coastal Wildlife Refuge would harm the animals, particularly nesting migratory birds, that seasonally inhabit the flats and adjacent woodland corridor.

The proposed project has splintered the Anchorage community in unusual ways. Conservationists, for example, are split on the issue. And the divide is deep and wide. People whose opinions I respect stand firmly opposed to one another, while offering reasonable arguments for their differing perspectives. Dave DeLap, for example, is an active member of the local Audubon group and was the organizer of its annual Christmas Bird Count for more than three decades. He's convinced the Coastal Trail extension would be a good thing, even though it would diminish, if not eliminate, his ability to wander around the refuge's flats. (If it were to approve a designated path through the refuge, the state would almost certainly restrict human traffic off the trail, whereas now you can pretty much wander wherever you wish.)

"I think Anchorage would really mess up if we don't extend the trail along the coast," he says. "With all the diminished access, something like that is really needed, or people aren't going to be able to even get in the refuge. Fish and Game says you're going to harm the wildlife, but I think they're way off on this one. A trail [through the refuge] won't hurt anything if you put it right against the bluff and then keep people from going off it. Look at the Coastal Trail we've got now. Opponents predicted it would cause big problems, but what has it harmed? Ask anybody; it's been a great thing for Anchorage. A trail will help build support for the refuge, once people see what we've got here."

My friend Dale Gardner, a "greenie" type who has closely followed the debate, is another who sees more benefits than drawbacks to a coastal route. He's especially annoyed by the bluff-dwelling opponents who've "got theirs" and now want to keep others out. Most, he's certain, are motivated by selfishness rather than any sincere desire to protect the refuge and its wildlife.

The opposition of state biologists is less easy to ignore or denigrate. Dale admits they legitimately worry about the potentially harmful impacts of increased human use, and the accompanying increased presence of dogs, on refuge wildlife. But he's confident their concerns can be adequately addressed. For example, "any worries about nesting birds can be handled through a seasonal rerouting onto the bluffs, like the one that Tony Knowles proposed [while governor]. For most of the year, there wouldn't be any conflicts at all with wildlife." Or at least no more than along the established Coastal Trail, where humans have had run-ins with moose in every season. (Over the years, several people have been charged, and a few stomped, by agitated moose. And one edgy guy, who'd previously been threatened by a moose, shot a young bull simply because it approached him and his dogs too closely.)

Dale points out that the refuge is hardly a pristine place. As I've already noted, its natural land- and seascape have been substantially altered by the clearing of bluff tops and slopes for houses and yards, the installation of sewage pipes and construction of a railroad berm, neighborhood runoff, scattered trash, the presence of a rifle range, and autumn waterfowl hunting. Of course much of that occurred before the refuge was established in 1988.

"If this was an unspoiled place some distance from the city, I'd be among the first to say, 'Leave it alone. It's no place for a trail.' But that's simply not the case," Dale argues. "Yes, it's wild; but it's not even close to wilderness. And it's already part of Anchorage's urban landscape. There's evidence of development almost everywhere along its edges."

To those who have proposed an alternate inland route, Dale responds, "Then it's not a coastal trail anymore, is it? An inland route has its own set of problems, including [motor vehicle] traffic, and it doesn't have the appeal of a coastal route. It would certainly be more dangerous to trail users, especially in winter, because of all the street crossings."

Dale, like Dave, is certain that the proposed extension will ultimately work to the refuge's advantage. "Much larger numbers of people will get to know the refuge and at least some of them will come to appreciate its wildness, so you'll be building a new constituency. More people will become advocates for this refuge; and I bet some would also become advocates for [wild] coastal environments in other areas."

I agree with Dale and Dave on nearly every point. I especially like the fact that a trail across the refuge would introduce many more people to what I'm discovering is a remarkable place, with its own sort of raw, undiminished wildness, even if it is on the city's edge and shows some fraying around its margins. Still, I'm not as confident as they seem to be that harm to the refuge can be so easily avoided. The coastal lands south of Kincaid Park are much different from those to the north, largely because the more widespread sedgeflats and associated network of ponds provide substantially more opportunities for nesting birds. And the marsh vegetation is fragile stuff. Can the wildlife and their habitat be adequately protected if a trail runs along the bluff's edge? Two of the people who know the refuge best say no, loudly and firmly.

One of the staunchest trail-extension opponents is wildlife manager Rick Sinnott. Rick is among the few people to seriously explore the refuge throughout the year and his interest in its well-being is both personal and professional. He is absolutely convinced that there's no way to put a trail through the refuge without doing some harm. And the damage could be considerable.

"The existing trail was specifically kept out of the refuge because of the problems it could cause, so that tells you something right there," Rick begins. "I just don't see how you can have hundreds or thousands of people a day going through there and control what they or their dogs are doing. There's going to be impacts on the birds and their habitat. Plus in building the trail, you're going to change the hydrology, and that will change the habitat, perhaps significantly. And the way the route is planned, it's going to move on and off the bluff, which means clearing tens of thousands of trees. There's going to be a massive amount of damage."

The second naysayer of note is Smiley Shields. An activist granddad in his sixties, he's lived along the bluff since the late 1980s, upon returning to Anchorage after many years away. In fact, his house on Shore Drive was among the first handful to be built in a subdivision that now includes hundreds. In that light, he might be pooh-poohed as just another NIMBY. But Smiley is also a passionate naturalist with a doctorate in biology. He watches the flats daily and walks through them regularly. Over the years he's brought along many groups of people—family, friends, friends of friends, local conservationists, schoolkids—interested in knowing more about Anchorage's wild coast. I've gone out with him a few times myself and his enthusiasm for the coastal landscape is both undeniable and infectious.

Based on what he knows about the coastal flats and human behavior, Smiley too says there's simply no way to put a trail through these flats without degrading them and harming their critters. "If you start moving large numbers of people through here, some are going to go off the trail, no matter how many signs you put up telling them not to. At some point, it's going to become disruptive. And what about the dogs? You think you're going to keep them from chasing birds?

"I'm really afraid people would overrun this marsh out here and I'd hate to see it ruined. There's already a place, right in my neighborhood, where people have made a trail through the sedges and that trail is becoming a ditch. I'm afraid that ditch is going to change the water flow and plant distribution."

Smiley also believes that a trail along the proposed coastal route will destroy the narrow, grassy transitional zone between the forested bluff and sedgeflats. Where present, the "ecotone" is only a few feet wide, if that, yet it supports a large population of meadow voles. In spring and summer, many of the voles migrate into the sedgeflats, where there's abundant food. They in turn become meals for all sorts of predators, from northern harriers to sandhill cranes, weasels, and coyotes. If the vole population is harmed, one of the marsh's major food webs will be disrupted.

Given all the risks, Smiley can't imagine why some local conservationists continue to push for a trail extension, and he's gotten into some heated arguments with people he considers friends and natural allies. "The thing that really bothers me about this whole debate," he says, "is that I'm on the opposite side of the fence from people with whom I'd agree on almost everything else. In some quarters, I've become a pariah because of the stand I've taken. That's been hard."

Smiley isn't about to give up the fight despite muddied relationships, broad local support for the project—including that of Mayor Mark Begich and several Anchorage Assembly members—and new funding that will jump-start stalled trail-location studies. Even with local government support, the state will have to approve any new development within the refuge and the governor's office has so far stayed out of the battle. Even the most optimistic projections suggest that work on any sort of trail extension is still several years away. A lot can happen in that time.

In the meanwhile, Smiley faces a conflict of his own. The same path-turned-ditch that he cites as evidence of the sedge marsh's fragility, in arguing against the Coastal Trail extension, can also be used to criticize one of his favorite activities: leading groups into the refuge and across the sedgeflats. Smiley can't imagine ending such excursions, but he says he'll cut back, rather than fall into that well-known trap of loving a place to death.

The ditch has become a reminder to me, too, to stay on the mudflats as much as possible when exploring the refuge, rather than wander through the sedge-marsh community, unnecessarily trampling plants. It's not something I thought much about, until taking a closer look at this trail-extension debate.

I FIRST MET SMILEY IN AUGUST 2001, though I'd read about him—and his determined opposition to the Coastal Trail extension—long before that. An acquaintance told me about the refuge walks he led, and I arranged to go along on one of them. This was before I made it my goal to seriously learn about Anchorage's coast, but I still brought a journal and pen and a nature writer's curiosity. Eight or nine of us gathered in Smiley's living room (several in the group already knew him), where we introduced ourselves and talked a short while before dropping seventy-five feet from his house down to the flats for a late-summer's evening stroll. What I remember most from that night are Smiley's resemblance to jolly ol' Santa, his effervescent and almost nonstop chatter, his homemade macroscope (still in an early monocular prototype phase at that point), which he encouraged everyone to try, my own first tentative steps across Cook Inlet's mudflats, and the rotting carcass of a baby beluga whale, which the tides had deposited among the sedges.

I've visited Smiley a couple times since, and now I'm back again, sitting on his living room couch while he holds court for me and a neighbor. I feel pretty confident saying this is a guy who loves welcoming people into his home; every time I've come, he's had at least one other guest. Or maybe he simply craves human company. It's that gregarious, jovial nature, in combination with his ruddy face, full white beard, receding gray-white head of hair, eyeglasses, and rounded (but not overly large) belly that stirs thoughts of Kris Kringle whenever we meet; though when he's speaking, his voice reminds me more of folksinger Burl Ives than St. Nick.

Dressed in a dark, long-sleeved shirt and khaki shorts over white long johns, Smiley paces around the house while sharing some of his personal history and scattered pieces of what he's learned about the coastal flats outside his home's back windows. He's someone who can't seem to sit still for long. Even when telling a story, he gets diverted by tangents that jump all over the map. His actively creative and mechanical mind makes him a consummate tinkerer and his basement is filled with tools and gadgets and inventions in various stages of completion. He's especially proud of the macroscope, which has earned him considerable coverage in the local media and is now being successfully marketed on the Internet.

"Let's see. I moved to Anchorage with my folks in 1953 and graduated from Anchorage High School in 1959. I grew up on Boniface Drive surrounded by woods, if you can imagine that [it is now a highly developed part of town]. But back then, I didn't appreciate Anchorage, I didn't understand what makes it special. It wasn't until after I returned and settled down here, along the bluff, that I began spending more and more time exploring the flats. The first time I walked out into the marsh, I had no idea what I was looking at. You know, salt marshes like this one are a very rare commodity. These sedgeflats are a very dynamic community. They're constantly changing with the tides, the seasons. The best time of year to see how dynamic it is is while the plants are maturing, and then right after seeding. That's when you can really see the diversity."

Smiley briefly returns to his personal history: he went to the University of Oregon, then grad school at UCLA, where he got a PhD in animal behavior with a special interest in small mammals. He moved around a bit after school, working and living in Southern California and Florida before finally returning north.

Turning back to the refuge, he reflects, "The thing about these flats is that virtually no research has been done on them. Sure, we know what birds come through here, we know the larger mammals. But we really don't know much at all about the plant communities, the invertebrates, the little guys. They're totally under-studied."

Though trained in mammalian biology, Smiley has become most enthralled with the refuge's "little guys." That's one reason he developed his macroscope: to better see the small stuff. He lists a few of the not-so-charismatic critters he's found in the flats beyond his yard: polycheate worms, spiders, "exquisite" red mites, tiny black beetles, brackish-water snails, minuscule crustaceans that resemble fairy shrimp, and pinky-fingernail–sized clams.

Those clams, which Smiley identifies as *Macoma balthica*, are super-abundant in the mud. Based on his diggings, he guesses that some parts of the refuge contain up to ten thousand clams per square meter. "There's a tremendous number of clams and they're food for many of the birds you see out on the flats. They may represent the greatest biomass in the Anchorage area," he speculates. "In some parts of the world, people would be out there harvesting the clams, boiling them up to make a broth." You won't see anyone digging for fingernail clams here, though. It's likely most Anchorage residents don't even suspect the local mudflats are thick with clams.

Actually, to say the mud is packed with clams and other life-forms is a bit misleading. Throughout most of the flats all, or nearly all, of that packing occurs within a half inch of the surface. Everything beneath that shallow layer is anaerobic. Notable exceptions are the tidal channels, or guts, where worms may dig down at least a couple feet.

Before we know it, a half hour has passed. "I could go on like this for hours," Smiley says, "but we should probably get out on the flats, and see some of this stuff firsthand. Get your boots on and follow me."

Macroscope hung around his neck and a clamming shovel in hand, Smiley leads me through the knee-high dandelions that have taken over his backyard. Then we descend through open forest to the edge of the sedgeflats, where he resumes his off-the-cuff narrative. "This strip of forest and the grasses and sedges just beyond it are filled with voles. In summer they colonize the intertidal zone and feed on the root crowns of the sedges, which are the most nutritious parts. If you look closely, you'll see their trails everywhere; there are hundreds of them. I've also found some of their nests, just these little piles of duff."

We begin our passage through the marsh, brushing aside waist-high blades of green and squooshing through organic-rich muck that releases foul-smelling methane with each step. Now and then we pass bleached driftwood stumps, which have been floated in and then dropped by the inlet's highest tides. Pointing to one such snag, Smiley says they are "really, really important" to this ecosystem for at least a few reasons. First, they serve as lookout perches for hunting or scavenging birds, including northern harriers, sharp-shinned hawks, bald eagles, ravens, and even certain shorebirds, such as yellowlegs (which hunt invertebrates and small fish). They're also used by some male birds to announce their territories or put on a show for the ladies. And they sometimes become temporary refuges for voles seeking to escape the highest tides that occasionally swamp their feeding grounds. Less obviously, the jostling of such stranded stumps by subsequent tides can create puddle-sized ponds that become homes for aquatic insects, snails, and sticklebacks (a small fish) that again help to feed coastal birds.

His discussion of driftwood stumps and the ponds they form prompts Smiley to emphasize again how unique this stretch of sedgeflats is. "And I don't use the word 'unique' lightly," he adds. This whole sedge-rich area exists because of Fire Island, a five-mile-long piece of ground a few miles off the mainland and ten miles northwest of where we're standing. The island casts a shadow on this stretch of mainland shore, one that encourages deposition of inlet sediments while inhibiting erosion by its often-raucous tides and scouring ice. "Fire Island slows down the currents; it makes this a collector beach. There's truly wonderful collecting out here. I come out after the salmon opener every summer and find all kinds of Pixies and cherry bobbers and other lures. I've also found five dead beluga whales and a couple of drowned moose. You never know what you'll discover out here."

We've now reached the far edges of the sedgeflats. Before proceeding onto the mud, Smiley gives his version of a safety talk. "Everybody's heard horror stories about Cook Inlet's quicksand-like mud and a lot of people are terrified of it, because of those stories. But in fact there are very few places where you'll get stuck. You just have to pay attention to the ground you're standing on. I've been out here hundreds of times and walked a mile out onto the mudflats and I've never found anyplace I was in danger of sinking into the mud. A bigger danger, probably, are the tides. You have to pay attention to what they are doing. But even then, I've never seen a place where a person couldn't outwalk a tide.

"I basically have two safety rules for being on the mudflats. No. 1, never walk uphill, because you could end up getting stuck when the tide comes in. No. 2, under no circumstances go into a tidal gut. Those are the danger spots; they can fill up with eight to ten feet of water."

I've heard Smiley's safety spiel before, but I'm happy to listen again. Thanks to his encouragement I have gained the confidence to wander around the mudflats, while paying attention to both mud and tidal conditions. This evening we won't be going far. Smiley mostly wants to visit a few of the mudflats' "tide pools"—really not much more than shallow pools of brackish water in the mud—and dig into the muck to show me some of the coastal "little guys" that fascinate him so.

We wander across rippled silt and mud, Smiley stopping now and then to push his shovel into the sediments and then, kneeling, to inspect the small mounds he excavates. He's not a guy afraid to get his hands dirty. The black mud, he explains, is anaerobic. See how thin the lighter, brownish-gray layer is? That's where the organisms are. Together we study wriggling segmented worms, two to four inches long. Cranes, gulls, yellowlegs, and other birds gorge themselves on the orange-brown polycheates. Next Smiley points out looping, curlicued tracks and says they're left by clams. He digs some out and they are indeed small enough to sit on my pinky's fingernail, though their numbers seem much smaller than one per square centimeter. Using Smiley's macroscope, we get an up-close look at worms, clams, and little black beetles.

We're forced to cut our field trip short when a squall moves in, bringing wind-driven rain that quickly soaks us. Blasted by thirty-mile-per-hour winds and unsure when the drenching will end, we agree to retreat. As we head in, Smiley tells me about the family of cranes that are nesting in front of his yard, the swans that stayed two weeks ("I'd never seen them before in this part of the refuge"), and the time unusually large swarms of swallows converged on the sedges. A walk onto the flats revealed the marsh to be teeming with an equally unusual hatch of beetles, which the swallows were gorging on. He repeats his mantra: "There's just so much going on in the refuge that we don't know or understand."

We get one final treat while ascending the bluff to Smiley's house. Perched on the limb of a birch tree, less than fifteen feet away, is a northern goshawk. Humans and raptor consider each other in quiet stillness for several seconds, as if unsure how to respond to this unexpected encounter. Then the bird takes off, with great, silent beats of its wings, and disappears into the forest. For a few moments, not even Smiley can find words to describe the encounter.

BESIDES THE FIRSTHAND KNOWLEDGE that he's imparted, Smiley has helped me along my learning path by introducing me to a couple of specialists. Botanist Katie Turner is one of a very few people to study the refuge's plant communities, while invertebrate biologist Jerry Kudenov is in the process of documenting its spineless wonders. While both emphasize that there's still much work to be done, their specialized knowledge has enlarged my own sense of place. Katie, for instance, has forwarded me a refuge plant list that numbers fifty-eight species, each with its scientific and common name. (Botanists, it seems, love to use scientific names when talking about plants, much more than wildlife biologists do when discussing animals.) The diversity is much grander than a visitor would ever imagine from a casual stroll through the flats. Some plants I can easily identify myself—for instance, tall fireweed, dwarf birch, Labrador tea, wild pea, goose tongue. Others I've never heard of: fennel-leaf pondweed, seaside crowfoot, glasswort, foxtail barley—the list of unknowns goes on and on. I've also learned that the predominant sedge community includes four types. The most abundant, by far, is *Carex lyngbyaei*, the lyngbye sedge. Spread across wide swaths of the refuge, this tall, sturdy sedge stirs images of Midwest grasslands as it ripples in coastal breezes.

Admitting he still has much to learn about the refuge's creepers and crawlers and plant communities, Smiley arranges an early-summer field trip with Katie and Jerry. By early June, green-up is sufficiently advanced that we can ID a variety of plants. Within minutes, Katie has taught me the names of several species I recognize but can't identify. On the dry-ground ecotone between forest and flats is dunegrass, a common grass often seen along roads (and one of at least nine grasses scattered through the refuge's freshwater habitats). Moving onto the moist, saltwater flats, Katie points out *Potentilla egedii*, the yellow-flowered Pacific silverweed, and *Potentilla palustre*, or marsh five-finger, with its handful of purplish-brown petals; these are two of the sedge community's few wildflowers. All around us is the predominant lyngbye, a hardy pioneering plant that can tolerate both fresh and brackish water, while here and there are scattered patches of *Carex ramenskii*, a smaller, daintier sort of sedge.

"You have to ask yourself," Katie says, "why is one sedge in this spot, and another type over there? Is it the salinity, the oxygen content, the type of sediment, or some combination? Or is it something else altogether? There's just so much we don't know. It seems I always leave with more questions than answers."

In between my own questions, I furiously scribble notes while trying to keep up with the others as we splash through the flats. By the end of our short walk I'll have the scientific and common names, plus brief descriptions, of more than a dozen plant species. But how much will I remember? Keeping track is hard enough as we move from plant to plant, but my information overload is deepened by a second ongoing conversation about insects, arachnids, and worms. Jerry has been running transects through the refuge to learn more about its invertebrate population and Smiley periodically engages him in excited talk about deerfly larvae, land and brackish-water snails that are small enough to fit easily on the tip of a pinky, water striders ("they're nasty predators"), and the vermilion mites that today are swarming the mudflats. Then, like flipping a light switch, Smiley turns the conversation back to plants. It's a bit like making several new acquaintances at a raucous party and later trying to match faces with names, except much worse.

After wandering awhile among the sedges, we venture out onto the mudflats. There I'm introduced to a couple of salt-resistant grasses, *Triglochin maritimum* and *Puccinellia phryganodes*, maritime arrowgrass and creeping alkali grass, respectively. Though creeping alkali grass looks fragile, it's a tenacious plant at the outermost edge of the refuge's plant community, with sediment-stabilizing roots that go deep into the mud.

Our attention now turns to polycheate worms, one of Jerry's chief research interests. His studies have shown Anchorage's mudflats to hold a previously unidentified species of polycheate, a type of marine flatworm. Not much is known about the worm's life, except that it inhabits the soft muds of the tidal guts that slice through these flats. There they dig tubes through the mud while hunting diatoms, a form of microscopic algae. In eating their way through the mud, the worms also aerate it to depths of two to three feet. The worms, in turn, become food for a variety of birds: yellowlegs, gulls, cranes, perhaps even geese and swans.

Stepping gingerly into a tidal gut, Jerry borrows Smiley's shovel and then digs vigorously into the mud. "Look at this," he says, dumping a pile of goo onto the flats. "The density of these worms is stunning. They're just packed in there."

Indeed they are. The shovelful of muck writhes with fifteen to twenty orange-brown polycheates, from one to five inches long. Jerry collects a dozen or so, which he'll take back to the lab for closer inspection. Right now he's especially curious about their reproductive organs.

Headed back to shore, Smiley can't help but wonder: would the presence of this newly discovered species of polycheate worm be reason enough to slow, or even halt, the push for a Coastal Trail extension, at least until it's determined whether the trail's presence might threaten Anchorage's polycheate population?

SEATED BEFORE MY COMPUTER on the last morning of May, I decide, for no clear reason, to call Rick Sinnott. More than anything, it's a simple check-in. He and I have talked now and then about the refuge's sandhill cranes and his occasional forays into the coastal refuge to observe the tallest of Alaska's birds. (Though they don't stand as tall, swans are larger and much heavier birds and have slightly larger wingspans; bald eagles boast the largest wingspan of Alaska's birds, up to eight feet across vs. the crane's six to seven feet.) And we've discussed the possibility that I join Rick on one of his visits. The third of my three primary guides to the refuge, he's the hardest to pin down, especially during the May–June peak of activity, because his wildlife-management position requires him to be on call at all times. Between moose calving and the seasonal movement of bears into the city, he is one busy guy.

The timing of my call could have been better, but not by much. Over his cell phone, Rick tells me that he is in the midst of his almost-annual crane-nest hunt. He and field assistant Jessy Coltrane have been splashing across the sedgeflats since 8 or so, and it's now nearly 11. After apologizing for neglecting to tell me, he says I'm welcome to join them for the rest of the day's survey. After agreeing on a rendezvous point, I grab my field gear, jump in the car, and drive to the end of

John's Road, about a mile from where I once lived. I spot the pair through binoculars, then descend the bluff, cut through the woods, and slosh among the sedges.

Three hours into their survey, Rick and Jessy's findings are two nests and four eggs (three of them in one nest). That's about normal, Rick says. Cranes average two eggs per nest. And in the half-dozen years that he's been doing these refuge counts, he has never found more than five nests in a season or three in one day. Given the hit-and-miss nature of the survey and the crane pairs he's observed, Rick guesses that eight to ten couples breed within the Anchorage Coastal Wildlife Refuge each year. The majority nest along the refuge's southeastern border, not far from where the Coastal Trail extension is projected to pass. They would be among the animals most threatened by the trail.

Hundreds of other sandhill cranes pass through the refuge each April and May en route to more northerly nesting grounds. The most I've counted here at one time is fifty, but Rick and Dave DeLap have told me of gatherings that numbered in the hundreds. One of the migrants' favorite staging areas is within a half mile of the John's Road overlook, along the edges of a "ghost forest."

The 1964 earthquake that violently rattled much of Southcentral Alaska also dropped the region's shorelines as much as seven and a half feet. That subsidence swamped many coastal spruce forests with saltwater, killing the trees. Gray skeletal forms remain scattered along many coastal flats, including parts of this refuge. The cranes seem to use the dead trees as cover, often hovering along its fringes while they feed. Like humans and bears and chickadees, cranes are opportunistic omnivores that consume a variety of food. Along Anchorage's coast they can often be seen poking through the mud to get at clams and worms, but they also eat insects, snails, small fish, and the soft green shoots of emerging plants.

As with the refuge itself, I only recently began learning about the cranes that come here. Now I take great delight in tracking their passage through Anchorage each year. And I enjoy the wonder they seem to stir in humans. From conversations and random observations, it seems clear that these large gray wading birds with blood-red crowns have a widespread appeal that extends to people who don't normally consider themselves bird-watchers. I think that's partly because of their great size. Contemporary Americans, who've become so obsessed with "more, more, more" and bigger-better-faster-grander, like their animals big. Of course large wild animals are now uncommon throughout most of the nation (with the notable exception of deer and, in some areas, black bears), but not in Alaska. Thus the appeal of the Last Frontier's charismatic mega-fauna, like bears, moose, Dall sheep, caribou, and wolves.

There's something of a parallel in the bird world. Everyone notices raptors, especially the biggest of them; in Alaska that means bald and golden eagles. But other large birds also gain our attention, especially if they're elegant, noisy, or aggressive.

Consider swans, great blue herons, gulls, loons, geese, and, yes, cranes. Sandhills are loud birds, with strange, roarking voices that have a primeval nature. Their bugled calls, large, skulking bodies, and great flapping wings seem to stir thoughts of prehistoric times. And when cranes fly past, shouting their cries and flapping their large wings, people inevitably stop what they're doing and turn toward the sky. They pull us out of our routines, out of ourselves, and into the larger world, in a way that few other birds seem capable of doing.

Besides their intriguingly ancient forms and voices, cranes have elaborate "dancing" courtship displays that have, I've read, inspired artists and choreographers as well as birders and naturalists. I've only seen bits and pieces of the dances from afar, with leaps and bows and much wing flapping, but even that has been a rush.

Before I join the search, Rick gives me brief instructions: "The nests really aren't much more than matted mounds of grass. Some look distinctly nestlike, with a shallow bowl, but others don't look like much more than matted grass. To our eyes, they seem to be pretty much randomly placed, except that they're most commonly beside pools of water. So finding them is mostly luck. Most of the ones we do find are near past nest sites [which have been given GPS coordinates], or sometimes we happen to spook a crane off the nest. If you find one, just give a holler."

We split up, fifty to a hundred yards apart, and continue the sweep. The afternoon is sunny but breezy, with temperatures in the fifties, so mosquitoes aren't yet the nuisance they will be later in the summer. The muck beneath and between the sedges tugs at my boots and the inside of my pants' legs become soaked with the muddy water that I splash through. I see lots of orb-weaving spiders, iridescent green beetles and water striders, and savannah sparrows. From off in the distance come the voices of Canada geese, mew gulls, and ducks. A hunting harrier passes by, gliding low over the sedges. And a handful of cranes show themselves, either flapping and roarking overhead or skulking across the flats. But bird nests of any sort are few and far between in this section of the sedgeflats. We find two duck nests, belonging to pintail and mallard pairs, and another built by snipes. That's all, for the next four hours.

PERHAPS FEELING BADLY THAT HE didn't invite me from the start, Rick offers to show me a nest with eggs that he and Jessy found two days earlier. It's in another part of the refuge, below Kincaid Park. Again, how can I refuse?

We meet at 8 a.m. on a drizzly but calm Saturday. From our parking spot we cross the grounds of a recycling center, then follow the Coastal Trail a few hundred feet before cutting through the woods and dropping down to the flats. Rick expects us to locate the nest quickly. After all, only two days have passed since he found it. On Thursday the female crane jumped off her nest as the two biologists approached. But this morning, though the male watches us from a distance, his mate hunkers down and refuses to budge.

Rick goes to a bleached log that he remembers from two days earlier and uses it as a reference point. The nest should be within one hundred feet. But as we split up and then circle and recircle the log at different distances, we still can't find any sign of the female or nest. (He didn't bring the GPS information, figuring he would easily re-locate the nest.)

Shrugging, I kid Rick. "I guess this just shows how well they camouflage their nests."

"Yeah," he replies unhappily. "They're darn good at it."

Rick is both befuddled and frustrated. The nest has to be here somewhere. But where, exactly? We continue inscribing arcs in the flats for nearly half an hour. We know we're close and it seems we've covered all of the nearby terrain at least once, some places twice; I'm starting to recognize spots I've already passed. Now and then I stop and peer through my binoculars. Even as we circled the bleached stump, the male crane had circled us, his body hunched. But now he's off in a pool of water, probing its muddy bottom for food. Apparently he figures we're no longer any danger.

"I can't believe this," Rick mutters. "I know we're close. She's probably covering the eggs, with her body and wings spread flat across the ground. We could be within twenty feet and not know it."

I stop again, wipe the misted lenses of my binoculars, scan the flats. Putting the glasses back down, I look around and notice a rounded reddish-brown–and–gray lump off to my right. At first it looks like a rusty rock. But then the lump becomes the body of a crane. Gradually I make out the bird's head, her long, pointed beak, red crown, outstretched wings, and yellow eye.

"I see her," I yell to Rick, pointing. "Over there."

Eyes squinting, brow furrowed, he looks hard. Then, "OK, I see her. Good job."

Slowly, we approach. As we do, the crane stands on her long, black legs, runs off several yards, and watches us in what I assume is intended to be a threatening pose: body hunched, wings spread, mouth open wide. We go up to the nest. It's a slightly matted mass of brown sedge with a small depression, hardly distinct from the surrounding vegetation. Inside it are two eggs, slightly larger than goose eggs. Mostly a muddy tan, they are a darker rusty brown at their larger, rounded end. "It's to make them less obvious, help them blend in," Rick explains.

We stay at the nest only a few moments. The female encourages our retreat. Mouth still open, she scampers ahead of us, crouching, wings open and dragging along the ground. The male follows at a distance.

"She's trying to lead us away," says Rick. "It's the old broken-wing routine."

Neither of the parents has "spoken" the entire time, though Rick says they sometimes squawk harshly when upset. A couple hundred feet from the nest the female crane begins circling off to the right and back to her nest. We continue our retreat as the parents converge. Any day now, their eggs will hatch to reveal large, downy chicks. Within a day or two of hatching, they'll leave the nest and follow their parents around the flats. The offspring will then stay with their parents through the fall and following spring migrations, then separate.

I take one final glance back as we regain the woods. I make a mental note of the setting and wonder how easily I would find the nest if I were to return in a day or two, even while knowing it's unlikely I'll come back anytime soon, given my busyness and scheduled trips in the weeks ahead.

I'VE BEEN LUCKY TO HAVE so many teachers and guides while getting to know Anchorage's coastal refuge. They have accelerated my education, offered insights and perspectives I might never have reached on my own, inspired me to learn more, and reminded me that even the "experts" know only a tiny bit about the functioning of this wild ecosystem. In a very real way, they've become part of my coastal landscape, every bit as much as cranes and sedges and polycheate worms.

Yet this mentored learning is only one piece of my education and must—for me, at least—be balanced by firsthand discovery. Nearly every time I visit, I return with some new piece of information, some new understanding. Or new questions. In the end, if I persist in my studies, the landscape and its inhabitants will be my primary teachers. Over time, they'll reveal patterns, relationships, seasonal cycles, oddities, and hints of larger mysteries.

By the end of my second full summer spent exploring the refuge, I've already begun to learn when and where I'm most likely to find swans, white-fronted and snow geese, arctic terns, yellowlegs, and other species of coastal birds; I've followed a family of cranes, off and on, for several weeks, as the chicks grew into juveniles and learned to take flight; I've watched ocean-bright coho salmon swimming through Campbell Creek's intertidal waters, bound for spawning grounds on the far eastern side of Anchorage; I've tracked coyote, moose, and weasel footprints across the mud; I've witnessed a raven mercilessly harass an eagle, then in turn be dive-bombed into fleeing by a protective arctic tern parent; and I've found a place where northern harrier mates hunt the sedgeflats for voles and other prey.

In the coastal refuge I have finally learned to identify the songs, markings, and habitat of savannah and Lincoln's sparrows. Here too, after years of procrastination, I've begun to recognize the many different ducks that pass through Anchorage each year, though I have a long way to go. And I have come to know more about the language, hunting techniques, and territorial behavior of arctic terns.

LONG FASCINATED BY THE FEROCITY and beauty of these amazing long-distance flyers, I enter the Anchorage Coastal Wildlife Refuge on an early July day, keeping watch for terns, seeking further glimpses into their lives.

Crossing a meadow of sedges, I skirt some ponds inhabited by several families of Canada geese, mallards, and American widgeon, while goslings and ducklings cluster about their parents on an early-morning swim. Gulls screech loudly as they circle and swoop above the ponds and their green perimeters, while families of violet-green swallows cut arcs through the calm air in their hunt for insects. In the distance, a fuzzy, gangly sandhill crane chick already bigger than an adult goose follows its parents, mimicking their slow, deliberate pace. Noticing me, one of the cranes calls loudly—*quoark . . . quoark*—in its rusty-door-hinged way and the cinnamon chick disappears into the sedges.

A hundred yards away or more, a couple of arctic terns hover over small tidal guts that wind through the mudflats. I sit upon the bleached trunk of a cottonwood that's been carried here by Cook Inlet tides and I watch the terns through binoculars. They are such handsome, streamlined birds and seem to carry themselves through the air with effortless grace on their slender wings.

Such flying talent is needed for their remarkable migrations. Arctic terns are the world's long-distance flying champs; some members of their species make annual migratory flights between the high Arctic and the Antarctic, a round-trip distance of nearly twenty-five thousand miles. Those that spend their summers locally arrive from late April into early May. Mates will breed sometime in May and chicks hatch in June, reaching fledging stage in July. Most parents and offspring will then begin their southern migrations sometime between late July and mid-August.

As I sit, a tern flies in and perches on a nearby bit of driftwood. Now and then the bird makes a cheeping sound, one note at a time. Has the watcher become the watched?

I admire the tern's sleek form, its black cap and striking blood-red bill and feet, which contrast so sharply with the white cheeks, neck, and breast, the pale gray wings and back. After several minutes, the bird lifts off and heads farther out onto the mudflats, where it joins another hovering tern. Mates, perhaps, engaged in hunting. I decide to follow. And in a matter of moments, an alert is sounded. The two terns approach, yelling loudly in a shrill, raspy voice. In field guides, the tern's alarm call is usually described as some variation on *keee-eer*, though to my ears it sounds closer to *eee-aagh* or *kee-aagh*.

Soon the couple is joined by other terns. I count five, then ten, then a dozen. It's as if they have appeared out of nowhere. I must be getting close—but to what? I can't imagine the terns would try to raise a family out on the mudflats, where the inlet's highest tides would swamp their nests. I've read that they will sometimes defend feeding territory. Is that what's going on? Or do they indeed have nests—or chicks—hidden among the salt-tolerant grasses and goose tongue plants that grow along the mudflats' meandering gullies?

My walk onto the mudflats is shortened when a pair of terns starts dive-bombing me. Now uttering clicking sounds, the birds come straight for my head, then lift or swerve at the last moment. Occasionally they swoop in close enough for me to hear the whoosh of their fast-moving bodies.

Arctic terns have been known to defecate on intruders and peck heads or hands uplifted to ward them off, sometimes drawing blood. Somehow my baseball cap doesn't seem enough protection. As the swooping birds increase their attack, I retreat back to the cottonwood. Almost immediately, the terns disperse. Content to keep my distance, I scan the coastal flats. Though some terns continue flying across the mudflats, others hover above the ponds, hunting sticklebacks and sculpins.

There is magic in the way a tern hunts. Hovering in place, with its long, forked tail spread wide for balance, the bird lifts its wings high above the body and beats them rapidly. Seen from below, the body is mostly white. And in that hovering whiteness, with the blood-red beak and black skullcap, the bird becomes a heavenly apparition.

If angelic, however, the tern is undoubtedly an angel of death. Sometimes hovering at thirty feet, other times just a few feet above the water, the tern zeroes in on its prey. Closing its wings, it then goes into a dive and plunges into the water with a splash. Terns also feed by skimming the water, delicately picking prey at or near its surface. If successful at either plunge or skim methods, the bird emerges with a fish, or insect, or crustacean, which it quickly swallows or carries to its mate or young.

Still curious about the terns' mudflat attacks, I return to the refuge later in the week. Crossing the flats seaward from the sedge meadows and ponds, I notice that most of the terns fly above, or near, the pools and surrounding marsh, though they occasionally make forays out to the mudflats. As long as I avoid the area I entered a few days earlier, they leave me alone.

Playing a hunch, I return to the spot where I'd been dive-bombed. Again, one loudly *kee-aaghing* tern zooms toward me, quickly followed by another. Others are drawn by the alarm, but they are content to hover and swoop high above me. Only a couple birds actually attack.

Now confident that this is a nesting pair, I skirt the tidal gut, looking closely among the grasses and goose tongue that grow above its banks. Finally I find it:

an oval nest of dried plants and mud, nestled into a patch of goose tongue. Inside the grassy bowl are two eggs, beige oval forms speckled with dark brown spots.

It's late in the season for unhatched eggs. I lean in close, extend a finger, and touch one: still warm. Then I back off, so the parents will return.

Though their mottled color matches guidebook descriptions, the eggs seem large for terns and I wonder if they instead belong to a mew gull. I'd seen one from afar, sitting near this locale. But with my attention turned toward the terns, I hadn't kept close track of the gull's movements. Perhaps it abandoned the nest as I approached. That would also explain why the terns have temporarily eased their attacks: their nest and offspring aren't being threatened.

Whether this is a gull or tern nest isn't so important; clearly, some birds, for whatever reasons, are nesting out on the mudflats, risking the tides. I've solved the riddle. I turn toward shore to make my retreat, still checking the ground but moving faster now. The terns return and escort me across their territory, diving at my head. One of them lets loose and splashes my shirt with watery guano. Finally they leave, attention turned to other potential intruders, still loudly *kee-aaghing*.

I HAVE ALSO OBSERVED BEHAVIORS that produce more questions than answers. Several times in late summer or early fall, for instance, I've noticed large groups of magpies leapfrogging their way across the sedgeflats. Never venturing far from the woodland fringe, they stop here and there to engage in loud, squawking conversations. Then, as if by some shared signal, they'll suddenly fly off. It's as if they're on a social outing, raising a good ruckus. Magpies most often travel alone, in pairs, or in family groups. When do they join together in these large bands? And why? Why do they periodically invade the coastal flats? And what prompts them to leave?

Even more curious is the midsummer mudflats walkabout of two yearling moose. I first notice the moose as they browse the edges of a pond. Nothing peculiar about that; I frequently see moose within the sedgeflats or along its wooded border. The next time I look in their direction, the moose are headed outward through the sedges, toward Cook Inlet's expansive mudflats. One moose stops, but the other continues several yards onto the mud. Then he turns his head and waits, as if beckoning—or daring—the other to follow. From their size and behavior, I guess that they've recently been weaned from Mom. Left to their own devices, they're out for a romp.

Like two teenagers in search of adventure, and maybe a little trouble, the moose head out onto the flats and keep going. And going. And going. Finally they're so far out I can barely see them without binoculars.

They must be well over a mile from shore. What are they doing out there? There can't be anything for a moose so far from shore. Or can there? Could I be witnessing some form of ungulate curiosity? Playfulness? Again I'm reminded how little we humans know about other creatures. As the saying goes, "the more you know, the more you know you don't know."

Rather than trying to interpret their actions, I decide simply to enjoy the moose's wild walk. It can't be an easy ramble, given the mud's soft, squishy nature. Now they're so far out that they've become tiny specks even with binoculars. The day's warming has produced a heat-wave mirage and it appears the moose are walking on water. A miracle, indeed.

They walk, they trot. They slow and walk some more, then stop and stand awhile. I begin to wonder if one, or both, has become stuck. What would happen if they got caught by an incoming tide? Could they outrun the water? Smiley Shields has told me he's occasionally found dead moose on the flats, but there's no way to know if they got caught in Cook Inlet's tides and drowned, or died some other way.

Eventually the moose return, after doing a large loop. They've been out on the mudflats for nearly two hours. Walking with a steady gait, they leave the mud and recross the sedgeflats, then casually enter the woods and disappear, as if they've done nothing strange.

THERE'S MORE THAN LEARNING INVOLVED here, of course. I delight in my solitary walks through the refuge, "alone" among the winnowing snipe and coyote tracks and screeching gulls. If guided walks have added immeasurably to my knowledge of Anchorage's coastal flats, then to a similar degree, my solo visits have deepened the emotional and—dare I say it?—spiritual bond I've come to feel with this place and its wild inhabitants.

The refuge is important to me now. It's important not only because of the amazing and diverse coastal life that I've learned it protects, but also because this narrow expanse of coastline adds richness and depth to my life. Now, when I'm at home or hiking in the Chugach foothills and look toward Cook Inlet, I recognize specific spots along the shoreline; I recall walks and memorable encounters. Memories are stirred, connections strengthened. I see more of the bigger picture that is Anchorage.

My building relationship with the refuge has motivated me to learn more about the existing Coastal Trail and the habitats it crosses, from mudflats to estuary to forest-covered bluff. In spring and early summer I've gone downtown to Westchester Lagoon on guided, early-morning bird walks. In winter I've gone skiing with local naturalist John Wenger, who's showed me a spot where a northern saw-whet owl persistently sings its single-note *too-too-too-too-too* song. I've explored the Fish Creek estuary with good friend and fellow writer Ellen Bielawski, who shared childhood memories of the summer nights that she and neighborhood friends would sneak down to the estuary and walk barefoot through its mud and sedges, and, at low tide, jump across the creek. I've gone "walking and wheeling" with my arthritis-crippled mom, pushing her in a wheelchair along the paved path. On our outings together we've identified local birds and wildflowers and berries and shared the trail with moose. And I've gone on many walks alone, just to see what I might notice.

The refuge brings me joy. And, sometimes, peace. Morning walks, especially, seem to lift my spirits. The day is still young, the light soft, the air often calm or only gently stirring, the background city noise quieter. As I walk to the edge of the bluffs, the first things I notice are the voices of birds. The animals themselves are sometimes hard to find, hidden among the trees, bushes, sedges, and other plants, but their songs and calls liven the landscape with screeches and cries, honks and squawks, peeps and chirps. The voices pull me out of my modern, rush-about urban world into their more timeless one. And the shift is a pleasing one.

It's not that I imagine an unrealistic harmony among the refuge's wild inhabitants; I understand that they are engaged in their own life-and-death dramas. All manner of creatures are eating and being eaten. I realize too that summer, for migratory birds at least, is in some ways more frenzied than for humans, with all the breeding, nest-building, rearing, and feeding to be done in a few weeks' time. Yet here my own busyness washes away, along with the routines and pressures of city life. And on most visits, especially when the refuge is rich with life, I'm pulled out of myself. As I become more tuned into my surroundings, a kind of forgetting occurs. I'm more in the present and more in my body, less in my head (where I spend altogether too much time). At times, I suppose, my hikes through the refuge are a walking meditation. That too is a good thing. As I write these thoughts, I realize that this refuge has become another sanctuary for me.

MID-OCTOBER. IT'S A RAW, leaden, blustery day, much like the one in mid-May when I happened to meet Dave DeLap, except much colder. Bundled up against the chill, I stand on the bluffs near Resolution Point and scan the flats. The sedges are brown once more and the ponds below are skimmed with ice, a reminder that winter is fast approaching. This will likely be my last visit for quite awhile. Soon all of the migrants will be gone. And within a few more weeks the landscape will be a frozen white. I'll come here only a few times during the winter, sharing the flats with an occasional raven, eagle, moose, and, if I'm lucky, coyote, and not much else. With winter's scarcity, the coastal flats just don't have the same allure.

The ponds' diminishing open waters are occupied by several dozen ducks. Nearly all are mallards, though I spot one misplaced merganser. A few gulls fly around the ponds and others are scattered on the mudflats. Three magpies fly along the bluff edge and a single raven is perched atop a snag. There's also a surprise: a family of trumpeter swans swims in one of the ponds.

Later, crossing the flats at low tide, I notice that the swans have taken to the air. There are six in all: two white adults and four cygnets, the palest of grays. The swans fly in a wide arc, looping toward the south, then swinging back north, over the distant water. They're so far away that I can't easily see them with the naked eye, so I follow the family with binoculars. All the birds flap their wings strongly; I can't distinguish the adults from their young by wingbeats alone.

The swans land near the mouth of Campbell Creek. I wonder what draws them there. Food? I also wonder if this might be the same family that Dulcy and I encountered in September at Denali State Park's Byers Lake, a hundred air miles to the north. Wherever they began their autumn journey, they're unlikely to stay here long before pushing on. Seeing them during today's brief visit was a bit of good fortune.

Turning my attention away from the swans, I face into the gusting breeze and pull my wool cap tighter. Walking again, I savor the sticky pull of mud on boots, the raw slap of wind, the distant screech of gull.

SPRING 2007. FIVE YEARS SINCE my own guided introduction to the refuge, I am now a regular who's introduced several friends to the coastal flats. Those visiting for the first time almost always express joy—and surprise—at the fecundity of this still-overlooked wonder. And the fact that they can walk here without getting hopelessly stuck in the mud or risk drowning.

For now the proposed Coastal Trail extension has been put on indefinite hold, much to the relief of Smiley Shields and Rick Sinnott and other opponents, and to the dismay of many other residents, like my friend Dale Gardner. The longer the project is put off, the less likely it is to happen. Though I remain somewhere in the middle, I'm happy enough that no trail will run along the edge of these flats. The more I visit, the more I agree with Smiley and Rick that a trail could be disruptive. Certainly it would impinge on the solitude that people like Dave DeLap and I find here.

The access issue has been at least partially resolved, with the opening of Discovery Hill's fenced-in field, now called Carr-Gottstein Park after the Anchorage developers who have unlocked this entryway. Now dog walkers, hang gliders, bird-watchers, and others can enter and cross the neighborhood's open space to the landfill spit. Most people go no farther; but I've noticed more boot tracks—and more people—exploring the flats. Still, on most visits I continue to have the refuge to myself, for as far as I can see. Of course I'm not really alone. Even in the depths of Anchorage's coldest and darkest season, I'll usually notice a raven or two. And once spring returns, the place is uproarious with life.

NINE

Chugach State Park

Wilderness at the Edge of Town

Spring

Friday afternoon, the end of a busy work week—so busy that I've kept myself sequestered indoors, despite six straight days of bright blue skies, glorious sunshine, and springtime warmth. Today, finally, I leave my hurried, too-much-to-do city life and head for the hills east of town. After too long away, I return to Anchorage's backyard wilderness, Chugach State Park, back to visit an old friend: Flattop Mountain.

Huffing and puffing, sweating heavily in the fifty-degree air, I slog my way up Flattop's still-snowy trail. At lower elevations, new shoots are poking their green heads through the soil and tree buds are opening, but here in the alpine, winter stubbornly resists spring's flirtations. Following bootprints of other hikers through mud and slush, I experience a strong sense of déjà vu. The feeling, however, seems less eerie than inevitable; I have indeed passed this way many times before. Enough times that my feet have almost memorized the trail's twists and turns. Moving steadily upward, I leave the slush and traverse talus piles of mostly bare rock, then, with the help of an ice axe, scramble up the final wall of sun-softened snow.

Within forty-five minutes, I'm on the mountain's 3,550-foot tabletop summit and gazing across a huge chunk of Southcentral Alaska: far to the north, beyond vast swampy lowlands and humpbacked foothills, the skyline is dominated by the Alaska Range's twin giants, 20,320-foot Denali and 17,400-foot Sultana (officially known as Mounts McKinley and Foraker), while nearly a hundred miles to the southwest is Mount Redoubt's volcanic cone. More immediately below me are the greening flatlands of the Anchorage Bowl and the gray, soupy waters of Cook Inlet.

At my back, walling the eastern horizon, are the Chugach Mountains: alpine wilderness on the doorstep of Alaska's largest city. It won't be long now before these hills and valleys are graced by brilliantly colored wildflowers and the bright songs of warblers, sparrows, robins.

A strong wind usually roars across Flattop's summit, but today the air is calm. It's so still, so quiet, that I can hear the snowpack melt: faint slumping noises reflect audible shifts in crystal-liquid interfaces, as snow yields to water. No other sound but my breathing until a flock of honking geese flies overhead, newly arrived from southern wintering grounds. Once the geese pass, there's not a creature in sight. No Dall sheep. No ravens. No people. All the solitude I could ever desire.

Time passes. From somewhere out in the mountains come human voices. Three hikers on a neighboring ridge glissade down a steep snowfield, their shrieks and laughter sliding across the still air. I'm content to sit and relax, skin caressed by gentle April sunlight and busy mind melting into tranquil contentment.

My reverie is briefly interrupted by the buzzing arrival of another warm-weather celebrant. A mosquito circles around my head, then lands softly on my arm. I watch it step across my shirt, doing its mosquito thing: probing, prospecting for blood. It's early enough in the season that I tolerate—even appreciate—the mosquito's surprising presence, one more reminder of summer's approach.

As afternoon gives way to evening, a few other hikers join me on top. Later, returning to the trailhead, I meet at least a dozen people bound for the summit, a hint of what's to come in the weeks ahead. Within a month or two, such a warm and sunny day as this will lure crowds of people to Flattop. By September, some ten thousand people—preschoolers, senior citizens, solitary hill runners, entire families, curious tourists, and hard-core mountaineers—will have scrambled up its trails.

In a state with nineteen peaks above fourteen thousand feet and seventeen of the nation's twenty highest mountains, Flattop is a mere bump, an ordinary hill. But locally this sawed-off mountain has an extraordinary allure. Less than fifteen miles from downtown Anchorage and visible throughout the city, Flattop is easy to find, easy to reach, and, as mountains go, easy to climb. From the main trailhead, it's only one and a half miles and 1,350 feet in elevation gain to the summit. And in summer no climbing expertise is needed; the ascent is more of a strenuous hike, with some rock scrambling necessary near the top. (That's not to say the mountain can't pose dangers; a handful of people have died on its slopes, in falls and snowslides.) Most people can be up and back in two or three hours. Nearly all of Anchorage's residents, it seems, have climbed Flattop, or at least tried. And enough succeed to easily make this drab brown hill the most-climbed mountain in Alaska.

For many, including me, Flattop was the initial lure to the 495,000-acre "accessible wilderness" east of Anchorage. I first scrambled up its slopes in the early eighties, a sports writer newly settled in Anchorage intent on exploring some of the city's fringes. I've come back to this hill and its neighbors again and again to clear my head, exercise my body, reconnect with this marvelous wild landscape so close to home.

Established in 1970, Chugach State Park encloses the western edge of the Chugach Mountains, a three-hundred-mile-long coastal range that arcs from Cook Inlet almost to the Canadian border. Measured in absolute numbers, the Chugach Range is not especially grand; its tallest peak, Mount Marcus Baker (east of the park), is only 13,176 feet high, nearly a mile and a half shorter than Denali. But measured from base to summit, the Chugach is Alaska's second-highest coastal range. These mountains also give birth to long rivers of glacial ice, more than a quarter of the state's total.

Though neither as high nor as remote as its eastern extension, the western Chugach beyond its civilized fringes is a wild and rugged mountain kingdom, rich with wildlife, jagged spires, forested valleys, rushing streams, tundra meadows, and alpine lakes. Within Chugach's park boundaries are 155 peaks (the highest is 8,005-foot Bashful), dozens of glaciers, two thousand Dall sheep, five hundred mountain goats, four hundred black bears, three hundred moose, twenty-five grizzlies, and at least two wolf packs. A place of expansive alpine tundra that's fringed by boreal forests and coastal waters, the park is seasonally inhabited by nearly fifty species of mammals—from orcas to little brown bats and five species of shrews—one hundred species of birds, nine species of fish, and one amphibian: the wood frog.

Largely unknown outside the state, the park is visited more than a million times annually, 90 percent of those by Alaskans, and is regarded by many locals as Anchorage's "crown jewel," a wild playground that adds immeasurably to the quality of life. If you live here and love the outdoors, the city and adjacent park are inextricably linked.

Anchorage economist Gunnar Knapp once determined that nearly three-fifths of Alaska's population resides within forty miles of the park. And those nearby residents use the park heavily, in myriad ways: camping, picnicking, berry picking, taking photographs, viewing wildlife, backpacking, hiking, sightseeing, rock and ice climbing, horseback riding, mountain biking, hang gliding, boating, fishing, hunting, snowmobiling, snowshoeing, mushing, skiing, and quiet reflection.

For all of that use, most people never venture more than a mile or two into the park and probably no more than a few dozen have explored Chugach's most remote ridges and valleys.

Summer

Wrapped in my sleeping bag, I am immersed in Captain Ahab's crazed rantings about an evil white whale when the high-pitched whine of a zipper pulls my attention to the front of the tent. Ellen, my friend and fellow writer, pokes her upper body inside the door. Then, appraising my bundled body, she smiles wickedly and gushes, "It's glorious out here."

Glorious? *Waterlogged* is what comes to my mind as I stare at the wetly pulsing tent fabric and bedraggled figure before me. Or perhaps sea-battered. Her face reddened from a slashing wind and water pouring from her hair and rain suit, my happily soaked friend could easily be a crew member on Ahab's storm-wracked *Pequod.* And she's been outside for all of ten minutes.

In a sense we are being blasted by an ocean gale, though camped miles from the coast in alpine wilderness. Both rain and winds were born where whales cruise and frolic, the Gulf of Alaska.

By late afternoon, the storm has demanded my attention for much of the past twelve hours. It has never strayed far from either conscious thought or my dreams since late last night, when high winds out of the southeast began pummeling our tent during a late-summer backpacking trip into Chugach Park. Joining the wind sometime after midnight, rain has beat a steady staccato against the nylon fabric ever since, sometimes with a soft tapping, other times with a deafening vengeance. At its peak, the rain noisily splatters against the tent as if someone were pelting us with sand or blasting us with a fire hose. I sink deeper into my sleeping bag, instinctively ducking the blows.

The wind, meanwhile, shakes the tent wildly, snaps it back and forth, pushes and pulls at the metal tubing that gives the tent shape. During brief lulls, our shelter rustles and crinkles like a plastic shopping bag that's being squeezed into a ball; but those lulls are inevitably followed by stronger, sustained gusts that make the tent shudder, sway, and flap wildly. Whipping back and forth, it rumbles like distant thunder. After one especially long and ferocious blow, I glance at Ellen and yell "Nasty stuff," my shout barely audible above the mad cacophony of air and water. She simply winces in response. Holding a conversation at such times is like trying to talk while plunging through a whitewater canyon.

Hoping for relief, we stuff soft orange plugs into our ears. But even with the roar muffled, my body vibrates with the turbulent tossing. Even the earth beneath us seems to quiver. The relentless pounding sets me on edge.

It's true that tents magnify the sound of rain and wind. But this fury inside speaks to a tempest outside. Just a few feet away, mountain hemlocks, like our tent, are being whipped into a side-to-side frenzy while surrounding mountain walls drop loosened rocks with sharp cracks and bangs. Whitecaps have formed on the small alpine lake below our tent and the alpine stream that feeds the lake has grown uproarious.

With temperatures in the forties, a person caught without shelter in this storm would risk hypothermia, even death. Yet the conditions are hardly extraordinary for these parts: the Chugach's valleys often act as wind tunnels, channeling streams of saturated air inland from the outer coast, sometimes at speeds of one hundred miles per hour or more. Caught in the turbulent flow of such a stream, we more fully appreciate the naming of this valley's lakes and nearby mountain: "Williwaw" honors the mountain gales that frequently spill across the Chugach's mountain passes.

We've made matters worse by our tent placement. Tunnel-like in form, it should be oriented parallel to the prevailing winds. Ours is nearly perpendicular. Limited by the terrain, we set it roughly north-south in a swale, figuring it to be largely protected from any blow that might pass through this east-west valley. In fact the swale provides little protection from the southeasterly winds. They pound the tent broadside, bend its poles and press its fabric in upon us. At times it seems our shelter will surely be blown away or collapse, but so far it has admirably absorbed the body blows administered by these alpine gusts. A good test for the tent, though in truth I'd prefer less testing and more peace.

We're in no immediate danger. Still, I worry when the wind throws its hardest punches: how long will this last? What if the weather worsens? If the winds build? Do we remain here and endure two more nights of this? Or call it quits?

Needing to pee, Ellen has no choice but to leave the tent twice. The second time out she's gone a half hour or more. She returns with hot camp-stove coffee, delighted by the day's somber, gray beauty. Armed with a pee bottle and a supply of distractions, I haven't left the tent all day. I remain inside my sleeping bag, content to write in my journal, share storm stories with Ellen, or bury myself in *Moby-Dick*.

As the hours wear on, Herman Melville's frenzied passages offer less and less shelter from the storm. I toss the book aside. And I wonder: instead of hiding, should I more willingly embrace the fury, venture into its grasp? I think of naturalist-writer John Muir, who disregarded even the most inclement weather—and on many occasions, even sought it out. Once, while camped in the Alaskan wilderness during a "wild, stormy, rainy night" an expedition mate awakened him to say that deep puddles were forming inside their water-logged tent. Muir's response: "Never mind, it is only water." Another time, in the Sierras, Muir climbed a tree to more fully embrace the power of a mountain gale. He perched there for hours, exulting in its ferocity, and descended only when the storm began to ease.

I think too about the wildlife—Dall sheep, grizzly, hawk, ptarmigan—that so regularly endure such weather; how, unlike humans, they remain so well adapted to wind-driven rains and other natural hardships. Do I wish too much for comfort? Do I shy too much from hardship? Our tent has no leaks. If I leave awhile and come back sodden and chilled, I can dive into a warm, dry sleeping bag.

At home in Anchorage I wouldn't have to face such questions. More completely insulated from the rain and wind, I'd go about my routine, barely considering—if at all—the day's stormy nature and my relationship to it. Here the storm engulfs me, even when I snuggle deep into my nylon-and-down cocoon. It rattles my psyche even as it shakes the tent.

Inspired by both Muir and Ellen—and perhaps even the maniacal Ahab—I set my journal aside and exchange my sleeping bag for rain gear. It's time to soak in the weather. Outside the tent I discover a diaphanous, monochrome world of light and dark grays. Dense clouds hide mountaintops, while swirling wisps of vapor soften the sharp angles of craggy towers and dance along the valley bottom. Newly reborn creeks form silvery necklaces against the dark, drenched skins of rock walls, gleaming in their wetness. And somewhere high above, moaning torrents of wind squeeze through mountain passes, rush along alpine ridges.

As I turn into the wind, cold mountain rain stings my face and an insistent surge of air pushes hard against my body—a shoving and throbbing presence that's invisible yet surely physical. Inhaling deeply, I breathe in the discomforting yet enthralling power of the ordinary Alaskan summer storm that now washes over and through me.

Fall

The stains on my pants are steadily growing in both number and size. Spreading and overlapping, they form an archipelago of dark, rounded islands on the tan nylon sea that covers my legs. The color of deep muscle bruises on the mend, these bluish-purple blotches come from the bodily juices of squashed blueberry fruits, which I've been hunting in the mountains east of my Anchorage home. The stains are most abundant around my right knee, reflecting my habit of kneeling on it when my lower back begins to ache from too much bending over.

Pants stains are a crude measure of my success at finding local berry crops. Lots of stains, lots of ripe blueberries. Of course I have other, more dependable, ways of documenting success: most obviously, the number of quarts I collect or the number of pies and berry-pancake breakfasts that my picking yields. Yet there are more subtle measures too: the stiffness in my back after hours spent hunched over ground-hugging tundra bushes; the joy of discovering a rich "new" patch that other berry pickers have ignored or overlooked; the invigorating pleasure of inhaling crisp mountain air while caressed by warm August sunlight and serenaded by redpolls or sparrows.

Though a half-century old, I am new to berry harvesting. Certainly I've picked and gobbled these tiny wild fruits for as long as I can remember, whenever walks have taken me through berry patches. But only in recent years has such casual picking become a more formal seasonal ritual. Now, in late summer and early fall, I sometimes head into the backcountry expressly to collect wild berries. Even in this northern climate, the variety of edible types is remarkable: salmonberries, watermelon berries, high- and low-bush cranberries, nagoonberries, gooseberries, cloudberries, crowberries, huckleberries, strawberries, raspberries, lingonberries. Blueberries are my favorite target, because of both their taste and their widespread abundance; they're everywhere, it seems, from Alaska's lush coastal rain forests to high alpine meadows and expansive arctic tundra.

I try to recall what caused the shift to serious collecting. Gradually, the memory takes shape: in the mid-nineties, while exploring Alaska's wild coast, I'd stumbled across an incredible profusion of juicily delicious blueberries. The last day of the trip, I filled two quart-sized water bottles with purple-blue fruits larger than peas and brought them home to share with Dulcy. We gobbled fresh blueberries, then blueberries with milk, and, finally, I tossed blueberries in pancake batter. Forever hooked by my experiments in berry pancakes, I asked Mom (a most excellent baker) for pie recipes. Her easy-to-follow, step-by-step instructions deepened our berry delight. And so I became a berry gatherer.

In just a few years, this harvesting has evolved into a valued ritual. One place I inevitably check is aptly named Blueberry Hill, a gently rounded knob in the Chugach Mountains a few miles from home. A short walk from the trailhead, the hill is an invigorating place of high winds, alpine meadows, and grand views that take in much of Southcentral Alaska. Kneeling on Blueberry Hill's pale brown soil, crawling among yellow, orange, and reddish-purple bushes, and grabbing berries one by one or in small bunches, I can't help but become more grounded in the local landscape. And by collecting and consuming the berries that grow in my wild "backyard," I more fully participate in the seasonal cycles; I digest and absorb the fruits of my homeland.

Last year, my best harvest ever, I picked three gallons of blueberries. This year, surprised by an early ripening and faced with smaller "crops" in my favorite picking spots, I will likely only gather two gallons, maybe less, by autumn's end. In one sense, I suppose, my picking is a token effort. In another sense—and the way I choose to see it—my harvest is a symbolic act, a personal reminder that *all* my food comes from the earth, not from supermarkets and food-packaging producers. Just as these wildly delicious berries from nearby mountains feed my body, so the act of picking them feeds my spirit.

Early Winter

Hiking through the mountains above Anchorage, I notice a large brown lump in the snow, about seventy-five feet off the trail. Curious, I move closer. And the lump becomes a moose. Lying sprawled in a snow-covered meadow, beneath a solitary spruce tree, its still body is growing cold in the twenty-degree chill. Its stomach is already taut with gases, and tiny ice crystals circle its mouth.

It isn't a big moose: three hundred pounds, give or take. And there are no "bumps" signaling the start of antler growth. My best guess is that it's a female calf, one of this year's offspring.

In its dying moments the calf had collapsed onto its left side, legs outstretched and head tilted so that its right eye now gazes, in an unfocused way, up into a pale blue sky. That wide-open eye, still a clear, dark pool of chocolate-brown tissue, is what tugs on me most, pulls me in close. Not a hunter of wild game, I have never been this close to a dead moose before. I wave my hand across its face, some part of me expecting the eye to blink or the moose to flinch. Nothing moves.

Eyes, Aristotle said, are windows to the soul. For moose as well as humans? To someone raised a Lutheran and later schooled in the sciences, such a notion might be quickly dismissed as ridiculous, if not blasphemous. But growing older, I find myself heartened by the ancient—and, in some parts of our modern, Western culture, resurrected—belief that everything has a spirit, a soul: moose, ravens, spiders, spruce trees, snow, clouds, rocks, mountains, Earth, stars. I find it arrogant that we civilized, industrialized, and ever-more-computerized humans are so certain that we know better than more primitive and intuitive peoples, while assuming that either we alone are soulful beings or that there is no soul at all. As I consider these notions, a shift occurs: it becomes she.

This particular eye offers no revelations, except to tell me that the calf's physical life has very recently ended. Eyeballs are a delicacy to ravens, usually among the first scavengers to discover and pick at a carcass. Ravens on their daily winter commute between Anchorage and the Chugach Mountains—morning flights into town and evening trips back to the hills, as though playfully mimicking the area's human residents—would soon spot a lifeless moose stretched out in the snow and rush in to begin their feast.

Gruesome, the thought of an eye being pecked. I've seen the same behavior with gulls feeding on dead or dying salmon: the eyes are gobbled first. Still considering the notion of eyes as windows to the soul, I whimsically wonder if the scavengers' choice might have something to do with their wish not to be observed by the dead animal's spirit while picking at a carcass. Biologists offer a simpler, more organic explanation: eyes, being soft tissue, are easy pickings to scavengers. Plus they're among the more nutritious body parts. It makes good sense for opportunistic feeders to go immediately for soft, nourishing spots like the eyes, for the same reason that larger scavengers, like bears, go for the guts: easy entry, easy feasting.

Circling the body, then kneeling beside it, I find no signs of predation or injury. Beside the calf's head is one discolored patch of snow, pinkish-yellow and silver-dollar-sized. The fluid could have come from nose or mouth. But there are no apparent wounds, no blood on the fur. And no tracks that hint of other animals, no tufts of hair pulled loose, no sign of a struggle. Starvation and exhaustion are other possibilities—but so early in winter? The weather has been mild in recent days and less than two feet of snow covers the ground. Down in Anchorage, internal injuries might be suspected, from a run-in with a car or truck. Here the nearest road is more than a mile away and it seems unlikely that a crash victim would head for the hills to die. Besides, I see no outward evidence of trauma.

What, then? Perhaps some illness, though local biologists say there's little in the way of moose diseases here. Maybe an injury that my untrained eye doesn't notice. Or some genetic weakness. Goaded by uncertainty, I wonder about the calf's final days and hours. What brought her to this place? Was she alone? Sick? Abandoned? Did she simply collapse, too weak to regain her feet? Backtracking along the moose's trail, I see no evidence of other falls or stumbles, no sign of other animals. But there may be much written in the snow, in the calf's posture or her body, that I don't notice. The more I look for evidence, the more I realize how little I know about moose specifically and wildlife in general. Again I wonder: what am I missing here?

More questions float past, moving beyond science and simple observation. Did the calf's mother know she was dying? And when did the cow leave her offspring? Do moose in any way grieve? And why does all this seem to matter so? Has the moose calf touched some fear I have of dying alone, abandoned? No good answers today, only more questions. Some days it's that way.

Kneeling beside the moose, I stroke her fur and touch her face, back, hooves, and ears. And I stare again into the fathomless depths of that dark, unblinking eye. Seeking some connection, not certain what I've found. I don't stay long, ten or fifteen minutes is all. But before returning to the trail and my afternoon hike, I offer a prayer—a simple bow of respect—to the moose, the circle of life and death, and the magnificent mystery of it all.

Chugach Christmas

Christmas is coming: season of good cheer, season of darkness; holiday spirit, holiday blues; time of endings and fresh beginnings; overly commercialized Christian celebration, with pagan roots. Mix in winter solstice, New Year's, the anniversary of Dad's death, my approaching birthday and the next few weeks promise sensory overload. And, if I'm not careful, emotional disconnection.

Already my mood swings have seemed wilder than usual. Reflective of our Anchorage weather, perhaps. Blue-sky days of inner calm, blown apart by stormy lows. Meltdowns, freeze-ups. Rapid shifts, back and forth. It's had me wondering about "the winds of change." Wondering, too, about my connections. To people, to nonhumans, to my adopted home, Alaska. Among the many wonderful gifts I received one recent Christmas was a book of paintings and poetry called *Spirit Walker*. A Nancy Wood poem that immediately touched me was one titled "My Help Is in the Mountain." It begins: "My help is in the mountain/where I take myself to heal/the earthly wounds/that people give to me."

So it is with me and the nearby Chugach Mountains. Place of healing, comfort, release, rejuvenation, connection, joy. I don't often go there in winter, and I sense this needs to change. There is magic to be found there.

DECEMBER 1. The thermometer outside the house reads four degrees Fahrenheit at 2 p.m. Skies are blue, the air is calm, and Rusty Point—a Chugach landmark visible from my yard—is bathed in golden light. A good day to be among the mountains, to visit Chugach State Park.

Walking along a forest trail, I welcome the cold as it engulfs me, presses in on my heavily clothed body, makes my wind pants stiffen and crinkle. I drink mountain air like chilled elixir, feel it swirl through my mouth, rush down my throat, cleanse my lungs. I feel it on my nose and cheeks, first as a coolness, then a tingling, a burning. The cold seeps through mittens and boots, lightly touching fingers and feet, and sends a wave of shivers through arms and shoulders. So nice, for a change, to simply be with the cold, to appreciate it.

Looking for wildlife, I see only tracks—moose, snowshoe hares, and voles—until a flock of pine grosbeaks passes overhead. I count fourteen of them dipping, swooping, chirping, and wonder if they are among the group that regularly visits my feeders. Male grosbeaks are mostly red, females gray with yellow to olive-green splotches on head and rump. These robin-sized birds are year-round residents of the Anchorage Bowl's spruce forests, yet I never noticed them until setting up some feeders a few years ago. Now they add pleasure to both my home life and my winter walks. Perched atop spruce trees, whistling brightly, they ornament the Hillside forest with holiday cheer. How did I miss them for so long?

Chickadees, magpies, ravens, and a small swarm of redpolls—tiny, sparrow-like birds distinguished by their black chin spots and red patches on their heads—also chatter among the trees. They, like grosbeaks, are new acquaintances of mine, welcomed guests at my feeders.

My walk now takes me into alpine tundra. Feathery clouds have drifted across the sky, but enough sunlight filters through for me to watch its changing hues on the mountains. Mid-afternoon's soft yellows subtly yield to peach, rose, and then lavender as day's end approaches. Slowly, almost imperceptibly, the sunlight dims and disappears. In its wake is a fiery sunset that casts a purplish-pink afterglow on the Chugach Range and prolongs day's passage into night.

Ravens, returning to their nighttime roosts, are silhouetted against the evening sky. Some fly alone, or in pairs. Others come in bunches; I count fifteen ravens in one group, twenty-two in another. The two flocks join above Blueberry Hill and the ravens engage in a swirling, spiraling winged dance. Then the dance abruptly ends and the birds resume their evening commute from city into mountains. In all, I see hundreds of the big black birds. A local biologist has been studying their movements, but their nighttime roosting habits remain largely a mystery.

Across Cook Inlet, Mounts Redoubt and Iliamna stand dark against a blood-red sky, while below me Anchorage is a mass of shimmering lights. It's all beautiful, all connected. Mountains, sky, forest, city. Alaska's winter cold. Grosbeaks and redpolls and ravens. And yes, me.

DECEMBER 13. Ten days have passed since my last visit to the Chugach foothills. Fighting off a flu infection, I stare out my window at spruce trees, snow, and a darkening sky and try to fit the pieces together, so they again make sense. Failing to gain the desired clarity, I settle for something else: appreciation. In a time of gift-giving and receiving, I appreciate the gift of nearby mountains. More than ornamented Christmas trees, Yuletide carols, or Nativity readings, they remind me, this holiday season, of the wonder in this world, my life.

Return to Spring

Friday evening, month of April. I have come to celebrate Alaska's change of seasons with a walk along my favorite forest path, the Turnagain Arm Trail. The route I follow predates Anchorage by several years. Cut across a wooded hillside, it was built in 1910 as a telegraph line and later served as a winter mail trail. Nowadays, it's a popular hiking trail in neighboring Chugach State Park.

I've hiked here, off and on, since the late 1980s and across the years this trail has become a place where I note the passing of seasons and continue learning about the plants and animals that inhabit Anchorage's wild edges. Even when nothing "special" happens, it's a place of solitude and great delight. And there's always the possibility of surprise.

The entire trail is nine and a half miles long, but ambling along at a leisurely pace I normally do only the first mile or two, then turn around. Several years ago I began keeping a journal to record observations and discoveries, but many are etched deeply in my memory as well. Numerous spots along the way have become personal mileposts. Leaving the trailhead, I recall the furtive movements of a young black bear as he passed through dense summer foliage, a fleeting forest shadow. Along another stretch, Mom and I looked for four-leaf clovers during her July visit in the early nineties, then surprised—and were surprised by—a browsing cow moose with calf.

Deep into April, the woods are nearly free of winter's grasp. Only a few patches of white slush remain scattered through the mostly brown and gray forest. Here and there, green sprouts poke through leaf litter. Gray, fuzzy catkins soften the ends of willow branches and spring's first mosquitoes buzz slowly through the air.

It's been a marvelous evening, with temperatures in the high forties—Alaskan T-shirt weather after winter's deep chill—a faint swirling breeze and the sun playing hide-and-seek among the clouds. I've been serenaded by the welcoming *fee-bee-bee* songs of black-capped chickadees and scolded by loudly chattering red squirrels, their bodies twitching nervously upon birch limbs. I've watched bald eagles spiral above the mudflats of Cook Inlet's Turnagain Arm and flocks of gulls skim the chocolaty water.

Now, as I head back to the trailhead just before 9 p.m., the sky thickens with gray clouds and the forest slowly edges toward darkness. My mind is drifting among memories of other hikes when I notice movement along the forest floor, a hundred feet ahead. Putting binoculars to eyes, I see what appears to be a furred, beige foot jutting from behind a cottonwood. I imagine it belongs to a snowshoe hare, in the midst of its seasonal change from white to brownish-gray.

Advancing up the trail, I look again and a form takes shape. I can't believe it: I seem to be looking at the face and body of a lynx. Part of me won't accept this fact. Lynx are so secretive, so elusive. I consider the possibility that the animal is a coyote, but the face is distinctly feline. Perhaps it's a house cat that's gone feral. I shift positions to gain a different perspective. Now I see the telltale sign: tufted ears, tipped in black. I've hoped for so long to see a lynx in these woods. Now that it's happened, I can scarcely contain my glee.

Hopeful of an even closer, clearer look, I walk to where the trail bends toward the cat. I don't attempt to hide my approach, because the lynx is all too aware of my presence, but I do my best to appear casual, nonthreatening. I stop again and now the lynx fills the field of my lens. Even knowing where it sits, I see how wonderfully it blends with the forest. Remaining still, the lynx is perfectly camouflaged. The cat's fur is tawny, grizzled, a blend of white, brown, and gray-black hairs. The face is whitish-beige with thin black streaks outlining the mouth as if delicately painted by a make-up artist. I can also make out the sleek, black whiskers and the black-edged ruffs that flow along the lynx's face like huge bushy sideburns.

The lynx's caramel-colored eyes watch me intently. I wonder what it makes of me and how often it sees people along the trail. Far more often than hikers see lynx, of that I'm certain. In the hundreds of times I've walked this trail, tonight is the first I've seen any sign of this northern wild cat.

The lynx sits on its haunches, once crouching low as I shift positions. Its eyes are alert, yet show no alarm. I sense caution, but not fear. Once the cat blinks, closes its eyes slightly, as if sleepy. We watch each other ten, maybe fifteen minutes. The lynx seems content to remain still indefinitely and I have no pressing need or desire to leave. I wonder if I'm keeping the cat from its evening hunt—or a mate, perhaps. This is the courting season for lynx.

I'm the one who finally yields. Brightened by this unexpected pleasure, I resume my walk, not looking back. Back home, I'll describe the meeting in my journal. But already I'm recalling details, firmly imprinting the lynx on my memory and connecting it with this spot. Already, it's become part of my relationship with this forest, this trail. A Friday night, month of April, along my favorite forest trail in Chugach State Park . . .

TEN

Wonders of the Night Sky

If the stars should appear one night in a thousand years, how would men believe and adore, and preserve for many generations the remembrance of the city of God!
—Ralph Waldo Emerson

LATE EVENING IN THE PETERS HILLS. THE SEPTEMBER SUN HAS been swallowed by the Alaska Range, and only a thin, faint purplish glow now marks its passing. As day gives way to night, I stand on a northwest-facing ridge and search the landscape for lights. In the distance are a few scattered cabins and a mining camp, barely visible in the deepening dark. But no points of light.

Higher on this ridgeline, I could look east and see the Parks Highway, with its lights of cars and lodges. Or, turning south, I would see the faraway urban glow of Anchorage. But where I'm camped, the surrounding hills shield me from highway and city. Here, in the far western corner of Denali State Park, I've serendipitously chosen a site where artificial lights won't disturb my wilderness nights.

Above me, wispy clouds have moved in from the southwest, and no stars are visible as I crawl into my tent. Several hours later, feeling chilled, I awake; it's much colder than my first night in these hills. I add another layer of clothes and then, sensing that the temperature drop reflects clearing skies, I open the tent door—and am greeted by the universe. Never have I seen such an Alaskan sky. No moon, no aurora, and no city glare. Thousands of brilliant stars sparkling in deep blackness. How to describe such an unexpected and overpowering sight?

I'm reminded of a wonderful story I read many years ago, the 1941 science-fiction classic *Nightfall*. Using the Emerson quote to begin his tale, Isaac Asimov explored how humans might react if they experienced darkness and stars only once every two thousand years. Would we experience spiritual rhapsody? Or go insane? On this September night, the heavens hold promise, not danger. Lured skyward, I'm pulled from my drowsiness and out of the tent. Still in my sleeping bag—and no longer chilled—I lay my head on the frosted tundra and face the night sky. So many stars. Such immense, unfathomable distances. A taste of infinity, an escape from ego.

In Anchorage, I seldom gaze for long at the nighttime sky, except to watch sunset afterglows, northern lights, meteor showers, or, perhaps, a full moon hanging low over the mountains. Hidden by clouds and summer's late-night sun, or dimmed in winter by urban glare, the stars hold little allure. Not enough, certainly, to draw me out of the house and into the cold.

Tonight is different. I wander in a dreamlike trance among the Milky Way, the Big and Little Dippers, the Gemini twins, and the seven sisters of the Pleiades. I wish I recognized more constellations. I want to know their ancient names, their legends, their origins. What is the story of Orion, the giant hunter? Or Taurus, the bull? And where are they hiding? So many stars fill the sky that I have difficulty seeing shapes and forms. Perhaps if I'm patient enough, ancient patterns will reveal themselves. As writer and human ecologist Paul Shepard once explained it, "[T]he spectacle of stars seems at first formless and chaotic. But it is far too large a part of the world to accept as randomly structured. . . . We discern or make there organic figures."

More than anything, humans have used animal forms to shape their universe and give it meaning. I like the idea of mythic creatures inhabiting the sky above this wilderness landscape. The constellation I know best is the Big Dipper. Yet it is part of a much grander figure, one I wasn't taught to recognize as a boy: Ursa Major, the Great Bear. In *Secrets of the Night Sky*, stargazer Bob Berman suggests, "It's odd, to say the least, that so many ancient civilizations discerned the shape of a bear in this region of the sky. . . . A bear is stretching it, and yet that is exactly what Native Americans, ancient Greeks, the Germanic tribes of middle Europe, and others saw in this formation. Why such disparate civilizations should all project the same unlikely bruin onto these northern stars remains a mystery."

I like that too: the fact that modern scientists can't figure out why several cultures, widely separated by time or distance, identified essentially the same Great Bear in the heavens. What could they see—or imagine—that we can't now? The myths explaining the origins of Ursa Major vary greatly, yet those of many North American Native groups are similar in that bear is "born" in the heavens and later becomes an envoy connecting the physical and spiritual worlds. It seems the perfect story for a magical night spent in grizzly country.

While most cultures have reveled in the images, stories, and meaning apparent in the night sky, ours has largely blocked it out with city lights and, consequently, learned to ignore it. This seems a paradox, given our nation's great interest in space exploration and odysseys. While the masses watch *Star Trek* and *Star Wars*, the heavens themselves have become the domain of astronomers, physicists, and other scientists who, with their high-tech instruments, probe, dissect, and analyze the universe as they "figure out" its mysteries. In the process, something has been lost. As with so many things nowadays, there's too much science and analysis, too little myth and magic. Too much arrogance, too little humility. Too much separation from the rest of creation, too little connection.

Here in the Peters Hills, on a starry Alaskan night like no other I've known, I reconnect with the wonder I felt as a boy while gazing at Connecticut skies. I shrink in size to an insignificant speck, yet I'm part of the glorious enormity that this extraordinary spectacle reveals. My imagination stirs, takes flight among far-away blazing suns and the power they reveal. Gradually I realize it was no accident I chose this place to camp. I have no idea how long I'm caught up in this reverie. Maybe ten minutes, maybe an hour. When I finally check my watch it's nearly 4 a.m. Already, the stars' brightness has begun to fade, and a pale glow lights the eastern horizon. I drift back to sleep, my spirit cleansed by starlight.

ANOTHER TRIP INTO THE DENALI region, this time on the cusp of winter. I spend my days exploring the park's northern foothills and my nights in a log cabin along the park's eastern edge. Each night, before retiring, I check the sky. Denali isn't widely known for its beautiful night skies simply because most people visit in summer, when the sky never fully darkens. But local residents know, and I have learned firsthand in recent years, that for eight or nine months of every year, many of the park's most inspiring spectacles are to be found overhead. What grabs a sky gazer's attention on most of these clear, dark nights—like mine in the Peters Hills—are the sparkling stars, the familiar constellations, the Milky Way band. On moonless nights, the ink-black sky grows vibrantly alive with uncountable numbers of sparkling stars. With no urban glare to dim their intensity, they blink brightly, wildly, like Christmas-tree lights or fireflies. Occasionally, however, Denali's night sky holds other luminous mysteries.

One evening toward the end of my stay, the sky is moonless and clear, filled with sparkling stars and the faintest trace of northern lights. I watch awhile, hoping for an auroral burst, but the lights fade and I head to bed.

Hours later I awaken from a restless sleep. Remembering the earlier display, I stumble, blurry-eyed, to a large picture window that faces west. Just above the darkened Alaska Range foothills, a pale green band arches gently across the sky, like a flattened rainbow. The arc seems to be flickering, but at first I'm not sure if it's the aurora borealis or my eyes. I rub them and watch more intently. Now there's no question: the band is slowly wavering. This goes on for five or ten minutes. Then the aurora explodes and fills the whole western sky. Bright green curtains of northern lights, tinged pink along their edges, ripple wildly above the hills. I've seen northern lights many times, but I am shocked by the deep, flashing brilliance of these.

The bright curtains abruptly vanish, leaving as suddenly and mysteriously as they first appeared, but faint patches and bands remain. Paler than the original green arc, they nearly disappear, then grow more intense. Now they are shimmering and jumping around the sky. My mind tries to put words to what I'm seeing, to make them more comprehensible.

The lights shimmer, flicker, pulsate. They ripple, explode, undulate. At times they are the embers of a heavenly fire, flickering on and off. At other times they are flames, leaping across the sky. There are moments when they remind me of exploding fireworks. An electric arc. Cannon fire. Or psychedelic lights, of the kind used in discos. Now they are rippling waves that appear at the horizon and move upward across an oceanic sky. They are the shimmer of sunlight on a river or a lightly rippled lake.

These northern lights hypnotize me in a way that few others have. I lose track of time. How long have I watched? An hour? Two?

I recently finished John Muir's *Travels in Alaska*, which includes a chapter on the aurora. Never one to avoid discomfort—or an adventure—Muir in 1890 witnessed an unusually dramatic aurora borealis display in Southeast Alaska: "Losing all thought of sleep, I ran back to my cabin, carried out blankets, and lay down on the [glacial] moraine to keep watch until daybreak, that none of the sky wonders of the glorious night within reach of my eyes might be lost."

I too think about going outside. But the view is good from here and I don't wish to pile on clothes or head outdoors to watch the sky in tonight's twenty-degree cold. I'm content to sit inside, with bare feet, short-sleeve shirt, and sweatpants. I lean against the window for several minutes at a time; when shoulder and upper back muscles stiffen, I move to a nearby armchair.

I tell myself to simply sit and watch and appreciate the aurora. No description, no analysis. It's hard to do. Words and images keep coming to mind. I think about the origins of northern lights and the science that explains them. Researchers tell us that these auroral apparitions are atmospheric phenomena, produced when a stream of charged particles from the sun, known as the solar wind, intersects the Earth's magnetic field. While most of the solar particles are deflected, some filter down into the planet's upper atmosphere, where they collide with gas molecules such as nitrogen and oxygen. The resulting reactions produce glowing colors. The aurora most commonly is pale green, but at times its borders are tinged with pink, purple, or red. Especially rare is the all-red aurora, which appears when charged solar particles collide with high-altitude oxygen. The science is complex and difficult to comprehend, but the results are pure beauty.

I appreciate the insights that scientists have gained in recent years and their improved ability to predict auroral events. Our Anchorage newspaper presents nightly auroral forecasts and directs readers to an aurora website. But on a night like this, with wild fiery lights burning across the Denali sky, I eventually—perhaps inevitably—choose rhapsody over rational thought, poetry over physical phenomena. These lights hint of forces larger than we can imagine, of worlds beyond our physical one.

In my watching, I begin to see a rhythm in the flashing, flickering, shimmering lights. Or at least I imagine one. I can also imagine why the peoples of so many northern cultures have created myths to explain the aurora. The lights take on a life, an energy, of their own. What began as patches, arcs, bands, curtains, and spirals has been transformed. Now the lights are wispy, vaporous, humanlike figures in the sky, drumming and dancing and singing. At other times, lights exploding along the horizon are the traces of distant battles.

The lights are still flashing and pulsating when I return to bed. While I don't have Muir's all-night stamina, like he was more than a century ago I've been touched in unforgettable ways by the "sky wonders" of a glorious northern night. Shining beacons, they urge me to pay attention to the wildness and mystery that surrounds me—both here in Denali and back home in Anchorage—and also lives inside me.

BACK HOME IN THE HILLS above Anchorage, month of November. I am sitting in my backyard hot tub, looking for meteors, when shortly before midnight a pale green glow appears on the northeastern horizon. The light brightens and sharpens into a distinct auroral band. Then it begins to curl and flow, spreading in undulating waves to the west, where it merges with Anchorage's more yellowish nighttime glare.

The aurora shape-shifts again; parts of it metamorphose into bright, sharp-edged curtains of light, still mostly green but now with rose-tinged edges. For a few minutes the curtains wave and dance. Then the aurora gradually loses both definition and intensity, becoming once again a faint green patch above the Chugach Mountains.

I smile and thank the heavens for this northern lights display. Short but deliciously sweet to both eyes and spirit, it's the best I've seen so far this winter from my Hillside home (which fortunately sits high above tonight's fog-blanketed Anchorage Bowl).

Settling back into my meteor watch I feel triply blessed: northern lights, shooting stars, and a performance by a group of Tibetan monks, all in one night.

Is this simple coincidence or are more powerful forces at work here? Whatever the reasons behind this confluence of spectacles, I hope our guests from the Drepung Loseling Monastery were able to witness the aurora: they'd be touched by its beauty, its mystery.

Among the sacred music and dances the monks performed for their Alaskan audience this evening was one called *Seng-geh Gar-cham*: the Snow Lion Dance. If I understand it correctly, this dance recognizes our role, as humans, in helping to create and maintain a healthy, harmonious environment; the Tibetan monks do their part through sacred purification rituals and healing music. When such harmony is achieved, all living beings—here symbolized by the snow lion—rejoice.

Carrying these thoughts and images with me into the night, I now imagine the northern lights to be another symbol of celebration, with a local twist: our Alaska skies are lighting up with joy at the monks' appearance.

Some would probably consider this idea to be nothing more than my projection, my fantasy. It's true that I welcome and celebrate the healing energy that the Tibetan monks bring to Alaska, where (as elsewhere) we human residents too often care more about what the environment can give us—through its so-called "natural resources"—than what we can give to our world. So maybe this entire auroral episode, or at least my interpretation of it, is a dream. Pure fantasy. But maybe not. Why not consider the deeper possibilities? Who can say for certain that auroral displays are nothing more than upper-atmosphere phenomena easily explainable by science? On a night when I've been touched by mystical traditions, I'm willing to believe that science can't explain it all.

I turn my attention away from the aurora and back to the meteor shower. Here too, there's an easy explanation for the six or seven bright streaks of light I'll see tonight. In answer to reports of bright blue flashes seen in the southern sky Friday, this morning's paper explained that the Earth and its atmosphere are now passing through an old comet stream. In other words, we're running into a belt of rock debris left by a comet that long ago passed through our solar system. When our atmosphere hits the rocks, they burn up. And if the rocks are big enough, they leave beautiful streaks across the sky while flaming out. Tonight's shower is part of a predictable event that lasts several nights. It's even got a name: the Leonids meteor shower.

Yet watching the night sky, I'm not thinking about the mechanics of the meteors. I'm out here for their beauty, the delight and sense of the unknown that they inspire. As a young boy, long before their origins were explained to me, I used to know these bright nighttime streaks as "shooting stars." Later I would learn they weren't stars at all. But I still love the expression: shooting stars is so descriptive, so lyrical. So mysterious.

That, to me, remains the essence of the night sky, with its moon, stars, constellations, comets, shooting stars, and deep impenetrable blackness: it's about the mystery of the universe. Now there's something that science can describe and perhaps even explain, at least in part: the universe. But science will never capture its essence. That requires a greater leap of faith, a sense of the mystical, the sacred. The same, I think, may be true for a full appreciation of northern lights, shooting stars, or any natural phenomenon. Besides science, there must be room for music and dance, for ritual. And a celebration of what we may not know.

ELEVEN

Going Solo Through
Gates of the Arctic

LATE JULY IN THE CENTRAL BROOKS RANGE. CAMPED ALONE A FEW miles from the Arctic Divide, I huddle in my sleeping bag while wind-driven sheets of rain soak the landscape, pelt my tent. It's been pouring like this, off and on, for at least ten hours. Five of the trip's first seven days have now been mostly rainy and overcast. Very strange weather, it seems, for a so-called "arctic desert." And depressing.

I began the day with ambitious goals. But plans to scramble up a nearby mountain were themselves scrambled by prolonged torrents that quickly waterlogged my aging and not-so-water-resistant rain gear. With no strict schedule to keep, I retreated to my comfortably dry and snug shelter, which has so far proved marvelously rainproof. Instead of ridge walking, I've napped, reread parts of Robert Marshall's Brooks Range classic, *Alaska Wilderness*, written copiously in my journal, and fretted about my journey.

I hate to admit it, but Dad was right: I am a worrywart. "Just like your mother," he'd hasten to add if he were here with me. Too much time holed up in a tent, especially when alone, inevitably leads to too much thinking and consequent anxieties. I worry that I haven't brought sufficient food and fuel for my two-week trip. I worry that animals—ground squirrels as much a grizzlies—may discover and invade my food stash. I worry that my blistered feet will worsen. But mostly I worry about the difficulties of fording the rain-swollen North Fork of the Koyukuk—a major river crossing still four days away. Bob Marshall, I'm certain, wouldn't be plagued by such uncertainties. In fact he would probably be out exploring this valley right now, soaking wet or not.

Thoughts of Marshall are interrupted by muted conversation that drifts into the tent with the steady splash of rain. I've already heard human voices, or something like them, a number of times while marching alone through these mountains, so I figure my imagination is acting up again. Until I hear shouts.

Craning my neck, I peek out the tent's mosquito netting and glimpse four ghostly shapes approaching from the south—an amazing sight. They seem to be zeroed in on me. "Hey," one yells, "anybody in there?" A couple minutes later, four bedraggled guys stand beside the tent. Normally I feel let down when meeting other parties in remote wilderness, my desire for solitude compromised. Not tonight, though. I'm intrigued by any group of trekkers traveling on a stormy night like this. And these guys seem a good-natured, jovial bunch, even in their drenching.

Poking upper body through the partly unzipped door, I introduce myself, then ask their names and where they've come from, where they're bound. The answer shocks me: Thor Tingey, Phillip Weidner, Sam Newbury, and Dan Dryden are in the midst of a five-hundred-mile, forty-six-day expedition. They began their Brooks Range crossing July 3 at the Arctic National Wildlife Refuge's Canning River and will end it August 19 at the Eskimo village of Kobuk, far to the west.

Led by Thor, a recent college grad, the group's primary aim is to see lots of country while going light and fast. "We're taking what you might call a minimalist approach to gear," he explains. "And we want to see how fast we can push ourselves." A series of food drops allows them to carry forty-to-sixty-pound packs, loads that include small pack rafts and two firearms. My gear, to start, totaled nearly seventy pounds—minus any raft or gun.

Backpacking and sometimes floating rivers, they're moving eight to ten hours a day, averaging twelve miles. With few planned rest days, the group doesn't have the flexibility to sit out storm-wracked days (or nights), unless conditions become severe. Even then, it depends on how you define severe. Tonight, for instance, is pretty darn miserable, but these spirited twentysomething guys are shrugging it off. I'm impressed. And thankful I don't have to be anywhere else in this downpour. Never a gung-ho backpacker, I've become even less enthusiastic as a forty- and now fiftysomething traveler. I like to take in my surroundings, and paying attention to the landscape is much harder to do when lugging a big, heavy pack. Plus there's all that bodily pain. My preference is to set up base camps and do day hikes in various directions. Such base camping eliminates heavily burdened packing. I may not cover as much ground, but I become more intimate with a smaller piece of the landscape.

This trip into the Brooks Range—one of several I've done over the years—is a backpacking–base camping hybrid. With nearly two weeks to travel fifty miles, I can more easily remain tentbound when the weather gets nasty or take an extra day when tempted by side trips. Ironically, my increased options sometimes unnecessarily complicate things. Marginal weather provokes internal debates: should I go or should I stay?

We compare notes, exchange tips. I tell them what I know about the Anaktuvuk River Valley, which they'll reach just a couple miles from here. They tell me not to worry about the North Fork; there's a braided section where the river didn't come much above their knees, even after several days of rain.

A half hour quickly passes. Now cooled and shivering, they're eager to get moving again. I watch them merge into rain and fog, four phantom figures walking slowly, stoically, side-by-side, bundled up against the storm. Finally they top a rise and drop out of sight, as if swallowed by the gloom and wilderness. Something akin to an eerie, haunting loneliness rises in me as they disappear. We've had a momentary crossing of paths, then resumed our separate journeys and destinies. Yet I feel a kinship with them.

My quest is modest by comparison, though it poses its own set of challenges and risks. At fifty years old, I am doing the longest backpack of my life, across mostly untrailed wilderness, much of it wet and tussocky. And I'm doing it entirely alone. Never have I gone so long without human company (though once, in graduate school, I considered becoming a hermit). So I'm pushing personal borders, entering new terrain.

The landscape is new to me, too. Much of my route roughly retraces Bob Marshall's explorations in 1929 and 1930, though I'm approaching from the opposite direction, north instead of south. Marshall began at Wiseman, an early 1900s gold-boom town along the Koyukuk River's Middle Fork. My starting point, the Nunamiut village of Anaktuvuk Pass, didn't even exist then.

Marshall is one of the big reasons I've come here, along with a desire for solitude and adventure, and a wish to explore new ground within my favorite mountain wilderness. I want to see for myself the places he mapped, named, and so vividly described in *Alaska Wilderness*, places like the Valley of Precipices, Mount Doonerak, Boreal Mountain, Frigid Crags. This is the heart of Marshall country, a landscape that fed his wilderness-preservation vision for the Brooks Range—and now it's one of the grandest areas protected by 8.2-million-acre Gates of the Arctic National Park and Preserve. If I am to know the magnificence of Gates, I can hardly ignore Marshall's "Koyukuk country."

When Marshall came here, few people had ever set foot in these valleys. Those who did were usually Nunamiut hunters or solitary prospectors, sometimes never heard from again. Nowadays, dozens of wilderness adventurers pass this way each year—a small number by Lower 48 standards, but heavy usage for Alaska's Arctic. A portion begin their travels at Anaktuvuk Pass, the only community inside the park's borders and the only remaining settlement of Alaska's Nunamiut people, inland Eskimos whose nomadic ancestors followed caribou herds across the western Arctic.

REWIND TO JULY 19. I BEGIN my trek by following two-wheeled tracks out of Anaktuvuk Pass, headed roughly east along the Anaktuvuk River. The Nunamiut, like rural Native residents throughout Alaska, have adapted new technologies to their hunting ways and ATV trails lead out from their village like spokes from a wheel, finally petering out where Native land gives way to parkland.

Where the tundra is soft and wet, the tracks become deeply rutted and muddied. In places, they are also littered with machine parts and trash. To an unsuspecting wilderness adventurer, the trails and debris can be a jarring eyesore. I already knew about them, so they aren't a complete shock to my wilderness-seeking spirit. Besides, the trails are not entirely loathsome: in drier areas, their hard-packed surfaces can be preferable to tussock stumbling, particularly when starting out an expedition lugging a pack that weighs mightily on a not-yet-tundra-toughened body. In a sense, they present a bridge from twenty-first-century Native culture to unspoiled wildlands.

For two and a half days I stay on the ATV trails as much as possible to ease my passage. Across dry terrain, I keep a good pace, maybe two miles an hour. But the route often crosses wetlands, slowing me down and keeping my feet soaked. Mosquitoes are the most aggravating part of this tough and tiring slog. At every step, dense, frenzied clouds of them rise from the tundra and attack my steaming body. I coat and re-coat my flesh and clothes with DEET-laden repellent, but that is only a temporary fix. Continued harassment eventually forces me to take an extreme step: I don a head net. I hate head nets. They make me claustrophobic. But in the Arctic, in July, a head net proves a blessing. It keeps the mosquitoes off my head and neck, though they continue their maddening buzz around my ears, bounce off the head net's mesh. The mosquitoes are clearly excited by my presence, but I could do without such an enthusiastic welcome.

I notice little other wildlife my first few days, except for birds. Songbirds are concentrated in streamside willow thickets: white-crowned and savannah sparrows, common and hoary redpolls, even a robin. The robin is a big surprise; until now, I never would have suspected they might inhabit remote Arctic mountain ranges. More birds: ravens, gulls, long-tailed jaegers, and American golden-plovers. The latter are shorebirds that winter in South America and breed on tundra throughout much of Alaska. The ATV trail must pass through prime golden-plover nesting grounds, because several of them scurry about and whistle alarms at my approach. Breeding males are exceedingly handsome, with mottled golden-brown back, black belly and face, and a narrow stripe of white that curls, in the form of a question mark (minus dot), from the head down the neck.

No mammals, but lots of signs, especially of caribou; mostly bleached antlers, sometimes still attached to skulls. Also fur, assorted bones, and one nearly complete skeleton. The abundance of caribou parts reflects the valley's importance as a migration route and its frequent use by Nunamiut hunters. I also see evidence of the Arctic's two other large terrestrial predators: wolf tracks and grizzly scat, plus some diggings that could only have been made by bear.

About fifteen miles from Anaktuvuk Pass, I leave the last vestiges of the Nunamiuts' ATV trails and parallel a rushing clearwater tributary called Graylime Creek. The name alerts me that I'm about to enter Robert Marshall country. Fed by gullies and brooks that flow off the Arctic Divide, Graylime is the first landscape feature I've encountered that was labeled by Marshall, an enthusiastic mapper responsible for dozens of names in the Central Brooks Range.

I set up camp on a tundra bench above one of Graylime's wide gravel bars, within two miles of Ernie Pass. The ground here is firmer, drier, smoother. Already I've backpacked farther than ever before, about twenty-one miles by map. The muscles in my shoulder and back are gradually adapting to the load, but now my feet are hurting: my left heel and right middle toe have been rubbed raw. Happily, my feet will now get a break: I'm staying put for the next couple of days, while exploring the area on day hikes.

ASCENDING A RIDGE NORTH OF CAMP, I am met by strongly gusting wind. Instant bug relief! Perched on a high bench, I can see miles down the east-west-trending Anaktuvuk River Valley. It is broad, green, and gently U-shaped, almost pastoral in its appearance, except for the one sign of people: the double-tracked ATV trail. The flanks of limestone hills dip gently toward the river, but their ridgetops are contorted into fantastic shapes. Layers of rock once horizontal are now thrust steeply upward, the jagged teeth of some primordial rock beast. In other directions are ridge upon nameless ridge, most barely touched by humans, some not at all.

Above the mountains, rafts of billowing clouds float through a deep blue ocean of sky. The day is a beauty, bright and dry, the nicest so far. The terrain, like the weather, adds to my enjoyment. There are moments on this ridge walk when my heart sings. I don't know how else to put it: I feel bursts of joy that I can't explain. Nothing specific seems to trigger these moments; no special revelations accompany them. It is, I think, the entirety of this day, this landscape. I am touched by wildness—and perhaps my own responds.

The wind picks up in late afternoon and clouds the color of bruises build to the south, so I begin an unhurried descent. On my way down I discover wolf scat, rich with hair and small bone fragments. Near the top of this same limestone rib are caribou antlers. It's nice to know I've shared the ridge with wolf and caribou. I imagine wolf traveling here, perhaps stalking prey or gazing across the same landscape that I've been relishing. Maybe howling to pack mates. I howl my own pleasure.

Tent-rattling winds and hard, drenching rain hit my part of the valley a half hour after dinner. The downpour is the sort you might expect in a rain forest, not an arctic desert. Fast and furious, the storm passes twenty to thirty minutes after it hit. In its wake is patchy blue sky and streaks of molten light that fall on distant peaks.

The next morning a light rain begins to fall after breakfast, but I head out with my daypack, bound for Limestack Mountain, which Marshall named and climbed in 1930. But the weather soon washes away my plans, as a monsoonlike downpour drives me back to the tent, where I curl up with journal, maps, and books for most of the day and night, 'til interrupted by the group of four (a most pleasant interruption). Shortly after they depart, the rain briefly lets up and I go for a late-evening tundra walk. On my return, I feel a deepening sadness but it has less to do with my earlier meeting than something emanating from the landscape itself. Life is hard here, in marginally productive conditions. Yes, there's an "explosion" of life (particularly mosquitoes) in summer, but that explosion is short-lived. Perhaps two months, maybe less, in some of these high alpine valleys.

I'm still struck by the paucity of mammals, big or small. Even the bird life, though ubiquitous, is not abundant, except in small areas, like creekside willow patches. Life seems to be concentrated in valley bottoms and occasional lush alpine meadows. Many people, even Marshall at times, have called this Arctic tundra landscape "barren." I don't see it as that. Spare, yes. But barren implies sterile, lifeless, empty, unattractive. The Central Brooks Range is none of those things.

JULY 24. Time to resume my journey. That means breaking camp, something I hate to do in the rain—and it's pouring again. I think of Marshall, who relished challenging weather and terrain, and of Thor Tingey and his buddies, on their five-hundred-mile trek. Thor was so matter of fact about it: "We're wet almost every day, all day. Staying dry is not a possibility." At least not 'til evening, when they gather wood to build a roaring fire. Wishing to limit my impact, I choose not to build any wood fires.

Despite the soaking rain, I feel energized as I head for the Arctic Divide and thirty-five-hundred-foot Ernie Pass. On the one side, Graylime Creek flows north and west into the Anaktuvuk River, which feeds the Colville, and finally the Arctic Ocean. To the south, Ernie Creek's waters eventually find their way to the North Pacific's Bering Sea.

I take one final look to the north, offer a goodbye salute, then descend into the broad, green, soggy bowl of upper Ernie Creek. Bounded by gray and brown hills, the saucer-shaped basin is covered by wet tundra. Resigned to my fate, I plunge ahead into a quagmire that oozes H_2O.

My path eventually brings me to a broad, rolling bench. Reaching its southern edge, I am suddenly and stunningly greeted by Marshall's famed Valley of Precipices—and a whole lot more. Seven hundred feet below, Ernie Creek meanders in braided channels through a steep-walled enclosure that rises more than twenty-five hundred feet, to summits shrouded in clouds. The northeast wall is higher, but those on the southwest—the precipices—thrust more steeply and starkly above the valley bottom. The contrast is deepened by the green valley's pastoral nature and the black, brooding aspect of the cliffs.

Two other magnificent watersheds open up from my vantage point and I can't imagine a more sensational seat to take it all in. To the southwest is Kenunga Creek, where a narrow unnamed cascade drops several hundred feet, in a series of waterfalls that form a gleaming silver necklace on the mountain's black body. Farther upvalley are immense slab-sided walls rising to six thousand feet or more, their dark cliff faces now powdered white with fresh snow.

Immediately below me and to my left, Grizzly Creek cuts a gorge through conglomerates and other sedimentary rocks, which have dropped huge boulders, some the size of trucks, into its narrow bottom. Flushed with recent rains, the creek tumbles wildly between canyon walls, a froth of whitewater.

I want to camp here, but a fierce wind howls across the bench and there's no place that provides sure shelter if another violent storm moves through. Reluctantly, I work my way down gullies and scree slopes to Grizzly Creek. The frothing stream I saw from above is a roaring, menacing rush of runoff that bounces wildly among conglomerate boulders. Normally this creek wouldn't be a fording problem, but with this much water, and the bouldery bottom, it's a potential death trap. After much searching I find a place where the river widens and is largely boulder free.

The creek's shockingly cold water comes up to mid-calf, splashes above my knees. Some small rocks roll beneath my feet. But I go slowly and, using my trekker's pole, stay balanced. Along the far bank, the creek rises above my knees and pushes harder at my legs. But one more step and I'm across.

I still have to find a campsite, set up the tent, put on warmer, drier clothes, and make dinner. Afterward I pick a few blueberries—they're just now ripening—and retire to the tent just before midnight. And the rain keeps falling.

Morning brings more mist, fog, wind. And cold: just after 10 a.m., my mini thermometer reads in the low forties. This will be another rest day, mostly tent-bound.

My second morning at Grizzly Creek I awaken to a foggy, windy day—and snow! A light flurry of snow "balls," more rounded than flaky, falls from dark skies. Temperatures are in the low to mid-thirties. The chill has a pleasing side effect: mosquitoes have all but vanished.

After breaking camp I initially stay high on the tundra hillside, above the heavy brush that borders Ernie Creek. I can't entirely avoid the "green hell," however; side gullies and swales are lined by dense willow and alder thickets, some more than head high and so dense I can see only a couple feet in any direction. For the first time on this trip I go into my bear chant.

"Yo, bear! . . . Yo, bear! . . . Hello, hello."

I feel a bit silly, chanting so. Yet any embarrassment fades in the face of this fact: a high percentage of grizzly maulings occur in just this sort of thick brush, where humans and bears surprise each other at close quarters.

An especially thick and ominous patch of near-impenetrable willows forces me to the river after two and a half or three miles of bushwhacking. There I discover long open stretches of gravel bars that ease the walking. Many others, it turns out, have come this way. The bars are tracked by caribou, wolves, bears, and even a few sets of boot prints.

Another saving grace: game trails. Used by wolves, caribou, bears, moose, and smaller critters, the trails come and go, distinct in places then fading out and later reappearing. Where present, they make travel across wet, hummocky tundra so much easier. I might have floundered several hours more, if not for these pain-saving paths.

I end my day on a small gravel bar beside Ernie Creek, now bordered by mixed tundra and open forest. A light rain falls, as it has for nearly all the past four days. I'm now within two miles of the Koyukuk's North Fork and the building anxieties of recent days deepen into dread as I imagine the worst: I won't be able to cross this major Brooks Range river; I'll be stranded and require rescue. Or I'll attempt to cross despite high water and lose my balance, lose my gear, maybe even lose my life.

NOT LONG AFTER BREAKING CAMP on July 27, my river-fording fears are temporarily pushed aside by more pressing matters. I'm headed across a gravel bar when a blonde, fur-wettened grizzly sow steps out of the forest and starts to dig in the stream bank, less than two hundred feet away. The stream is raucous and the wind blows toward me, so she can't hear or smell my approach and she hasn't looked in my direction.

After digging furiously a minute or two, the grizzly disappears back into the woods. Wishing to track her whereabouts, I head to a clearing near the edge of forest and tundra. Soon I see her, headed toward me but attention drawn elsewhere. It's time to act. I shout: "Hello bear, hello."

The bear stops short, half stands, pauses, then lopes forward a few paces. She's not charging, but I guess that her adrenaline is now pumping fiercely through that powerfully muscled body, just as it is through my much frailer one. More softly, I shout again, a now-familiar line: "Hello bear. It's just me, a human passing through."

The bear stops again, stands on her hind legs. She's trying to get a better idea of who, or what, is talking to her in such a way. I guess she's a young adult, maybe 200 to 250 pounds. Her shape, as much as anything, suggests maturity. She's fuller bodied, less gangly, than "teenage" bears I've seen. Back on all fours, the bear retreats twenty or thirty feet, moving at a lope. Then she begins to circle toward the tundra bench above us. "That's it," I encourage her, "no need to come closer."

The grizzly glances my way now and then while loping uphill in an arc that gradually takes her farther from me. I'm impressed, once more, by how easily and swiftly bears move through terrain that's so rugged and difficult for us humans. She passes over a rise and is gone.

Angling across mixed tundra and forest, I reach the North Fork–Ernie Creek confluence in early afternoon. There's absolutely no chance of crossing here without going for a swim. I search upstream and find a place where several braids pour into one main channel. They all look doable—except, perhaps, for the one along the near shore. Fast and deep, its waters pile against a cut bank, eroding the forest floor. I skirt this channel several hundred feet, to a place where it widens.

The water is a murky bluish-green, but where shallow I can see the bottom. Once I'm in the water, fear gives way to total focus. I'm engaged in the act of fording, making constant choices, moving ahead. Moving diagonally upstream, I stay in ankle-high water for fifty feet. Then it deepens. Still, along one line I can make out the bottom. It looks even, gravelly. No apparent holes. The water is now midcalf, now at my knee tops, splashing higher. And *cold*. The numbing water pushes hard at me, but the footing is good and my pole adds balance. A few more feet and I'm across. What relief!

The rest of the channels are easy to negotiate. Seven or eight in all, most of them narrow and shallow. Reaching the far side I nibble on cheese and beef jerky, relax. I'm past my biggest obstacle. I'm going to be OK.

Thor's group, it turns out, had a much more exciting time along the North Fork, including some dunkings in class III rapids while rafting the river between its headwaters and Ernie Creek. "Nearly everybody fell out of the rafts and took a swim somewhere on the trip," he'll tell me weeks later, back in town. "That part wasn't so much fun, getting dumped in icy water, but no one got seriously hurt. Hypothermia was the scariest part and we had to build some fires." I can't imagine it, swimming down this river.

Now only ten miles or so from my rendezvous point, I'll be staying here three nights, so I want a good campsite. I find one at the edge of spruce-birch woods, in a mossy clearing. Nice and flat, out of the wind. The sand and gravel bar that borders my temporary home is filled with tracks: wolf, caribou, bear, moose, hare, squirrel, bird, human.

The evening is a calm one, after a blustery day. The stillness seems to reflect my own inner peacefulness, now that I've passed my biggest hurdle. Adding to my contentment is the continued absence of mosquitoes. For the second straight day I've needed neither head net nor bug dope.

JULY 28. Drawn outside my warming tent, I bask awhile in sweet sunshine, then tend to aching feet. My left heel and right middle toe are blistered badly and hurt with every step. I've survived grizzlies and stream crossings, but blisters may be my undoing.

My feet feel better after a day in camp, so I head out to visit 7,457-foot Mount Doonerak. One of my desires has been to approach—and perhaps walk upon—the mountain that Marshall once called "the Matterhorn of the Koyukuk." To reach Doonerak's flanks, or even see the peak, I must first hike to Bombardment Creek, about three and a half miles east of camp. I sidehill through open spruce forest, gradually ascending into subalpine tundra meadows. I keep turning corners in the terrain, expecting a full view of the mountain, but there's always one more spine to block the peak. Then, finally, I round one last bend—and I'm greeted by an over-whelming presence.

Even after reading and rereading Marshall's enthusiastic descriptions, I wasn't prepared for such a starkly magnificent landscape. Desolate, yet sublime. It's not only Doonerak that overwhelms me, but also its neighbor, Hanging Glacier Mountain, and the chasm—Bombardment Creek—that both separates and connects the two. A deep gash between looming, steep-sided rock walls thousands of feet high, this narrow gorge is unlike any I've seen. In its shadowed, bare-rock bottom are remnant snowfields, cascading whitewaters, landslide and avalanche debris, and, near its head, a stairstep waterfall fed by gleaming snowfields.

East of Bombardment, tan limestones form Doonerak's lower reaches (any notions about walking upon them have been erased by the chasm below me). The limy rocks give way to a succession of dark spires and pinnacles that ascend to Doonerak's ultimate heights, with a final black tower as its throne. The mountain's lower flanks are whiskered by green tundra plants but its upper slopes are bare rock, blanketed by recent snows that accentuate the sharply angled rock forms. Uphill from me, Hanging Glacier Mountain thrusts upward on massive rock walls and great towers, weathered and broken into pyramidal shapes.

The combined effect of mountains and gorge is one of extreme verticality. The landscape sweeps sharply upward, more than a mile into the sky. I can easily understand why Marshall estimated Doonerak's height at more than ten thousand feet. It seems such a soaring mountain must be at least that tall. It's as if somehow I've been transported to the "throne room of the mountain gods," to borrow a phrase from nature photographer Galen Rowell. This sense of being on the threshold to a more transcendent realm is accentuated by the gentler, greener landscape below me to the north: the broad, forested valley of the Koyukuk's North Fork and the rounded, more subdued mountains across the valley.

Stomach growling, I end my mountain reverie and descend to camp in golden evening light. The sun dips below the western ridgeline at 9:38 p.m. just as I'm finishing dinner under blue skies.

Thin wisps of clouds move in during the night, cutting the chill, and by midday a steady, light rain again falls gently upon river, forest, tundra, and my rain gear. I find a favorite spot along the North Fork and listen to its music.

JULY 31. A beautiful morning to pack up camp. Clear blue sky, gentlest of breezes. Warm, after a chilly night, yet remarkably mosquito free. My spirit, like the day, is bright and calm, though I'm sorry to be leaving this spot. By late morning a stiff southerly wind has kicked up and tendrils of clouds rush upvalley.

I pack six miles in just under six hours, with symphonic and choral tunes playing in my head and birdsong all around me. Boreal chickadees, juncos, robins all serenade my passage, while gray jays and ravens squawk and caw.

I'm nearing the end of my day's march, resting on a river bar, when four people appear out of the woods. We wave greetings and they come over to chat—my first conversation with people (other than myself) since July 23. Part of a ten-member British expedition, they, like me, are headed for what Robert Marshall long ago named "The Gates of the Arctic" formed by a pair of massive mountains that flank the North Fork. They'll float the Koyukuk; I'll join up with Dulcy and some friends for more Brooks Range adventures.

If I pushed it, I could reach my rendezvous point late tonight. But I'm already bushed and the Brits reported that a small tent city has formed at the site (the only gravel bar on which planes can safely land in this part of the Brooks Range). I choose solitude over crowds, rest over ambition, and stop at a sandbar for one last night of solo camping.

The first morning of August brings sunshine, mostly blue skies, and steady, dry winds to the North Fork. Maybe it's because I know the end is near, but my pack seems heavier and my muscles feel achier today. As the hours pass I grow weary of detours, from river bars to forest and then back again, simply to avoid cutbank channels and soaked feet. Finally I decide the most direct route works best, even if it's the wettest. Slogging through slow-moving side channels and crossing river bars, I see and hear growing signs of a human presence. Dozens of boot prints have been pressed into the sand and increased numbers of aircraft roar through the sky. By day's end I'll have counted five planes, the most I've seen or heard on this trip.

Just when I'm beginning to wonder if I've somehow missed the rendezvous point, I spot two tents and two people on a large gravel bar. Even from a distance, I recognize Patti and Nancy. Friends from Anchorage, they've come to float the North Fork. Hallelujah! My endless last-day trudge is over. I wander into camp, beaming and waving. I've survived my two weeks alone in the wilderness. It's time for some hugs, stories, and food.

Dulcy arrives a couple hours later, flown in from Bettles, south of the range. She jumps out of the plane bringing big bear hugs and sweets hauled from Anchorage: orange, tomato, roast beef sandwich, Pepsi, fudge brownie. Words pour out of me. It seems I can't stop talking—about the weather, Doonerak, encounters with bear, the magic of river songs, the splendid solitude, the terror of stream crossings. No more worries now about rendezvous points to reach, miles to go, or rivers to cross. No more need to be alone. I am a happy pilgrim.

TWELVE

Encounters with the Other

Arctic Wolf

CAMPED ALONE, DEEP IN ALASKA'S BROOKS RANGE WILDERNESS, I find a comfortable spot along the North Fork of the Koyukuk. Then, placing my head beside the river's churning aqua waters, I listen closely to its fluid play of sounds. I've heard beautiful Celtic-like chanting, off and on, for the past few days. The songs seem to come from outside me, from the forest and tundra and especially the river, but I suppose it could all be in my head. I've even put words to some of the music: "Holy, ho-o-o-ly, holy . . . " I wonder what combination of landscape and wind sounds mix with my own memories and thought processes—and several days of solitude—to produce these voices, this music.

My musings are interrupted by an unmistakably "real" voice that has nothing to do with my imagination: a howling comes from the forest, behind my tent. It is a loud, clear, resonant wail of alto key that rolls across the valley. The howl triggers an immediate physical and emotional response. My heart races, pulse quickens, spirit lifts. I'm amazed, excited, and curious, all at once. I instinctively turn from the river, binoculars in hand, and face the wooded hills above camp. With all the tracks and scat on this river bar and across the North Fork, I've anticipated—and sometimes imagined—wolf howls throughout my three-day campout here. Each morning and night I've swept the hillsides with binoculars, hopeful of a miracle. Now one has come to me.

I peer at two tundra knobs a few hundred feet above camp, then scan the spruce forest below. Even as I do, the howling resumes. The first baleful voice is joined by a second that's higher pitched. This one is more of a soprano. The trembling howls blend and shift key. Are there more than two wolves? Hard to tell. Wolves are known to mix their voices in a way that produces a magnified sense of numbers.

I wonder if the wolves have seen me on the open gravel bar, or noticed the tarp or tent. Are they protesting this intruder? Announcing my presence—or theirs—to other wolves?

Rain is falling hard now, but I barely notice. Or care. The wolf songs last a minute or two, but resonate much longer. This is what I dream about, to share the wilderness with howling wolves. I wish Dulcy were here to share this moment and ask myself: which is more desirable, to see wolves or hear them sing? There's no simple answer, but there is this fact: over the years I've seen wolves a half-dozen times, yet heard them howling only once. Those songs came from a distance, in these very mountains (though in another valley, miles to the west).

I don't think the wolves would disturb anything in camp—they're not notorious camp raiders like bears and squirrels and jays—but I go over to the tarp, where I've placed my food cache for lunch, just to be sure. Then back to the water's edge for more looking. Even before I reach my "lookout," I see her: a whitish-gray animal, upstream from camp and halfway across the braided North Fork, not far from where I crossed the river three days ago. Maybe two hundred yards away. If I had to name a color, I'd say white wolf. But that ignores the subtleties of her coat. Bringing her into focus with my glasses, I see she has a mostly white face, with some gray atop her head and on her neck. Her flanks are a light gray, legs are white, tail a very light gray, becoming darker at the tip. In her wettened coat, the wolf appears lean but not skinny, and I assume, for no sure reason, that she's in good health.

The wolf skulks across the mid-river sand and gravel bars, crouched low as if to avoid detection. She glances now and then in my direction. I'm sure she sees me. Moving slowly, she reaches the final, deepest channel. She steps gingerly at first, splashing as she angles downstream across the milky green river. Then, for the final few feet, she plunges and swims across. The wolf stops at the forest's edge and looks back intently—but this time not toward me. I've already swung the binoculars back and forth across the river two or three times, expecting another wolf to appear. But none follows. Was I wrong about two wolves howling?

The she-wolf melts into the forest and as she does, a large brownish bird is flushed from a spruce: a northern goshawk. I assume our encounter's over, but the wolf reappears, walking slowly along the woods' margin. Once she steps into the open, bends and smells something on the bar. Then back under the trees. She takes one last look across the North Fork and turns away. Her walk becomes a trot and she's gone, melted into the forest's shadows.

Minutes later, there's more howling—from my side of the river, though farther downstream. Perhaps the second wolf was unwilling to cross the stream within sight of me or the camp. The white wolf sings back, briefly. Then silence returns to the valley, except for the rushing, rattling, humming North Fork and tapping of rain. In a growing downpour I stand still another thirty or forty-five minutes, maybe an hour. I listen and look, upstream and down, along the forest's edge and up higher, along tundra terraces. I wipe the lenses of my binoculars. It's become a cold, hard Arctic rain but today I don't mind being out in it. Finally I give up my watch, grab shelter under the tarp. I notice I'm shivering—from the wet chill, yes, but also from the song of *Canis lupus*.

I love grizzly bears. They are one of my primary totem animals, maybe my most important. To share the landscape with grizzlies is always an honor and delight. But to be with howling wolves in the Arctic wilds—there is no greater magic. Beneath the tarp and later in the tent, I imagine distant, intermittent howling throughout the afternoon and evening. It's amazing how much a river or the wind can sound like wolves.

I've had a feeling about this place since first seeing the many wolf tracks along the river. I'm convinced there's a den not far away and have wished I might stumble upon it, or even see wolf pups from a distance while scanning the landscape. But I'm satisfied now. I've had my communion. Both body and soul have been stirred by songs that tell, without words, of mountains, of rivers, of mysteries as ancient as music.

THIRTEEN

Encounters with the Other

In the Company of Bears

I USED TO HAVE NIGHTMARES ABOUT BEARS. THEY ENTERED MY dream world in the mid-1970s, shortly after I'd come to Alaska, and they roamed the forests of my subconscious for many years after. A geologist then, just out of graduate school, I spent my first Alaskan summers in some of the state's wildest, most remote grizzly bear country. And each year, usually toward the end of the field season, phantom grizzlies would stalk me, chase me, attack me. They lurked in my dream shadows, ominous and haunting. I now sometimes wonder if those nightmares were omens. Perhaps they spoke of things to come, of a summer afternoon in Shuyak Island State Park, at the northern end of Alaska's Kodiak Archipelago. . . .

FIVE OF US HAVE SPENT the morning in kayaks; now it's time to stretch muscles and explore one of the many small islands that border Shuyak's northern coast. The islet we choose is inhabited by Sitka black-tailed deer; from the water, we see several animals feeding in open meadows. It's also home to a brown bear female, with three tiny cubs. We spotted them earlier in the day, though the bear family has since disappeared into the forest.

I've seen many grizzlies over the years, but that was my first sighting of brown bears, the coastal cousins of griz. Alaska's brown bears tend to be more chocolaty in color and have less distinctive humps and shorter claws than their Interior relatives. On average they're much larger animals, mainly because they have access to more plentiful, energy-rich foods, especially salmon. A large male grizzly may weigh six hundred to seven hundred pounds in fall, when it's fattened for hibernation. But the largest brown bears are twice that size. And nowhere do brown bears grow larger than on the Kodiak Archipelago, home to the subspecies *Ursus arctos middendorffi.* Even here, researchers say, adult females rarely reach seven hundred pounds, though this mother bear appeared much bigger.

We beach our kayaks, then split up. I go with Sam, one of the expedition's guides, following a game trail that begins in a meadow, but soon borders a thick stand of spruce. Sam calls out to announce our presence: "Hooyah . . . hooyah." Eventually the trail peters out, where the forest reaches the island's edge. We have a simple choice: return down the trail or cut through the woods. Sam chooses the trees and I follow, despite some misgivings. He's the guide, after all.

The spruce are twenty to thirty feet high, spindly, and densely packed. We can't easily see more than ten to fifteen feet ahead, sometimes less. We're walking slowly, talking loudly, when suddenly my worst nightmare comes true: a bear charges out of the forest's shadows. She must have tried to hide her family in this stand to avoid the strange two-legged invaders of her island. But we've entered her sanctuary and threatened, however innocently, her offspring. Retreat hasn't worked, so her only option now is to defend her cubs by force.

Things begin to speed up and, simultaneously, move in slow motion around me. Less than twenty feet away, the bear is a blur of terrible speed, size, and power—a dark image of unstoppable rage. Her face is indistinct, and I sense, more than see, her teeth and claws. Two giant bounds are all it takes for the bear to reach Sam, five feet in front of me. Somewhere, amid the roaring that fills my head, I hear a cry: "Oh no." I'm certain that Sam is about to die, or be seriously mauled, and fear that I may be also.

The last thing I see is the bear engulfing Sam. Then, despite everything I've learned about bears, I turn and run, breaking one of the cardinal rules of bear encounters. But my instincts are strong, and they tell me to get out of sight, out of the woods. Climbing one of these slender trees isn't an option, and without any weapon, there's nothing I can do to help Sam. The only question now is whether the bear will come after me when it's done with him. I run out of the forest onto a narrow stretch of beach; I must find the other three members of the party, get Sam's rifle from his kayak, and try to rescue him.

Back in the forest, Sam is doing what he must to survive. As the bear charges, Sam tells us later, he ducks his head and falls backward. Falling, he sees the bear's open mouth, its teeth and claws. Hitting the ground, he curls into a fetal position, to protect his head and vital organs, and offers the bear a shoulder to chew on instead. And with the bear breathing in his face, he plays dead.

The bear grabs Sam in a "hug," woofs at him, and bats him a few times like a kitten playing with a mouse. But she strikes him with her paws, not her claws. There's no sound of tearing flesh. And when, after several moments—or is it minutes?—there is no response from her victim, the bear ends her attack just as suddenly as she began it. The threat removed, she leaves with her cubs.

I'm still standing on the beach, listening and looking for any sign of the bear, when, incredibly, I hear Sam shout: "The bear's gone.... I'm all right." Miraculously, he's uninjured, except for a small scratch on the back of his hand, which he got when falling backward into a small spruce. For someone who's just been attacked by a bear, Sam is taking the incident much more calmly than I. Perhaps, I'll learn later, this is because he's had lots of experience in such matters. He'd been "false charged" by bears three times previously.

"Thank goodness it was a friendly bear," Sam says after recounting his story. "It wasn't looking for a fight; it was trying to make a point: 'Leave me alone.'" Hours later, when we're rehashing the attack, he'll add: "I felt no sense of aggression or panic. I believe animals can sense a person's energy. If you're projecting aggression, or if the adrenaline is flowing, they know it. I was very calculating as to what I should do." It turns out he did everything right—once the bear attacked. Listening to Sam's story, still pumped with adrenaline, I can only shake my head and marvel at our escape.

Heading across a meadow to warn the others, we see the sow a hundred yards away, still greatly agitated. She stands up, then falls back to all fours and runs around in circles, and stands up again. She's looking down the island, and we guess that she has seen or smelled our companions. The bear stands one final time, then turns sharply and lopes into another, larger spruce stand. Strung out in a line, the three cubs run hard to keep up with Mom.

We rendezvous with the others, quickly retell our story, and leave the bears' island. Back in camp, we talk for hours about the encounter and second-guess ourselves. We agree it was foolish to visit the island, given our earlier bear sighting, even more foolhardy to cut through the woods. I'm reminded, again, to question authority and trust my own judgment.

The encounter also raises questions about firearms, which may be carried in all of Alaska's state parks. I have never carried a gun into Alaska's backcountry; I'm not a firearms expert, have no desire to be, and believe that guns cause more trouble than bears. Like Sam, I also believe that guns change a person's "energy," change the way a person relates to wild places, wild creatures. They offer security, but they also can prompt people to take chances they ordinarily wouldn't, sometimes resulting in confrontations that might have been avoided. The usual result is injury or death, most often for the bear.

For awhile, after the Shuyak attack, I questioned my philosophy. It's often said that bears, like people, are individuals. Each one is different, unpredictable. As

Richard Nelson, an Alaskan writer, anthropologist, and naturalist whose philosophy I greatly respect, says in *The Island Within:* "All it takes is once in a lifetime, the wrong bear in the wrong place. Without a rifle (and the knowledge of when and how to use it), the rest of the story would be entirely up to the bear. . . . It's my way of self-preservation, as the hawk has its talons, the heron its piercing beak, the bear its claws. . . ." But as time has passed, I've become more convinced than ever that it's right, for me, to walk unarmed in Alaska's backcountry. It would be different, perhaps, if brown or black bears preyed on people. But they rarely do. In a sense, my choice is a symbolic gesture of respect to the animal and its world; I'm only a visitor in the bear's realm, passing through and intending no harm.

On Shuyak, we provoked the attack. A mother was being crowded, and she wanted to eliminate what she perceived as a very real threat. She was protecting her cubs, no more, no less. Playing dead, removing the threat, proved the best thing to do, not fight back. Shooting her would have been a tragedy.

BEARS CONTINUE TO WALK the forests of my dream worlds, but no longer are they a shadowy menace. This makes good sense to me. Over the years I've come to believe that the Shuyak bear was a messenger of sorts—and a gift in my life. Her attack was more fearsome than anything I'd imagined or dreamed. Yet the encounter ended well for both humans and bears. The bear's sudden and overwhelmingly powerful presence taught me lessons about foolishness and the need to pay greater attention to my own intuition. And, in a curious way, her brief passage through my life led to new pathways. In the years since the attack, I have spent many, many days in the company of bears and have learned that they are remarkably tolerant of people—much more tolerant than we humans are of them, certainly. Bears, especially the brown/grizzly, have been guides as I reconnect with my own wild spirit. Now I welcome their appearance in both my waking life and dreams.

FAST-FORWARD A DOZEN YEARS to the upper Alaska Peninsula, where I'm camped among several other bear lovers. . . .

We have barely finished storing away food and setting up tents among tall meadow plants, when a family of brown bears comes ambling down the narrow sand beach that fronts our camp. The bears are walking slowly, without menace, eating as they go. Still, they're moving ever closer. In the lead is a large female with a beautiful milk chocolate–colored coat that has not yet begun to shed. And trailing her in single file are four tiny cubs. Darker than their mom, the cubs were born in January or February. Only a pound or so at birth, the largest of the four in late July weighs twenty-five to thirty pounds. The runt of the litter weighs half as much; incredibly small and fragile-looking, he has the cute appeal of a real live teddy bear.

In most places, the steady approach of a brown bear family would be cause for concern, perhaps even alarm, because females with cubs are notoriously aggressive. The five of us who watch the bears—soon to be joined by a half-dozen others—would likely announce our presence by talking loudly, maybe while waving our arms and slowly retreating. We would crowd together, to increase our size, and worry that the bears might invade our camp. Someone in the group might reach for a firearm or pepper spray. None of that happens, however. Not here, with this particular female.

Newly arrived at Alaska's McNeil River State Game Sanctuary and accompanied by a Fish and Game bear biologist, we watch calmly and quietly from the edge of camp while the mom and her cubs forage among sedges that grow where beach sand gives way to expansive mudflats. We talk in whispered tones of our good fortune, as the bears come to within a hundred feet, then eighty, then forty. It's clear that their approach has nothing to do with us; it just so happens that the mother's beach foraging has brought the family in our direction. The cubs look toward us now and then with an apparent mix of curiosity and anxiety, but their mom hardly pays us any heed as she hungrily gulps down clumps of green blades.

One of dozens of brown bears to congregate at McNeil each summer, this female is recognized by sanctuary manager Larry Aumiller as Snow Bear. Known to be highly tolerant of humans and comfortable in their presence, she understands, in her own ursine way, that we humans present no danger to her or her cubs.

McNeil's staff has named nearly all of the sanctuary's adult bears—at least the regulars who come back year after year. Some people have criticized this practice, but Aumiller, who's run the McNeil program since 1976, notes that wildlife researchers often use naming to identify individuals: "With more than eighty or ninety adult bears here, you need a way to keep track of different ones. Naming them is almost like a mnemonic device to help you remember them. It doesn't imply human characteristics or qualities." In Snow Bear's case, the name was bestowed several summers ago, while she sat upon a patch of snow. Now in her prime, she weighs five hundred to six hundred pounds. That's a good-sized female. McNeil's largest males weigh twice that.

Snow Bear is only one of several females to bring new litters to McNeil River this summer, but she and her cubs dominate our conversations over the next four days. Partly, that's because she frequently forages near camp; but it's also because four-cub litters are so rare. Over the past quarter century, only four females have shown up here with four cubs. The usual number is two.

Brown bear cubs are usually weaned from their mothers during their third summer, at age two and a half. The chances of a cub surviving that long at

McNeil are fifty-fifty, says Aumiller. Some drown; others starve or are killed by disease, falls, or other bears. The runt's odds are even slimmer. A few days later, during a swim across McNeil Lagoon, he lags behind and for a few moments we wonder if he'll make it to shore. He does, but takes far longer to recover than his siblings. We find ourselves rooting for him to make it, a natural human response to underdogs.

ESTABLISHED IN 1967 AND MANAGED by the state's Division of Wildlife Conservation, McNeil Sanctuary protects the world's largest gathering of brown bears, the coastal cousins of grizzlies. The focal point of this gathering is McNeil Falls, where bears come to feed on chum salmon. During the peak of that July–August chum run, dozens of brown bears congregate. As many as 144 individual bears (adults and cubs) have been identified along McNeil River in a single season. And in July 1997, biologists counted seventy bears at the falls at one time.

Even more impressive than the numbers of bears, perhaps, is their acceptance of a human presence. Every day from early July through late August, ten visitors plus sanctuary staff spend seven to eight hours at the falls, while stationed at two gravel pads (one atop a knoll, the other right below it). "Think about it," Aumiller says. "You've got this group of people standing in the middle of forty, fifty, sixty bears. You're very close to where they want to be. And they tolerate you." Some will eat salmon, take naps, nurse cubs, or even mate within a short distance of the viewing pads.

The high degree of tolerance shown by McNeil's bears may be Aumiller's greatest legacy. More than anyone else, this sixtysomething naturalist with dark, silver-speckled hair, sparkling eyes, and an easy smile has demonstrated that bears can become habituated to people without also becoming food conditioned. And he's shown that such people-tolerant bears—Aumiller calls them "neutrally habituated"—are safe to be around. As he explains it, "At McNeil, humans are neither a threat nor a source of food. Over time it became clear from their actions that the more tolerant bears were perceiving us as neutral objects, maybe as innocuous as a rock or a tree."

Before the McNeil "experiment," most people—including many so-called bear experts—believed that habituated bears, particularly grizzlies (or browns), are extremely dangerous. McNeil proved the opposite is true, *if* food is removed from the equation. For that reason, all human food is stored and meals are prepared and eaten in a sturdy cabin that's off-limits to bears. The sanctuary's bears-come-first philosophy has also been a key to its success. Visitor numbers are restricted and human activities are kept as predictable as possible. As a general rule, people aren't allowed to wander outside the well-defined campground area without being accompanied by sanctuary staff.

Reflecting on the lessons he's learned in nearly three decades at the sanctuary, Aumiller readily admits that living with bears is not an easy thing, but McNeil is proof of what's possible when humans are willing to compromise: people and bears can indeed peacefully coexist, often in close company. "What goes on here is still news to a lot of people," Aumiller says. "They don't think it can happen. But it does. McNeil shows that if you learn about something that's different from you, and begin to appreciate it, then you'll figure out a way to keep it in your life. You'll learn to coexist."

THE NUMBER OF BEARS GATHERING at the falls is down this summer, reflecting a poor return of chums. Unless there's a sudden late surge of fish, the run is likely to be the smallest on record. In a good year, bears fishing the falls in late July and early August will pull a hundred or more salmon from McNeil's blue-green waters every hour. The hourly counts on August 1 are dismal by comparison: eight, ten, five, twelve . . .

With less food to go around, bears are less tolerant of each other as they compete for prime fishing spots. There's more tension, more fighting—and fewer scraps for the adolescents and females with cubs that roam the river's perimeter. The best fishing spots are hogged by large, mature males weighing a thousand pounds or more and bearing numerous pink scars from battles won and lost.

The lord of the falls this year, as he's been since the early 1990s, is a hulking, dark-chocolate brown male named Woofie. Now in his late teens, Woofie has a huge "fish gut." He also has a huge head, legs, and rear end, rippling muscles—and a long pink slash of a scar that cuts diagonally across his left side. Given Woofie's reputation, the scar leaves you wondering what happened to the other guy.

Among the largest of McNeil's bears, Woofie has an aggressive, intimidating personality among his own kind, though like many mature males he tends to shy away from humans. A decent salmon fisher, he seems to prefer bullying other bears and stealing their fish. Typically he'll arrive at the falls, take in the scene for a few minutes, then walk nonchalantly, in his swaggering way, to his chosen victim. With Woofie's reputation now well established, most picked-on bears give up their catch without a fuss. Occasionally, however, there is much growling, snarling, baring of teeth, and even front-leg jabs to the chest.

With little hope this year at the falls, many adolescents and females with cubs have taken to wandering the coastal mudflats, where they feed on sedges and other greens or chase salmon in tidal channels.

ONCE, AS WE'RE WATCHING from a remarkably close distance, Snow Bear rolls over onto her back to nurse her cubs. With her in this most vulnerable position—legs extended and her more sparsely furred belly and groin area revealed—I can more easily see, or at least imagine, a physical likeness between human and bear.

As David Rockwell explains at great length in *Giving Voice to Bear*, many Native American tribes—including some of Alaska's "first peoples"—have attached great meaning to the physical similarities of our two species. Bears, like people, can easily stand on their hind legs; they can even walk upright for short distances. And when a bear is standing, the animal's front legs hang at his sides like arms. As anyone who's seen bears catch and eat salmon knows, they are surprisingly adroit when using their front paws; even more impressively, Rockwell notes, "in captivity they have been known to peel peaches." And there's this fact: skinned bears look eerily human. Such resemblances, combined with similarities in diet and behaviors (strong maternal instincts, problem-solving abilities, playfulness) have led many Native groups to feel a special kinship with bears. Tribes throughout North America traditionally believed the bear to be half-human, or that humans were descended from bears.

I like that notion, just as I've come to relish the shape-shifting myths that tell of bears becoming humans or humans becoming bears, transformations back and forth. Something about those stories resonates. They hold a certain magic. And here things start to get tricky. How do you talk—or write—about such things without seeming New Agey? Without trivializing something that holds great power? Or without "stealing" from other cultural traditions? I don't know the answer, so I usually steer clear of such dilemmas, keep my more mystical leanings under wraps (except with dear friends who've come to accept my occasional ecstatic outbursts). But here I'll recklessly plunge ahead: bears, I've come to realize, are one of my totem animals. Though I come from a different cultural tradition, this white guy of European descent, Lutheran upbringing, and scientific training nevertheless finds meaning in the Native American notion of totems; and I've come to understand and identify them in my own, personal way. A totem animal is one that has caught or "demanded" my attention; one that "speaks" to me; one with which I sense some special connection or an inexplicable fascination. A teacher. A messenger. A guide. Bear is one. Squirrel, chickadee, wolf, and spider are others. Who can understand, let alone explain, such things? As weird as it seems, there's something to the kinship/totem idea, even for a recovering, born-and-bred fundamentalist Christian and ex-geologist educated in the sciences. This fascination with bears and the desire to know them better is worth pursuing. Bear brings me closer to wildness, closer to myself.

As to how and when the seeds of this strange bonding were planted, I can't say for sure. I recall no special interest in bears during my boyhood years in Connecticut. Bears weren't part of my world, though it seems they must have occasionally roamed through the woodlands my friends and I explored. What I knew of them I learned from sensationalized outdoor-magazine stories and "bear tales" books; namely that bears are dangerous, unpredictable, blood-thirsty critters that can— and will, if given the chance—tear you limb from limb.

Not until I came to Alaska in 1974 did I see a bear in the wild. And it wasn't until the late 1980s—after I'd left Alaska, switched careers from geology to journalism, and then returned to work at the *Anchorage Times*, eventually to become the newspaper's outdoors writer—that I truly became a passionate student of *ursus*. My education accelerated dramatically, and my affinity for bears deepened immeasurably, both during and after my first trip to McNeil in 1988, which I've had the good fortune to visit a half-dozen times.

Taught by both the bears and Aumiller, I've been changed by McNeil, as so many others have been transformed. I've come to understand bears as complex, amazingly adaptive, and intelligent creatures. And I've learned, as Aumiller learned years earlier, that bears are much more tolerant of us than humans are of them.

As the sanctuary's "take-home" lessons took hold, my fear of bears gave way to respect and reverence. Yes, bears—especially grizzlies—are large, powerful, and sometimes fiercely aggressive animals, particularly when protecting their young or food. They have the strength and "tools"—their teeth and claws—to do great harm. They can be dangerous. But they're not blood-thirsty killers of humans and rarely prey on people. If that weren't true, we would have plenty to fear when passing through bear country.

And, I've learned, they carry a power that goes far beyond their physical strength and size and ferocity.

SHORTLY BEFORE 11 MY LAST EVENING at the sanctuary, I stand above the sand beach in gray light that is dimming to darkness. The land and seascape beyond our small defined campground is once again a place only of bears, gulls, eagles, ravens, ground squirrels, foxes, and salmon. Watching from camp's edge, I count twenty-nine bears scattered from the mouth of McNeil River to the outer mudflats of Kamishak Bay. And I hear the sounds of night: the screech of gulls and eagles, the loud splash of bears chasing fish, the melancholy three-note song of a golden-crowned sparrow in alder thickets behind camp.

The bears are distant silhouettes. I see one family with two cubs, another with three. And then I see Snow Bear, still with her four. I am cheered by this, even while knowing the odds are small that they'll all make it through the summer.

The wildness deepens with the darkness as we humans shrink into our tents and sleeping bags, hiding from the night, the cold, the rain. Thick clouds shroud the landscape as salmon move through tidal flats toward McNeil River and bears hunt the salmon as they've done for centuries.

MID-AUGUST, THE BROOKS RANGE. Two years after meeting McNeil's brown bear quadruplets, I am alone, camped deep in the Arctic. For the past two weeks I have been keeping watch for bear. Partly that's to ensure I don't have any surprise encounters with a grizzly. Unlike their coastal relatives, grizzlies don't easily adapt to being around other bears. Or people. Researchers guess that's because they rarely, if ever, gather in large groups to feed on concentrated, energy-rich food sources. So they haven't evolved the "social behaviors" to be in close company with each other—or, by extension, with humans. My previous experience with grizzlies has been this: upon seeing, smelling, or otherwise sensing *Homo sapiens*, most skedaddle with little or no hesitation. They want nothing to do with us hairless bipeds.

Still, if you surprise a grizzly (or any bear, for that matter) at close range, all bets are off. The bear must make a split-second decision. It may flee, or it may choose to forcefully eliminate the perceived threat by attacking. Happily, surprise encounters are rare in the vast tundra expanses of Alaska's northernmost mountain chain.

There's another, deeper reason that I've been keeping watch: I wish to share the landscape with bear. In one respect, I have been doing so since arriving in the Brooks Range. Whether or not they're visible, or physically present, grizzlies regularly pass through the valleys I've been exploring. These "barren ground" grizzlies are almost constantly on the move in their search for food, not nearly as abundant here as it is along Alaska's southern coastline. For all its beauty, most of the Arctic is a place of scarcity—except for its mosquitoes. The living is not easy, especially for a large predator.

In the course of my travels, I've seen plenty of bear sign: tracks (some of them fresh), scat, and tundra diggings, where a grizzly has hunted ground squirrels. But no bear. So in my journal I wonder: will seeing a grizzly make my trip here more memorable? Is it not enough to know that bears frequent these valleys and ridges? I know the answer even as I write the question. I won't be disappointed if I leave without seeing a grizzly. But a bear sighting would inevitably enhance my stay here.

Sitting in camp, I imagine a grizzly walking across the tundra. Sitting on a tundra bench. Watching. Watching me? Might bear seek me? Am I becoming bear? Certainly

I've come to feel a more ursine presence within my psyche in recent years. Allowing my thoughts to roam, I ask myself again why I've come to this Arctic wilderness and its high alpine. What do I seek? Adventure? Revelation? Transformation?

There's no question that adventure is part of the draw. So is the wild beauty of this place. Since I first came here more than a quarter century ago, the Brooks Range has become my favorite wilderness. It's a place where wildness is manifested in wave after wave of rocky, knife-edged ridges that can be attained without climbing expertise, and which stretch to the horizon and beyond; in glacially carved basins that grow lush in midsummer with the rich greens of tundra meadows and the vibrant purples, yellows, magentas, and blues of alpine wildflowers; in wolves, Dall sheep, caribou, bears, and wolverines; in an unpeopled landscape where one can still travel for days—perhaps even weeks—without seeing another person, or even signs of humanity.

Not coincidentally, the Brooks Range is where I saw my first wild bear, in 1974, while working as an exploration geologist. The animal, a chocolate-colored grizzly, stood several hundred yards away, busily digging into the tundra for roots or perhaps ground squirrels, while I collected rock and sediment specimens from a mountain stream. I was deeply stirred by the presence of the bear; but what moved me initially was the grizzly itself, rather than anything it implied about wildness or vast, undeveloped landscapes. That recognition would come later, in bits and pieces, along with a passionate interest in the animal and a desire to know it better.

But more than adventure or memories are at play. I'm also seeking answers. I want to better understand what wildness means to me. And what "sacred" means. I want to embrace the wild Other that roams this Arctic world and also lurks inside, still mostly hidden.

Keep searching and wondering, I encourage myself. Sleep on it. Dream it. What's important? What's here for me? What's the essence of this journey? Stay open to possibilities, to miracles and revelations. Let the landscape speak. Pay attention to its inhabitants: animal, plant, rock, creek, mountain.

THREE DAYS LATER, bear comes to me.

Like the previous four, this August day has been gray, raw, windy, and wet, so I've spent most of the morning and afternoon hunkered in my dry tent and warm cocoon of a sleeping bag. Finally braving the storm, I grab my bear-resistant food container, duck under a small tarp, and slowly savor a meal of granola bars, cheese, oatmeal, beef jerky, and fresh coffee. Then, in my usual way, I scan the landscape.

Across the creek, on a gentle rise, I turn my attention to a couple of dark, hulking shapes. That's nothing unusual; I've seen dozens of "bear boulders" over the past two and a half weeks. But there's something about one of the rocks; exactly what, I can't say. Maybe it's the boulder's dark-chocolate-brown color; or the fact that I hadn't noticed this particular boulder before, among several other familiar ones.

After shifting my gaze to another part of the valley, I pull it back across the creek. And darned if that chocolaty boulder hasn't moved. A couple minutes earlier, it lay in an open meadow. Now it's beside a willow thicket, near the bottom of a gully. Just to be certain, I hurry back to the tent and grab my binoculars. Normally I carry them everywhere, but with the weather being so poor, I figured I wouldn't need them.

By now the boulder has moved again, so I'm all but certain what I'm going to see. The glasses confirm it: a chocolate grizzly bear is grazing on tundra plants directly across Giant Creek, maybe an eighth of a mile away. Well, this is what I've wanted. But now, miles from the nearest human on a dark and utterly dreary day, I can't help but recall the saying *be careful what you wish for*.

The bear's shape suggests an adult: heavily muscled body, large belly, and massive head. From here the grizzly easily looks large enough to be a male and that's what I guess the animal to be. The bear works his way uphill, out of the thickets and back into the tundra meadow, and I find myself encouraging this move. *Good bear; stay away from my camp.*

The wind and rain don't seem to bother him at all. In fact he moseys along, munching as he goes, as if he has no cares at all—which at this moment, and likely most moments in his adult life, is probably true. I wonder what he's eating, since berries are scarce in this upper valley. From what I can tell, he's consuming both greens and wildflowers. When the bear leaves, I'd like to go inspect where he's now grazing, but high, rain-swollen creek waters may prevent that.

Scribbling notes in my journal, I lose track of the grizzly. Ten or fifteen seconds pass before I re-locate him, though he's not hiding. That's how well he blends in. Now he's lying down among some cobble-sized rubble. An after-lunch nap? Out in the open, he faces directly into the wind-driven rain.

The grizzly hasn't looked my way once, that I can tell. I wonder if he's noticed me, or my purple-and-green tent, or this beige flapping tarp. From my own hikes, I know the tarp stands out, even from a distance. And now it's flailing about in the gusting wind. If the bear has noticed, what does he "think"? Or sense? What do his instincts tell him? Has he encountered humans before?

For the moment, at least, I'm much more interested in the bear than he is in me. That's good. That's what I want. Though I'm pleased to be sharing the valley with this grizzly, I wish to do so at a distance. Even having one this close to camp makes me a little nervous. One thing seems certain: the grizzly's experience of this valley is not enhanced by a human presence. Many residents of the nearest village would likely shoot the bear if they found him this close to camp, or even crossed paths with him on trips through the mountains. Whether or not he's had any past encounters with humans, the bear shows no anxiety about my presence.

It's cold out here. Fingers and toes are tingling. My small field thermometer reads in the upper forties, but with the gusting winds, the chill is probably closer to freezing. Classic hypothermia weather. So, here I am, behind a shelter and cloaked in wind shell, fleece jacket, capilene shirt, nylon pants, wool cap with rain hood pulled over it, and fleece gloves—and starting to shiver. Meanwhile the bear, lying on an exposed bench and faced into the wind, shows no discomfort at all. If he's not chilled at all on a day like this, does he overheat on the bright, sunny, warm days of summer (which admittedly seem to be few and far between here)?

The bear naps more than an hour before rising. Immediately, he resumes feeding. He does little else for the next two hours except chew mouthfuls of tundra greens. He barely lifts his head, except to see where the next patch of food might be, and seldom has to take more than a few steps to get there. He continues to ascend a rocky rivulet surrounded by low-lying but lush green plants, until reaching a rubbly pile of lichen-bearded boulders. He then tops a brownish knoll that apparently has little to tempt him, and ambles to another lush swale, where he resumes his feasting.

It would appear the grizzly has entered the late-summer phase that biologists sometimes call hyperphagia: an almost around-the-clock gorging, in preparation for winter's months-long fasting. At one point the bear finds a spot so luscious, all he can do is sprawl in the midst of it.

The more I watch the grizzly, the more I'm confident he's a heavily muscled mature male, perhaps in his prime. He has little to fear, except, perhaps, for a larger bear—which seems unlikely here—or hunters bearing guns. That's one good thing about this weather: no hunters are likely to come this way today.

IT'S EVENING NOW AND I'VE finished dinner except for a few bites of dark chocolate and some sips of coffee. My stinging-cold toes tell me not to stay out too much longer. Must be five hours, at least, since I first spotted the boulder that turned into a bear. Over that time it's become clear that much of what he's eating is Richardson's saxifrage, also commonly known as "bear flower" for good reason. The grizzly seems to be consuming it all: flowers, stems, and leaves. An eating machine, indeed. And havin' a ball. Again he sprawls out, head swiveling back and forth, mowing down those plants. It must be the closest thing to bear heaven, if you don't have access to berries or salmon.

Once, twice, the bear's attention is diverted. He stares down into the creek a few moments, then resumes eating. As strange as it seems, I wonder if backpackers might have come over from a neighboring valley and are headed down Giant Creek. Or, even less probable, that Nunamiut hunters have come up here, unnoticed by me in the howling and drum-beating cacophony of wind and rain. *Don't you dare shoot that bear*, I warn the imagined hunters.

I put away food and cooking gear, take some stuff back to the tent, then return for a final look. The grizzly is now on the move. Heading slowly toward the creek bottom, he stops now and then for snacks along the way. I take down the tarp and retreat to the tent with binoculars and sitting pad, setting up on the downwind side. Glancing at my watch, I see it's 8:30.

Just once that I can tell, the grizzly looks toward the tent. Then, still headed downstream—and away from my camp—he disappears into thick brush that lines the creek. There's no sign of him for several minutes. Finally he reappears, going up a gully that leads to a side valley. Moving beyond a thicket of shoulder-high willows, the grizzly heads out onto open tundra, walking slowly but steadily in a gait that is part swagger, part waddle. He comes to a rise and tops it, body disappearing bit by bit 'til he's gone.

I've spent six hours, maybe more, in the company of bear. It's one thing to do so at a place like McNeil, where you walk among bears in a guided group, within a structured system. It's quite another while alone, deep in the wilderness. I feel a vague emptiness in my gut as the bear disappears, a sadness to go with my great pleasure at this gift, this opportunity to gain an extended peek into a grizzly's solitary life.

On the surface, I suppose, it might be said that nothing special happened today. The bear didn't do anything unexpected or threatening, so my "encounter" with this grizzly won't grip friends and new acquaintances the way my bear-attack story inevitably does. And I had no breakthrough epiphany. And yet this has been everything I could have asked for, and more. There's little that could have kept me outdoors in such bleak weather; yet while engaged with the grizzly I largely forgot my own discomfort and moved more deeply into the raw power of this Arctic alpine valley. While on Shuyak Island I was an unschooled intruder, here I've slipped into the bear's world without threatening him or otherwise affecting his behavior that I can tell. Though each on his own path, we've shared something here today: a valley, a storm, an awareness of place.

Already I'm certain this wet, blustery day will remain as memorable to me as that afternoon on Shuyak. Ending the vigil, I crawl into the wind-whipped tent, curl up inside my sleeping bag, and drift into a deep sleep. Body calm and spirits lifted, I move through these mountains with bear.

FOURTEEN

Encounters with the Other

A Gift of Halibut

THE FRESHLY CUT HERRING BAIT HAS BEEN SITTING ON COOK Inlet's sandy bottom for only a few minutes when there's a sharp tug on my line. My first impulse is to set the hook, hard. Instead, I follow Mark Chihuly's instructions: I wait. "Don't be impatient," Mark has been telling us all afternoon. "Let the fish take the bait." It's the same advice my Uncle Peach gave me when we fished live minnows for bass and pickerel in Connecticut lakes more than thirty years ago. Patience usually paid off then, and it's worked so far today: already I've landed a seventy-pound halibut, the largest fish I've ever caught and the biggest our party has taken on this splendid mid-July afternoon of blue skies, sixty-something temperatures, and calm seas.

Waiting for the right moment to strike, I wonder what it would be like to catch a two-hundred- or three-hundred-pound fish. I've read stories, even written stories, about people who've caught such halibut, but it's not something I've fantasized about. Even today's seventy-pounder seemed huge; the idea of hauling in something three or four times larger is impossible to imagine. Yet this spot, we've been assured, sometimes yields giant halibut. How would I respond to such a monster fish?

Other, more disturbing, questions have drifted through my consciousness today, like fishing line through water. It's not the first time I've wondered about my decades-long desire to hook and "play" hard-fighting sport fish. But as usual, I've refused to take that particular bait, while caught up in the excitement of the chase and catch. Instead of insight, action.

Guided by Mark, five of us have been saltwater fishing from his charter boat, the *Suzy Q*, since mid-morning, first for king salmon, then for halibut, a member of the flatfish family. The king fishing had been slower than slow; no one in our boat got even a strike. "That's fishing," shrugged Mark, a stocky, muscular, good-natured outdoorsman and lifelong Alaskan who's spent much of his adult life guiding anglers and hunters. A favorite phrase, he'll repeat it a dozen times before day's end, as if to remind us—or himself—of the sport's vagaries. Still, I am disappointed. Allen, my brother-in-law, is visiting from Florida and his best chance of catching an Alaskan king is past. Like Mark, I believe that "going fishing" means more than simply catching fish, but on this day Allen and I had come to the inlet expecting to take home both sporting memories and meat. Heading away from the Kenai Peninsula coastline, I could only hope that halibut would salvage our day, make it memorable.

WE ANCHOR UP MILES FROM LAND, at a fishing hole where halibut of a hundred pounds or more are known to prowl the bottom. Back in the early eighties, Mark tells us, it was not uncommon to catch one-hundred- to two-hundred-pound halibut within a half mile of the beach. One year he pulled in a 325-pound fish and another weighing 250 pounds, "almost within stone-throwing distance of shore." But those days, he laments, are gone forever, ended by a saltwater sport fishery and charter industry that have grown precipitously in the past two decades. Trophy-size halibut are still being caught; but anglers and guides have to travel farther and expend more time and energy to catch them. Each summer hundreds of charter boats work the central waters of Cook Inlet, a long, narrow, glacially fed estuary that stretches nearly three hundred miles from the Gulf of Alaska to the Mat-Su Valleys north of Anchorage. And every one is after big fish: one hundred, two hundred, three hundred pounds. Any halibut that big is bound to be a breeding female. And the bigger the fish, the more eggs it produces: a fifty-pound female will on average release half a million eggs annually; a 250-pounder will produce four million.

Within minutes Mark has baited our hooks with herring and fish heads, and helped us to put our lines into the 160-foot-deep water. Joe, from Fairbanks, and I have fished for halibut several times before and know the routine. But Allen, Floria, and Kim—the latter two also from Fairbanks—have little or no halibut experience, so Mark emphasizes and re-emphasizes the two key elements to catching them: No. 1, keep your bait on the bottom. No. 2, "Don't set the hook too soon; let them really take it." Be patient, in other words.

Almost immediately, we get bites. Our first two fish are grey cod. Then a halibut takes my bait. I wait and wait and wait, then set the hook hard. And again. The fish takes off, stripping one-hundred-pound line from my bait-casting reel. I try to slow it by placing my thumb on the line, a foolish decision: it slices an inch-long gash into my skin. After its initial run, the halibut comes in slowly. Within fifteen minutes it's shot, gaffed, and pulled aboard. It's a good-sized fish, about seventy pounds, and someone offers to take a picture. Grunting, I lift it off the deck. I'm satisfied. Now if only Allen would catch a nice-sized halibut.

For the next two hours, Mark keeps busy untangling lines, baiting hooks, unhooking fish. By 3 p.m. our boat has landed more than a dozen halibut and kept about half, most in the twenty-to-fifty-pound range; Allen pulled in one of forty pounds, inspiring big grins and a high-five exchange. Not big fish, but large enough to satisfy clients who've spent $150 apiece for the charter—and good eating. Small halibut are juicier, tastier, and more tender than larger ones. Mark, who clearly knows his fish, rarely brings home anything over twenty pounds for eating. Still, it's hard to shake the sportfishing truism that "bigger is better." Given a choice, it's unlikely any of Mark's clients would trade a hundred-pound halibut for a twenty-pounder. I've come away from charters disappointed that I caught fish weighing "only" fifteen to twenty-five pounds. It's partly ego, but it's also the economics of guided fishing and a desire to fill freezers with halibut steaks.

Still looking for my second halibut, I feel a tug, wait, then set the hook. At first I think it's a cod, but it proves to be a small halibut, maybe fifteen pounds. With the seventy-pounder already boated, I'd be satisfied with this one to fill out my limit, but Mark tosses it back. Almost as an afterthought, he looks at me and says, "That was OK, I hope." It's as if he senses there's a bigger fish down there, ready to take the bait.

Again I let out my line. No more than five or ten minutes go by, when I feel the tug. It's a solid take, a steady, strong pull. I let the rod tip go down, let the halibut swallow the herring deeply. Then, finally, I set the hook: once, twice, three times, to be sure.

This fish doesn't run like my first halibut, but I can feel its heaviness. "I've got something," I say, feigning nonchalance, then begin a slow retrieve: lift, reel down; lift, reel down. This goes on for several minutes, until the fish decides to sit. I can't budge it an inch.

"Keep lifting," says Mark. "Stay with it."

I'm sweating now, grimacing. I'm surprised and a little chagrined that I can't move the fish. Where's that upper-body strength? On the boat's opposite side, Floria's line is doing funny things and Mark figures he's somehow become tangled with my fish. He tells Floria to give slack, then joins me. We work together, me lifting and reeling, Mark pulling the line, hand over hand, his heavily muscled arms and shoulders making my job easier. After five minutes of this, he looks at me and smiles: "You've got a big fish, maybe bigger than we've caught all year. We don't want to lose this one."

EVERYONE'S ATTENTION IS NOW FOCUSED on the fish at the end of my line. The others offer encouragement, tell me to keep at it. I'm lifting and grunting, working hard, but I'm also smiling, engaged by the growing drama. Slowly, reluctantly, the great fish is dragged upward until finally it is close enough to see through the murky water.

"It's huge!" someone shouts.

Guessing the halibut may weigh three hundred pounds, Mark says, "This is the kind of fish that will get you in the newspaper."

It's slack tide now, and the flat, diamond-shaped fish hangs from my line like a vertical slab of meat. Later, Mark tells me that most sport-caught halibut come up from the depths with their bodies in a more-or-less horizontal position. By doing that, he says, they actually help the angler, make it easier to reel them in. But occasionally a fish will come up vertically. When they do that, it's like hauling dead weight through the water.

There's another problem: halibut are powerful fish. Once boated, they're capable of doing serious damage with their flopping tails. In August 1973, the *Juneau Empire* reported the story of an Alaskan commercial fisherman who'd been killed by a halibut he'd caught: "The body of Joseph T. Cash, 67, of Petersburg was found lashed to the winch of his troller after a 150-pound halibut had apparently broken his leg and severed an artery when he hoisted it aboard his boat while fishing alone...."

Because of this and other tail-thrashing incidents, sport-fishing guides routinely shoot large halibut before bringing them aboard. Mark uses a .22-caliber pistol. The best place to shoot, he says, is in the spine, at the base of the skull. But when a three-hundred-pound halibut is hanging vertically, it's almost impossible to put a bullet in the spine. How do you lift a fish that size out of the water for a clean shot?

Slowly working the halibut toward the boat, we notice that another line, with forty-ounce weight, is tangled with mine. Complicating things even more is the fact that my line has begun to fray. Mark fires his pistol. But instead of the expected fury, the halibut just sits there in the water. Now it's time to spear the fish, using a small harpoon that's attached to a rope and buoy; that way, if my line breaks, we'll still have the fish. When Mark strikes, the halibut thrashes wildly, then dives deep—without the harpoon, which somehow pops free.

"Oh no," Mark moans. "Give it line." That's what I'm already doing, not that I have much choice. The fish disappears into the inlet's grayish-brown depths and we begin the process again.

The rod butt is bruising my inner thigh, so Mark digs out a harness. But we can't get it to fit properly and I keep the butt pinned against my upper leg and groin area, trying to leverage the rod as I work it up and down. Tomorrow I'll have deep purplish bruises to remind me of this battle.

With the halibut wounded by the bullet, perhaps mortally, landing it becomes a more serious task. As Mark says, "It would be a shame to lose it now."

Praying that the frayed line will hold, I haul it up as gingerly as possible, inch by inch. Arms, shoulders, and thighs aching, I again bring the fish within harpooning distance and Mark jabs it. Again the fish dives deep. And again the harpoon point somehow breaks free, leaving a weakening line as my only link to the fish.

I sense a frenzy around me. Mark's nerves, like the line, are fraying: he curses our bad luck and scrambles around the deck; his clients scramble to stay out of the way. At one point Allen comes over to pat me on the back, offer encouragement. I'm a point of calm within the growing storm; hopeful, but without expectations or anxieties. I'm exhausted, but focused on my role, which at this point means simply holding on to the fish.

We bring the halibut in a third time. Mark decides to shoot it again, before attempting to harpoon it. I winch the fish until its upper body is above the water, amazed that the shredded line continues to hold. He shoots once, twice, three times, four times. I wince with each shot and my ears ring with exploding gunfire.

This wondrously large fish now hangs limply. Holding the line, Mark asks Allen to harpoon the halibut. A quick, hard jab. "OK, it's in," says Allen, who looks my way and smiles.

THE FISH IS OURS NOW. Connected by the harpoon rope, it won't get away or sink from us even if the fishing line breaks. Allen sticks a large hooked gaff into the halibut, then, with loud grunts, he and Mark haul it aboard. We shout our delight, exchange congratulatory handshakes. Only our guide has ever landed a halibut this big and everyone marvels at the fish. Now that the fight is over, I'm dumbstruck. Exhausted. Relieved. How long has it been? A half hour? An hour? I feel as though I've been pulled outside ordinary time while connected to this giant fish by a thin thread.

I take some pictures then approach the halibut, lying on the boat's deck. The side that faces us is a brownish olive green, a predator's camouflage, while her underside, the side that faces the ocean bottom, is white. The skin is smooth and slippery—most would say slimy—when wet, but grows sticky with drying. I touch the skin of this great grandmother fish and something shifts in me: for a short while, at least, "it" becomes a "she." I watch her gills slowly expand, remain open for several seconds, then collapse. Is this a reflex, I wonder, or does some life force still flicker within? Except for the gills, she's still.

I'm drawn to her large, bulbous eyes, which protrude from the green upper side of the head like golf ball–sized knobs. Larger than a nickel, each black pupil is surrounded by a golden iris halo. Though unfocused, the eyes have an eerie depth to them. They pull me in, enchant me.

"It's a beautiful fish," says Allen, as though reading my mind.

"I'm glad you said that," replies Mark. "Most people think they're ugly, but I've always found them to be pretty fish."

Their comments make me consider how we so often label these large fish "monsters." So-and-so landed a monster king or a monster halibut—I used that phrase so many times when doing fishing reports as a newspaper writer. Later, a female friend will point out that such monster imagery seems a very masculine thing. Perhaps it adds drama to the hunt, accentuates the idea of doing battle with a large and powerful adversary. The paradox, in this case, is that such monster halibut are females. More than that, they're fecund mothers. I'm reminded that Western men's traditional attitudes toward hunting have sometimes been linked with their passion for sexual conquest. Both beasts and women become objects of desire, something to chase and conquer. So which is it: beauty or the beast? A little bit of both, probably, in halibut as well as humans. And where do I fit in as fisher, as hunter? Surely while "fighting" the halibut, I felt something close to desire. Now other emotions begin to intrude.

As others resume fishing, I fall into a cushioned seat, physically and emotionally drained. Earlier I'd been fully absorbed by the chase, the catch. Now I wonder if I should have given the rod and the experience to Allen, who in recent years has become an avid, if still largely inexperienced, fisherman. Traveling north with his wife and three daughters, Allen has enthusiastically spent most of his Alaska vacation on sightseeing and camping trips to Denali, Resurrection Bay, Kenai Fjords. We've caught a few small fish along the way, but this is the one day he and I have devoted solely to angling. What an Alaskan memory this great halibut could have been for the fortysomething businessman from Florida. But while I was hooked to the halibut, the thought of handing the rod to Allen didn't even cross my mind. Nothing in his actions or words suggests envy. On the contrary, he seems as excited as anyone about my catch. Later, heading to land with two fish in the twenty- to forty-pound range, Allen will voice satisfaction in his own harvest. Still I wonder: was I selfish?

I wonder too if killing this halibut was the right thing to do. Based on body measurements, a biologist later estimates her to be twenty to twenty-five years old. Something about her age, her size, her eyes, combined with what Mark has told me about the fishing pressure on female breeders, makes me question my own desires and attitudes. Perhaps it's the knowledge that, during our struggle, I was caught up in the battle and gave little thought to her life. Or death. She was something to be caught, a form of wild game—a slab of meat. I roll the words around in my head:

something to be caught, some *thing*. Before seeing her up close, the halibut had been an "it," a resource, not another being.

I think back three days, when Allen's young daughter, Emily, caught a fifteen-inch Dolly Varden char in the saltwater near Seward. Excited by the catch and charmed by the char's sleek beauty, Emily wanted to keep the fish. She would show it to her family, then we'd have it for dinner. I grabbed a rock and clubbed the Dolly, but not well enough to kill it immediately. The bloodied fish flopped on the beach. As I prepared to club it again, Emily had second thoughts: "Maybe we should let it go," she said softly. "It's too late," I told her gently. "It wouldn't survive."

Watching her stare quietly at the dying fish, I asked what she was thinking, feeling. She only shrugged, a half smile, half grimace on her face. Still silent, she bent and touched the fish, then slowly picked its limp body from the beach and carried it to her father. Later, Emily and I talked some about the fish's death, and how it was natural, OK, to feel such contradictory emotions: the initial rush of excitement when catching and seeing the fish, then sadness, even regret, at the taking of another creature's life. Killing is not an act to be taken lightly, I reminded her. When necessary, as for eating, it should be done with respect for the animal's life.

Now I'm having the same sort of second thoughts. It was only after I'd seen the old halibut's final breaths, looked into her eyes and felt her flesh, that I'd fully comprehended what I'd done: taken a life. It's strange how the earlier, smaller fish we'd caught didn't affect me this way. No brooding with them, no self-analysis. Even after considerable reflection, I can't explain the difference. Maybe it's because the smaller fish were so quickly dumped into the holding tank, leaving no time for connection or remorse. Maybe it took something as huge, as miraculous, as this great mother halibut to shake things up inside.

Could I have seen, somehow perceived, her life flickering away? Did the halibut speak to me in some way? I want to honor this matriarch somehow, to show my respect for her being, her kind. Sitting in my chair, I look again at the halibut's unblinking eyes, her huge and slightly opened mouth, with its rows of sharp teeth. In her world, she's at the top of the food chain, an aggressive bottom-feeding predator who eats crabs, shrimp, schooling fish, cod, even other halibut. Now she's become the prey.

THERE'S SOMETHING ELSE about the catch that bothers me: the "sport" aspect. We killed this halibut—all these halibut—for meat, but also for sport. For the thrill of the chase, the battle, the catch. Tutored by my Uncle Peach, a passionate angler who never showed guilt or second-guessed his motives, I've been a sport fisherman since I was eleven or twelve. Sometimes gruff, often playful, Peach was (and is) a boisterous, bearded Hemingwayesque character with a passion for the outdoors. Under his guidance I learned to catch nightcrawlers and minnows for bait and place them on my hook. I learned patience and the proper way to present the bait, to set the hook and play the fish. We were fishing buddies for years, sometimes filling our limit, more often getting skunked. Almost always we kept what we caught in Connecticut lakes and streams, the fish becoming food for the table. But sport, not food, seemed to me our main motivation.

Later, when I'd moved to Alaska and taken up fly-fishing, I became an avid catch-and-release angler. In the world of fly-fishers, catch-and-release is the highest, most ethical, and conservation-minded form of fishing possible. Anglers, biologists, and conservationists agree it has protected many fish populations that would otherwise be decimated by heavy fishing pressure.

There still are times when I enthusiastically embrace such "sport" fishing. But at other times—like now, on this halibut charter—I have second thoughts. The idea of harming another creature for sport, as opposed to need, is disgusting somehow. We have sport or game fish and we have big- and small-game animals. What it becomes is blood sport. A bloody game.

The questions go beyond simple killing. Nearly every sport fisherman and sport fish biologist I've ever met has accepted as truth the notion that fish feel no pain. At least not the way we humans do. Or even mammals and birds. That makes it easier to hook 'em, haul 'em in, and then either kill or release the fish "unharmed." I wondered about this even as a boy. But whenever I raised the question, Uncle Peach always assured me, "Fish don't feel pain." And that was that. But is it true? Or are we humans torturing and sometimes killing these critters for fun? For play?

Because they are cold-blooded, live in water, have fins and scales instead of limbs and hair (or fur or feathers), we don't identify with fish the way we do with our warm-blooded relatives, mammals and birds. It becomes easy to rationalize that they don't have feelings, can't experience trauma—or if they do, it's "no big deal." As philosopher and former angler Jack Turner has commented, "Imagine using worms and flies to catch mountain bluebirds or pine grosbeaks or maybe eagles and ospreys, and hauling them around on 50 feet of line while they tried to get away. Then when you landed them, you'd release them. No one would tolerate that sort of thing with birds. But we will for fish because they're underwater and out of sight." Yet for all of our rationalizing—and denial—there's increased scientific evidence that fish do in fact feel pain. One researcher, Michael Stoskopf, found convincing evidence that fish (and other nonmammals) had both biochemical and physical responses similar to those of mammals when subjected to pain. A growing number of other ethicists and scientists say its unthinkable that fish don't suffer when hooked and pulled through water. Should this matter?

Tied to the pain of catch-and-release fishing is the question of respect for other life-forms. Back in the mid-eighties, while working at the *Anchorage Times*, I reported on fishing conflicts along the Kanektok River in Southwest Alaska. Native residents of Quinhagak, a Yup'ik village at the river's mouth, had been protesting the increased presence of sportfishing parties and their impacts on local subsistence uses of the Kanektok. I've forgotten many details of that conflict, but one thing has stayed with me. I remember that the villagers were especially offended and outraged by the visiting anglers' use of catch-and-release techniques. To locals, the practice was disrespectful to the fish. It was, in essence, "playing with the food," a taboo in their culture.

Initially I found it strange that catch-and-release might be offensive, even "bad" or unethical. But after listening to the Native perspective and reporting on this clash of cultural values, I began to reassess my own beliefs and biases. The more I thought about it, the more the Yup'ik attitude made sense. Even the terms "sport" fish and "game" fish imply the notion of play. It doesn't take much of a leap in logic to see that this Western art form easily could be seen as playing with food, especially if the fish being "played" (as anglers like to say) is an important part of someone else's subsistence diet, a source of sustenance that's important for survival.

For all my growing doubts about the sport of fishing, it seems more honest to kill the fish and other animals we eat, rather than avoid or deny the loss of life by shopping in supermarkets for prepackaged products. So many in our culture—and I am certainly among them—have become distanced and disconnected from the food that gives us life. When done properly, fishing and hunting allow us humans to claim and perhaps even celebrate our role in the food web, our connection to the world that sustains us, instead of denying it.

Mark might respond, "That's fishing." At least for me such back-and-forth agonizing has apparently become a part of the ritual. A key to acceptance, I suspect, is to treat this halibut, or any animal, with respect; to have the humility to recognize this halibut as a gift, not a conquest. Many indigenous peoples believe that hunting success has less to do with any great skills than the fact that prey presents itself to the respectful hunter. Their traditions emphasize humility and restraint, a recognition of spirit and sacredness in all of nature, and a receptivity to mystery. More and more, such beliefs and mores make wonderful sense to me.

PERHAPS PICKING UP ON MY SOMBER MOOD or my questions about the halibut's size and age, Mark says he'd like to see a limit placed on the number of hundred-pounders that a sport fisher could keep. After one lunker, what's the need for more? He then recalls a story from the previous summer, about a fishing charter that brought in ten or twelve halibut weighing one hundred to three hundred pounds. Mark sees that not as some special triumph but as a waste. The big females are the ones that need protection, he again emphasizes. Why not have a system in which it's possible to arrange some sort of halibut trophy mount, without killing the fish? It's already done with certain species, like rainbow trout.

Fishery biologists who monitor Cook Inlet say the increased sport harvest of breeders isn't threatening the inlet's population. But their assurances don't ease Mark's worries. The inlet is home; it's where he has fished since childhood, and he sees a local problem developing if guides and anglers don't ease up on large female halibut. "Somewhere down the line, it's going to catch up with us," he frets. "We need to show some restraint."

But restraint is a difficult thing when you own a charter operation. Trophy fish make for good advertising. The walls, doors, and windows of charter offices are plastered with pictures of barn-door-size halibut. And at day's end, crowds naturally gather around the largest fish. "He who can get the biggest fish is he who will get the business," Mark says. "You'd be cutting your own throat if you didn't go after the big ones. But what's going to happen when they're gone?"

Mark then tells me about a halibut sport-fish tagging program run by the International Pacific Halibut Commission. Even as we're catching our limits, there's another Chihuly charter boat on which customers are catching and releasing large halibut: by day's end, several in the 80- to 150-pound range will be tagged and let go. The tagging program gives people another option. Guides buy tags from the halibut commission and, if clients are interested, they tag their fish, get an estimated size, and turn them loose. In return, tagging participants receive a pin and certificate; and if a tagged fish is eventually re-caught, that information is passed on to the original halibut catcher. Tagged-and-recovered fish, in turn, give the commission helpful data on halibut movements and growth.

Recognizing that his tagging clients might wish to preserve some record of their released fish, Mark has constructed a half-dozen plywood replicas of halibut. Each a different size, the plywood pieces are cut and painted to look just like the fish; they even have blood running out their gills. I'm not sure about getting my picture taken with a plywood halibut, but I like the tagging idea. Right now, I can't imagine myself ever again keeping a trophy-sized halibut; the idea of returning grandmother fish to their saltwater homes pleases me.

On our return to shore, Mark suggests I get a "tail mount" of my halibut. On my catch the fish's tail fin measures twenty-one inches from tip to tip. At first I'm repulsed by the idea: for years I've opposed the act of collecting animal trophies, whether fish or bears. Big-game trophy hunting especially bothers me. Killing for meat I can understand; but killing for heads or hide alone? Killing to place a prize upon a wall or floor? This deadly game reeks of self-aggrandizing pride and male ego, at the expense of another's life. I find it offensive, unacceptable.

Is a halibut tail mount any different from a grizzly bear mount? I eventually decide it is, at least partly because of intent: I didn't come here looking for trophies; I came to harvest meat. And yes, engage in sport. But there's something else: a tail mount would preserve the memory of all that's happened today, including the inner debate that has raged since I peered into the halibut's eyes, touched her skin. In a sense it could be my memorial to the great fish, a way of honoring her spirit. Placed on my wall beside a picture of the halibut, it will be a reminder of the day's ambiguities and revelations, and my own contradictory nature. This is not one in a series, but once in a lifetime. After still more agonizing—am I being hypocritical?—I decide to do it. For $125, a local taxidermy shop will prepare the halibut's tail fin, to be hung upon my dining room wall.

BACK ON LAND, WE WEIGH the halibut at Chihuly Charters. The scale reads only 220 pounds, which surprises us all. Mark explains that it's uncertified and only gives approximate weights. Next we measure the fish: she's eighty-two inches long. The International Pacific Halibut Commission has put together a table that correlates halibut length and weight; by its measure, an average halibut of eighty-two inches would weigh 299½ pounds. So I split the difference and figure my halibut goes about 298.

Chihuly's, like most charters, has a "hang 'em and shoot" ritual for its customers. Halibut are hung, white side out, on a fish rack and their catchers are then posed with the fish. As we bring in our catch, mine gets everyone's attention. It's strange to be at the center of this commotion, both exhilarating and embarrassing. Soon our images will join others on Chihuly Charters' office door and the big halibut in our Polaroid will grab people's attention. Mark may not like it, but that's part of charter fishing too. My trophy catch may symbolize the growing pressures on Cook Inlet halibut, but it is also good for business.

After the photo session, Mark and his guides filet the halibut. We catchers of the fish stand aside, curiously detached from this part of the harvesting process. Even after the head, guts, and bones are removed, Allen and I will take home more than 250 pounds of fish from our four halibut. I get caught up in the picture-taking frenzy, the meat packing, the preparation for our drive back to Anchorage, and the halibut, for awhile at least, again becomes an object—something for the freezer.

On Sunday, the day after our fishing expedition, Allen and I cut the halibut fillets into smaller, meal-sized pieces and bag them for refrigeration, a three-hour process that becomes part of our shared ritual. He'll take fifty pounds back to Florida; I'll keep the rest here, giving some to friends. It's satisfying, to have a fresh supply of halibut for the winter. Last year I didn't put any fish in the freezer.

I barbecue several pounds of the fish for Sunday dinner and seven of us hold hands as Allen thanks God for the halibut. Silently, I add my thanks to the halibut for giving herself to us. Then we eat.

FIFTEEN

In Search of the Wild Man

IN MY MIDDLE-AGED QUEST TO BETTER UNDERSTAND WILDNESS—
and my own nature—I came face to face with an unsettling yet fascinating creature in 1990. The encounter occurred not in remote wilderness, as you might expect, but in the heart of Alaska's urban center, while I was exploring that ill-defined and short-lived cultural phenomenon called the men's movement. I suppose it's more accurate to say I was formally introduced to the Wild Man that year. There's plenty of evidence that we first made contact decades earlier, on the opposite side of the continent, and then crossed paths several times afterward, in many different settings.

Like several of my Anchorage friends, I was drawn to the men's movement's promise of new possibilities, particularly that branch called "mythopoetic." Always something of a sensitive sort—but one who'd learned at an early age to stifle his feelings—I found it hopeful and exciting that, both locally and across the nation, a growing number of men were re-examining our culture's notions of what it means to be male. The men's movement offered alternative images of manhood, different ways of being and acting. Its leaders also uncovered many long-buried myths, including that of the Wild Man, whose story is told in poet and teacher Robert Bly's best-selling book *Iron John: A Book About Men*.

All of this resonated deeply with me and it came at just the right time: at the end of my fourth decade, when I was reawakening to the world and renewing bonds I'd ignored since my boyhood. Even as I re-embraced nature in the 1980s and 1990s, I became more fully engaged with the human community, less isolated from my own kind. Being one who tends to compartmentalize his life, I at first separated "men's work" from my nature explorations. But as time has passed, I've come to understand how parts of my life that once seemed distinct are in fact tightly inter-woven. This may seem obvious to more enlightened sorts, but it's something I've had to learn and re-learn, over and over.

Unfortunately, the mythopoetic men's movement that stirred me so has largely faded away, though remnants of it are scattered here and there, and its leaders—Robert Bly, Michael Meade, James Hillman, and others—continue to do healing work with men and boys. And women and girls, too. I still hold out hope for a future revival, in some form that more easily builds alliances.

So, you may wonder, what does all this have to do with us modern Americans and our relationship with nature? In a way, everything. A key symbol of the mythopoetic men's movement, Iron John *is* the Wild Man. And the Wild Man, along with a related mythic character, the Green Man, is an archetypal figure who symbolizes humanity's ties to the earth and wild nature. (There is a mythical Wild Woman as well, but I'll be sticking with the male figure because it's the one I know best and, naturally, most identify with.)

Because Iron John's story enriched my life and helped me understand my interior world and male connections to the wild earth and its more-than-human nature, I want to discuss this ancient tale in some depth and consider its relevance in America today. But first I'd like to introduce a related being with closer ties to my adopted homeland, a being whom at least some Alaskans know as a living, breathing part of the natural world.

OVER THE YEARS, MY IMAGINATION has been stirred by periodic reports of giant, shaggy primates roaming the forests of North America. Like many people, I've won-dered: are they physically real? Invented? Imagined? Until my own recent search for the Wild Man led me back into ancient, shadowed forests and a reacquaintance with Iron John, I never linked the two beings. Now I can't help but wonder how our modern Western culture's repression of the Wild Man ties into Americans' schizophrenic fascination with that hairy anthropoid variously known as Bigfoot or Sasquatch. It turns out I'm not alone in my curiosity. Among the dozens of books written about Sasquatch and his hirsute contemporaries is Robert Michael Pyle's *Where Bigfoot Walks: Crossing the Dark Divide*. Not only is Pyle's book a wonderfully provocative exploration of the Bigfoot phenomenon, it stands apart from most other works of the genre by considering the creature's mythical roots.

Only a few pages into his narrative, Pyle reflects:

Certain social anthropologists like to consign Bigfoot to the category of arche-typal myth: the contemporary expression of Beowulf's Grendel, the modern manifestation of the medieval Green Man—the wild counterpart to our domestic selves that all folk seem to need. Probably it works well for this purpose, for we do require bogeymen. But is there more to it than that? Looking at the traditions of Northwest Coast Indians, we see through the moss and the mist a furry figure who fits that deep myth of the monster-beyond-the-fire-circle, while clutching about itself a coarse-haired cloak of reality.

Pyle then tells us about the Kwakiutl tribe of Washington and British Columbia, whose world includes Bukwus, the Wild Man of the woods, and Dzonoqua, the Wild Woman. Roaming the forest's deep shadows, they are local, indigenous manifestations of Sasquatch, with one critical difference. The Kwakiutl accept these wild folk the same way they accept frogs, spruce trees, bears, and salmon: as part of their literal, physical world.

The Kwakiutl tribe is just one among many Native American groups who include wild people in their world. Here in Alaska, Interior-dwelling Athabascans share the boreal forest with the *nuhu'anh*—literally, "the sneaker," but nowadays more commonly called the Woodsman. And throughout the state's southern regions, residents tell stories of creatures who, by most accounts, are dark-haired, larger than people, reclusive, solitary, nocturnal, and forest- or mountain-dwellers. Almost always, these beings are "Hairy Men," not women. Sometimes gentle, other times menacing, they never seem to speak, but they may scream, whistle, or imitate animal sounds. To many southwestern Eskimos, this being is *Urayuli*. To Lake Iliamna's Athabascans, he is *Get'gun*; to Southeastern Tlingits, *Kushtaka*; to Bristol Bay's Yup'iks, *A-hoo-la-luk*; and to the Alutiiq, *a'ula'ats* or *a'ula'aqs*.

The best non-Native accounts of northern Alaska's Woodsman have been provided by anthropologist and nature writer Richard Nelson. Before settling in the Panhandle town of Sitka, Nelson spent years studying Alaska's Inupiat and Koyukon Athabascan cultures, and in the early 1980s he wrote *Make Prayers to the Raven: A Koyukon View of the Northern Forest*. Widely recognized as a classic work of anthropology and natural history, the book includes a section on the Woodsman. Like the Kwakiutl's Bukwus and Dzonoqua, the Woodsman, Nelson writes, "is as real as any other creature in the vast Koyukon wildland, but far more mysterious." With fur-covered bodies, long arms, and clawlike nails, they are superhuman beings who can vanish at will and who "stalk the wilds, hiding themselves almost completely from human contact, living more like animals than humans." Though they sometimes harass or steal from people, the Woodsmen are considered more tricksters than threats.

While I've come to know the Woodsman through Nelson's studies, I'm more familiar with the Hairy Man, whom I met, secondhand, in the early nineties—a period, it seems, when the Wild Man re-entered my life in a big way. I began hearing stories about the Hairy Man in 1993, while working on a project for the tribally run Bristol Bay Area Health Corporation. My job required that I talk with many of the region's Native leaders and elders. Besides sharing their memories of traditional healing practices, the influence of Christian missionaries, and introduced diseases that killed thousands of Native residents, a few storytellers shared tales of huge, hairy, humanlike creatures. I began collecting their stories in notebooks and on audiotapes and, over time, compiled an impressive record of encounters.

Ted Angasan is among those who immediately come to mind when I recall those Bristol Bay days. A Westerner listening to this Aleut's quiet but earnest accounts might say that Angasan truly believes in the Hairy Man. But that would be misleading and unfair, rather like saying that you or I believe in whales, or northern lights, or Jupiter. In the same way that Bukwus inhabits the Kwakiutl's homeland and the Woodsman roams the Koyukon landscape, the Hairy Man is as much a part of Angasan's world as are bears, birds, and trees. He requires no proof and offers none. But he has stories to tell that speak of the creature's existence.

In the late 1950s, Angasan told me, one of his teenage pals reported seeing a hairy, humanlike creature near the village of South Naknek. The friend, named Peter, had surprised the animal as it lay on some fifty-five-gallon fuel drums. Panicked and alone, Peter grabbed his gun, shot—and missed. The creature, in turn, screamed loudly, then took off running.

Peter ran too, and didn't stop until he reached the village, where he told of his meeting with Hairy Man. Most people remained skeptical. "They thought he'd seen everything but a Hairy Man," Angasan recalled. "But I believed. You can tell when a guy is lying or not. He was scared to death." He then paused a moment, as if sorting through memories, before adding, "I know the story is true, because I've seen it too."

Angasan saw Hairy Man in 1985, while on a commercial flight from Kululak Bay to Dillingham, the region's largest town. Passing over forested mountains near the village of Manokotak, he noticed an unusual form below: "There was this giant thing sitting in the trees. He looked like, not quite a gorilla, but dark and full of hair. I'd say, from the trees around him, he was between seven and ten feet tall."

When I suggested the creature might have been a bear, Angasan shook his head and replied, "Uh-uh. I'm color-blind, so I look for shapes. I could see his eyes and his head, his whole body. He was looking at us, watching us fly by; he didn't seem bothered at all. But he was a Hairy Man, all right."

Besides the stories themselves, what stands out in my memory is that Angasan told them in a dispassionate, matter-of-fact manner. There was no attempt to convince me or sensationalize the experience. If anything, he seemed reluctant to say any more than necessary. Yet the fact that they are his stories makes them all the more believable, because this soft-spoken man is a respected leader within his community. Among other things, he has served as the Bristol Bay Native Corporation's executive director and represented the region on Alaska's Inter-Tribal Council. From a Western perspective he's articulate, politically savvy, sharp. In both worlds, Native and Western, he's a credible witness.

Sam Stepanoff had a story to share too. An Aleut resident of Perryville and, later, Chignik Lake (villages on the lower Alaska Peninsula), he learned wilderness survival skills from village elders at a young age and felt no anxiety about camping alone even as a boy. "I was never afraid of anything," he recalled, "not even in the dark."

But once, at age fourteen, he lost his usual cool.

Out harvesting sea urchins with friends one night, Stepanoff heard a dog barking in the nearby mountains. Recognizing it as his dog that had run off four days earlier, he followed the howls into the hills and tracked it down. As he stooped to pick up the dog, Stepanoff recalls,

> The alders made some noise right beside me, and I saw a person. I thought it was the boys; we used to play around, scare each other. I said, "Knock it off—I know who you are." But it didn't move, so I shined a flashlight and it was a man, his face just pure wrinkles. I said, "Who are you?" but got no answer. He's just looking at me, not speaking. I got so scared, I dropped my dog and went down the cliff. I ran to where [the others] were gathering wood for a bonfire, and told them what I'd seen, and they took off running too.

Back in Perryville, Stepanoff shared his story with the village elders, who searched the hill but found nothing, not even tracks. The elders told him other "hairy guys" had been seen in the hills; occasionally they'd come into the village and rob fish from smokehouses.

"I've read all about the Abominable Snowmans and Bigfoot," Stepanoff says. "But the guy I seen was little, smaller than me. I never could figure it out; he just looked like a real old man, all wrinkled. He had a beard and was kind of hairy, but he was human."

More stories.

John Gumlickpuk, a Yup'ik elder, once encountered a Hairy Man near Togiak. Then in his early thirties, he went outside at sunrise and met a man covered with long hair. "He was as big as us, but hairy all over," Gumlickpuk recounted. "The only place he didn't have hair was his face."

Startled by Gumlickpuk, the man quickly ran away. Speedy exits are character-istic of many Bristol Bay Hairy Men, who by most accounts can run incredibly fast. They can also jump high and far, sometimes over rivers or trees. Case in point: John Gumlickpuk's wife, Elena, tells of a Hairy Man who was spotted by a woman washing clothes. When confronted, she says, "He jump off, way far. He could jump over high bushes and really run fast."

Numerous Hairy Man sightings have also been made in the Lake Iliamna area east of Bristol Bay. Myrtle Anelon, a lifelong resident of the area and former health aide who's now a grandmother, was seventeen when two "hairy things" visited her home in 1957. One October night, after everyone had gone to bed, the fami-ly's cat began meowing loudly, then scampered up a ladder onto the roof. Shortly after, there was a loud crash, like something had fallen through the ladder's steps. "While falling," Anelon recounted, "it broke the bedroom window next to Mom's bed." Anelon and two brothers went outside, where they found several tracks, "really huge, but narrow, with big toes. We knew that nobody around there had big feet like that."

Later that night, the family's dogs began barking, "like they're really scared," Anelon said.

Mom tells the boys to take a bright flashlight and shine it where the dogs are looking. When they did, they saw two real hairy things; they thought it was two bears standing on their hind legs. They come running in, saying, 'Give me a gun, a knife, anything,' but my mom says, 'Don't kill anything. You don't know what they are. They might be human.'

The boys go back out and don't shoot, but they start chasing those things all over the place. They said the things ran like humans, not bears, but were full of hair, and fast. They came around three nights in a row, even looked in our windows. Mom said they were probably wild people, and if we don't harm them, they won't harm us. So we never bothered them anymore, and they kind of quit coming around. I never saw them, but my brothers did.

Angasan, Stepanoff, Gumlickpuk, and Anelon are among the many people throughout Alaska—mostly Native and mostly rural—who acknowledge the existence of a large, hair-covered, two-footed creature that is human- or ape-like in nature.

Scientists and other researchers have so far shown less interest in Alaska's hairy bipeds than in Sasquatch or Yeti. Of the half-dozen Sasquatch/Bigfoot books at Anchorage's public library—books aimed at a general audience—I could find none that mentioned Hairy Man. From an academic perspective, the anthropologists who have documented Alaska Hairy Man stories have tended to treat them as Native mythical beings, rather than real creatures—not surprising, given their scientific bias. One notable exception is Anchorage resident Patricia Partnow, who studied the Alutiiq people of Southwest Alaska for her dissertation with the University of Alaska Fairbanks. In one section of her work, Partnow describes a group of outsiders known to the Alutiiq as *a'ula'ats* or *a'ula'aqs*, while avoiding judgments about their reality.

"*A'ula'aqs* are not human," she observes, "though it is possible for them to be mistaken for people and for people who go to live with them to take on their characteristics." Strong and hairy, they are dangerous beings who lure people away from human society. Much like Dracula, they can be warded off with crosses or holy water, but "the best strategy with *a'ula'aqs*," writes Partnow, "is to avoid them altogether."

Partnow notes that these "hairy men" are related to other dangerous beings, including *usillllraarpak*, a kind of "super child" or "baby with a big mouth," who "cries and lures people up its ravine whence they never return." In a similar manner, people I interviewed in the Bristol Bay region described "little people," who sometimes were merely mischievous—while resembling leprechauns in both appearance and behavior—and at other times presented a serious threat. Among their talents, little people can disappear at will, run faster than people, and jump long distances.

Not all Natives believe *a'ula'aqs* to be supernatural or "other than human." Several Southwestern Alaska residents interviewed by both Partnow and me believe such creatures to be runaways, ranging from members of their own tribes to AWOL servicemen and "hippies" who have "gone wild." But nearly all are similar in these respects: they are not normal; and they usually pose some sort of danger associated with what Partnow calls "an irresistible power which can only be countered by quick minds and feet and powerful religious (i.e., Russian Orthodox) beliefs."

The Alaska Department of Fish and Game has not undertaken a Hairy Man study, says Jim Fall, an anthropologist with the state's Subsistence Division. And yet he's often heard Dena'ina Athabascans—some of whom live in and around Anchorage—speak of *Nant'ina*: large, shaggy creatures that "are fairly malevolent and dangerous. One of the themes is that they [like the Woodsman] steal children and raise them in the wild." From a Western perspective, Fall adds, "One could speculate that the origins of these stories might come from outcasts or social misfits not subject to traditional norms, and therefore dangerous." That view, of course, is very much like the one that prevailed in medieval Europe.

"The thing you have to remember about Native beliefs," he notes, "is that boundaries between humans and other creatures are often blurred. There's no question that *Nant'ina* is part of Dena'ina reality."

THE PARALLELS ARE STRIKING. From Arctic boreal woodlands to Washington's old-growth forest—and perhaps as far south as California—the wild people of Native lore are as real as any creature that inhabits the landscape. But they're also mysterious beings that move through the shadows, only rarely showing themselves. They also may possess superhuman, or supernatural, abilities: they can disappear, jump across large rivers, run incredibly fast, sometimes leave no tracks, and possess unusual strength. Though no one knows their origins for sure, each region has legends that suggest these wild folk are social outcasts or misfits, people who left the human world for a more primitive or even animal-like existence. And while many stories describe them as tricksters or malicious beings who sometimes steal children, these wild men and women seem more shy than dangerous. In all of these aspects of the Wild Man, what seems important are the human ties and supernatural elements, which harken back to Western stories from the Middle Ages and more ancient times.

Because their experience of what's "real" has remained much broader than that of Euro-Americans, our country's indigenous peoples have kept more room in their worlds for the likes of Bukwus, Hairy Man, and their wild kin, even in this modern era. That may be changing, though, as older traditions and beliefs fade in a world where TVs, computers, and the Internet bring new realities and mysteries while increasing distance from wild nature.

Given my Euro-American, Judeo-Christian ancestry and the religious and scientific influences of the modern Western culture in which I've been immersed since birth, I naturally find the physical existence of such Hairy Men—and their acceptance by many Native Alaskans—to be incredible. Once upon a time, I would have said "unbelievable." But now I'm not so sure. Surely the Hairy Man is no more amazing than much of what's in the Bible. Or what scientists have discovered about the origins of the universe and life on our small blue planet. The older I get and the more I learn, the more room I leave for the mysterious, the fantastic, and the magical. I'm open to the possibility of Hairy Man and his kind, because I've come to realize there's so much we don't—and can't—know about this wide, wild world. In the same way, I've learned to understand and accept that different cultures experience the world in strikingly different, and equally valid, ways.

Despite the limits imposed upon me by both my fundamentalist Christian upbringing and the biases of mainstream American culture, my own world has expanded immensely in my middle-aged years, to include "realities" I once never imagined possible. One of my grandest and most hopeful experiences *ever* was the discovery, in my late forties, that Christianity has a mystical tradition. How many of our nation's Christians know that? None that I ever met, or at least no one who admitted it, until I stumbled across the writings of theologian Matthew Fox. And what about all the incredible "new" details we've learned about North America's Native peoples prior to the arrival of Christopher Columbus, as discussed at length in Charles Mann's recent book *1491*? Or what about the narrowing gap between science and spirituality and their notions of the "oneness" of everything that comprises the universe—or creation, if you prefer? The more I discover about life on this planet, the more it seems a miracle, whether it was created by a higher power or evolved over billions of years. And of course there are the birds, which on a very personal level opened up my own life in previously unimaginable ways. As I've said elsewhere in these pages, I often wonder what else surrounds me, waiting for my attention, my "discovery."

Which brings me back, in a roundabout way, to my Germanic, Judeo-Christian roots, and Iron John.

IN THE FRONT OF MY SLIGHTLY TATTERED and well-marked copy of *Iron John* is a note written in blue ink. Dated Christmas 1990, the short but heartening message is "For Bill" and is simply signed "Mike." We'd met in 1987, when I joined a small circle of men who were individually and collectively taking a hard look at what it means to be male in this culture. At the most basic level, we were healing emotional and spiritual wounds, including some that we'd carried for thirty or forty years, even longer for a couple of guys. Several of us were the sort of men that Robert Bly so aptly describes in chapter 1 of *Iron John*. We were "soft males": anti-war and earth-friendly, kind-hearted, willing to balance male strength and competitiveness with a more gentle and nurturing attitude toward life, willing to explore the feminine aspects of our psyches.

Meeting such soft males at men's gatherings, Bly reported, he was astounded by the grief and anguish they seemed to carry. Again and again, he saw them shy away from any display of ferocity. They didn't seem to understand that "[i]n every relationship something *fierce* is needed once in a while."

All of this resonated with me, in a deeply personal way. I was a "nice guy." My buddies and our female mates even joked sometimes about us being SNAGs: Sensitive New Age Guys. And all too often we were soft, in the way Bly described it.

By page four, I was hooked. So I eagerly jumped to the next page and the start of Iron John's story. Though it was first written down in the early 1800s by the Grimm Brothers in their famous collection of fairy tales, Bly muses that this story "could be ten or twenty thousand years old." Reflecting a much older and longer-lived wisdom, the tale explores the nature of masculinity, the passage from boyhood into manhood, and the role of male initiation in that transformation. Such a promise set the hook even deeper. And though I didn't understand, or necessarily agree with, everything that followed over the next 255 pages, *Iron John* touched me—and grabbed and shook me—as few other books (or other works of art) have. The story opened me up to all sorts of possibilities, while guiding me through the wilds of my internal landscape.

Over the years I've returned to Bly's inspired writing again and again, and even now, some seventeen years later, the book makes incredible sense. Each time I open it up, *Iron John* speaks to me, often in new and different ways, as evidenced by the abundance of underlined sentences, paragraphs now highlighted in yellow, orange, pink, blue, and green, my scratchings in the margins, and the many sticky notes attached to the tops and sides of pages.

Still among my favorite passages are those that tell the Wild Man's story and reflect upon his meaning. For those who don't yet know the tale, it begins deep in a forest, where several hunters have disappeared. Found at the bottom of a forest pond, Iron John is "a large man covered with hair from head to foot. The hair is reddish— it looks a little like rusty iron." Captured and brought to the king's castle, Iron John is locked in a cage and the key is put in the queen's keeping. There Iron John languishes, until one day the king's young son is playing nearby with his golden ball and the ball rolls into the cage. The boy of course wants his special ball returned; but in trade, the Wild Man demands his own release. Stealing the key from beneath his mother's pillow, the boy frees Iron John. Then, fearing the consequences of his action, he asks to be taken away. Iron John lifts the boy onto his shoulder and disappears into the dark forest, where they won't be found. Later, the Wild Man tests the boy. Failing the trial, the boy is sent out of the forest and on to other adventures, in a second king's realm. The two are later reunited, after the boy, now "quite grown," returns to the forest and requests Iron John's help. Transformed into a heroic knight, the young man wins the heart and hand of the second king's daughter and he is reunited with his own parents at a great wedding celebration. Iron John attends too. Freed from an enchantment by the boy's actions, he's been changed from a Wild Man into a "baronial King," who grants the boy all his treasure.

Like most (if not all) folk tales, the story is rich in symbolism and Bly does a wonderful job of exploring the symbols and their possible meanings. But here I'm most interested in Iron John himself. Bly has this to say after introducing us to the Wild Man, hiding at the bottom of a forest pond:

> When a contemporary man looks down into his psyche, he may, if conditions are right, find under the water of his soul, lying in an area no one has visited for a long time, an ancient hairy man.
>
> The mythological systems associate hair with the instinctive and the sexual and the primitive. What I'm suggesting, then, is that every modern male has,

lying at the bottom of his psyche, a large, primitive being covered with hair down to his feet....

As the story suggests very delicately, there's more than a little fear around this hairy man, as there is around all change.... Welcoming the Hairy Man *is* scary and risky, and it requires a different sort of courage. Contact with Iron John requires a willingness to descend into the male psyche and accept what's dark down there, including the *nourishing* dark.

For generations now, the industrial community has warned young businessmen to keep away from Iron John, and the Christian church is not too fond of him either.

The notion of an ancient, primitive Hairy Man hiding somewhere in my psyche makes sense to me. Intuitively, it feels right. So does the idea that this Hairy Man is frightening to most modern males and the culture at large, given the cultural associations we make with hairiness and hairy beasts. Bly identifies at least a handful. One is a natural, unrepressed sexual energy; beyond its passionate embrace of other humans, such healthy sexuality, in Bly's words, "resonates also to hills, clouds, and ocean." Another is the life of animals and hunting instincts in males, including young boys. A third is hot-bloodedness, as reflected in such things as fiery temperaments, passionate impulsiveness, spontaneity, and fierceness. Hair also suggests excess, "what is beyond all middle of the road civilization." Finally, hair hints of thoughts, particularly those that come when we are sleeping, or those intuitions that come unexpectedly, as if from out of nowhere.

As symbolized by hairiness and primitive instincts, Wild Man "energy" also reflects a friendliness toward wild nature, a draw to wilderness, the ability to see the divine in ordinary things, a willingness to take risks and follow one's desires, and an honoring of grief in self and the larger world.

You would think that anyone who loves the earth and its myriad inhabitants would delight in such traits. Yet many feminists have decried both Robert Bly and *Iron John* while mischaracterizing the story as a celebration of patriarchal values, despite the fact that Bly stresses the difference between the Wild Man of myth and the savage—or in our society, "macho"—male image: "The savage mode does great damage to soul, earth, and humankind. The Wild Man ... resembles a Zen Priest, a shaman, or a woodsman more than a savage."

In reflecting upon this Wild Man and the threat he poses to America's fundamentalist religious traditions, Bly reminds the reader that the story of Iron John is not anti-Christian, but pre-Christian, by a thousand years or more. And while the institution of Christianity does not embrace the Wild Man, "there is some evidence that Christ himself did." Bly offers one bit of evidence: at the start of his ministry, Christ was baptized by a "hairy John." Beyond that he doesn't elaborate, but I remember enough from my Lutheran upbringing to know that Christ occasionally demonstrated what I would call Wild Man energy. Here I must re-emphasize a distinction that Bly repeatedly makes: in contrast to machismo, such energy "leads to forceful action undertaken, not with cruelty, but with resolve." Picture an angry Christ at the temple, wreaking havoc with the moneychangers. Or walking alone into the wilderness to face his demons. Or sacrificing himself after the darkness of the Garden of Gethsemane.

While Bly comes at this idea of an internal Wild Man from a mythological angle, it's not so different, really, from what human ecologist Paul Shepard proposes in many of his writings, based on what's known about human evolution. In *Coming Home to the Pleistocene*, he argues, "We ourselves are genetically wild ... We are Pleistocene hominids keyed with infinite exactitude to small-group, omnivorous life in forest/plains edges of the wilderness.... Modern life conceals our inherent need for diverse, wild, natural communities, but it does not alter that need."

Whether in our genes or our psyches, the message is the same: we carry within us a Wild Man or Woman, attuned to and conversant with wild nature. But we've learned to suppress or hide or otherwise bury that ancient being. This separation has caused great harm, both to humans and to the larger world.

AND STILL THERE'S MORE TO KNOW about the Wild Man. As if dropping crumbs that lead ever deeper into the dark, primeval forest, Bly scatters bits and pieces of Iron John's nature throughout the book. Here's some of what I've taken away from my return trips to those shadowy woods.

Besides residing deep inside the psyche, the Wild Man is an invisible presence—whether being, spirit, or energy—that has existed for centuries outside human consciousness. In some cultures, he's been celebrated as a god of nature or heroic figure; in others, he's been scorned. Or denied.

For a long time now, we Westerners have largely denied the existence of Wild Man energy, both within us and outside us. In the United States and other modern Western societies, the Earth is considered feminine; by extension it "belongs" to women. The image of earth mother—or, if you prefer, Mother Earth—is a popular one, used extensively by environmental groups, the media, pop singers, advertising campaigns (recall "It's not nice to fool with Mother Nature!"), and in our day-to-day conversations.

The sky, meanwhile, belongs to men. While pop-culture images of "sky father" may not be so immediately apparent, consider that the Western vision of God is male. And He lives among the heavens. Most science fiction, too, tends to portray humanoid "aliens" from outer space as masculine, particularly if threatening.

While there's nothing inherently wrong with those earth and sky images, Bly says our modern perspectives ignore their ancient counterparts: earth father and sky mother. The Egyptians, for example, identified Ra as sky father and Isis as earth mother. "But prominent in every Egyptian moment were two other gods, Nut and Geb. Nut, the sky-mother, was painted on the inside of every coffin or mummy-lid, so that the dead person looking up saw a being bending down from the stars. Stars were shown on her body and around her body. Her hands and feet touched the earth, and the rest arched among the heavens. . . ."

Then there was Geb, the earth father, who in some images is portrayed "with his back to the earth, his stomach and erect phallus, earth-colored, reaching up toward the woman in the sky, or longing for the stars."

Even if Bly is correct that ancient myths included sky mothers and earth fathers, what does it matter now? It matters for this reason: "When our [modern, Western] mythology opens again to welcome women into sky-heaven and men into earth-water, then the genders will not seem so far apart. White men will feel it more natural, then, for them to protect earth."

In rejecting stereotypical images of the American male—and female—and seeking to find the part of them that's been lost or misplaced, a growing number of our nation's men are indeed (re)discovering their bonds with the Earth. Myths that reinforce an identification with the Earth can only promote a healthier, less abusive, male relationship with our planet. And with females. Any number of people who have taken a hard look at American culture have pointed out the parallels between male exploitation of "Mother Nature" and the exploitation of women.

Because the original Iron John story is pre-Greek, it doesn't polarize earth and sky. That, I think, has been part of its appeal since Bly resurrected the tale. Iron John the Wild Man lives deep in the forest, in the depths of a pond. As a mythological figure, he "lives wholeheartedly on earth; his wildness and hairiness in fact belong to earth and its animals." Part of the story's message, then, seems to be this: whether hiding or revealed, whether recognized by us humans or not, the Wild Man is always present in nature, as the Earth's male protector. Taking it even one step further, Bly suggests that the Wild Man can be seen as nature itself—as, of course, we humans are too.

IT'S ALSO POSSIBLE TO IMAGINE the Wild Man as a sort of mentor, the one who guides you into larger nature and reveals the nonhuman intelligence or awareness to be found there. As Bly suggests, there may even be a sense of eyes looking back, perhaps from a pool of water, or a forest of trees, or the mountains. For some people, this sense of eyes, of wild nature's own consciousness, "arrived early in childhood, when we were amazed by woods and gardens, and knew they were 'alive.'"

Gary Snyder is another who touches on this notion of wild intelligence, in *The Practice of the Wild*: "The world is watching: one cannot walk through a meadow or forest without a ripple of reports spreading out from one's passage. The thrush darts back, the jay squalls, a beetle scuttles under the grasses, and the signal is passed along. Every creature knows when a hawk is cruising or a human strolling. The information passed through the system is intelligence."

In recalling some of my own childhood memories—the hard stare of a snake's eyes; flickering starlight in the night sky; the purple brilliance of an amethyst crystal; the croaking songs of frogs—that sense of amazement flows back, bringing with it a dim remembrance of something greater, something I could not name. The nights that I looked out from my bedroom window upon that old, grandfather oak, I sensed a shared awareness, of nature "looking back" and maybe even whispering. I have no doubt now that I was in touch with the Wild Man at such times. And later, too, there have been passing moments when the ego slipped away and I've felt a hard-to-explain sense of being pulled out of myself, into a temporary connection with the Other, whether animal or landscape or cosmos, that creates a sense of oneness, wholeness, even holiness. That's not to say I can communicate with, understand, or become the Other, though I've read and heard stories, some of them shared by friends, that speak to such possibilities. Of course many cultures, including those of Alaskan Natives, have traditionally accepted that certain individuals are capable of shape-shifting or moving between the human and other realms.

While our Western tradition, with its scientific and fundamentalist Christian influences, remains largely closed to such "realities," we too have our mystics, those who move between realms or converse with other species. Most are denigrated by the popular culture, but a few maintain their credibility. I'd hold up celebrated naturalist Loren Eiseley as one who deftly moved between worlds. Introduced to Eiseley's writings in the 1990s (not long after meeting Iron John), I quickly became fascinated with his ability to interweave science with more mystical ways of looking at the world. His book *The Immense Journey* is exquisite proof of that talent. In "The Slit," which opens the collection, Eiseley alerts the reader that the book's essays are offered as "a somewhat unconventional record of the prowlings of one mind which has sought to explore, to understand, and to enjoy the miracles of this world, both in and out of science."

A few paragraphs later, Eiseley confides that the book is not so much a sharing of discoveries as it is

a confession of ignorance and of the final illumination that sometimes comes to a man when he is no longer careful of his pride. In the last three chapters of the book I have tried to put down such miracles as can be evoked from common earth.

But men see differently. I can at best report only from my own wilderness. The important thing is that each man possess such a wilderness [one might substitute wildness here] and that he consider what marvels are to be observed there.

Instead of sharing insights into some scientific model of the universe, Eiseley's aim was to share his personal universe, one traversed during his own immense journey: "If my record, like those of the sixteenth-century voyageurs, is confused by strange beasts or monstrous thoughts or sights of abortive men, these are no more than my eyes saw or my mind conceived. On the world island we are all castaways, so that what is seen by one may often be dark or obscure to another."

Among the three last chapters mentioned above is "The Judgment of the Birds," an exquisite story that immediately became one of my favorite science-and-nature essays and remains so. A few pages into the piece, Eiseley introduces the idea of seeing the world "from an inverted angle," a gift not merely limited to the human imagination:

I have come to suspect that within their degree it is sensed by animals, though perhaps as rarely as among men. The time has to be right; one has to be, by chance or intention, upon the border of two worlds. And sometimes these two borders may shift or interpenetrate and one sees the miraculous.

I once saw this happen to a crow.

After telling the story of his unnerving encounter with the crow, which turned out to be much more frightening to the bird, Eiseley hears in the crow's cawing "the uncertainty of a mind that has come to know things are not always what they seem. He has seen a marvel in his heights of air and is no longer as other crows. He has experienced the human world from an unlikely perspective. He and I share a viewpoint in common: our worlds have interpenetrated and we both have faith in the miraculous."

This was a scientist and storyteller in touch with the Wild Man, both inside and outside himself.

SOMETHING STRANGE AND UNEXPECTED happens to the Wild Man near the end of *Iron John*: in the wedding scene that ends the story, the primitive, hairy forest creature is transformed into a king.

"We have become used to seeing the Wild Man as wet, moist, foresty, ignorant, leafy," Bly comments, "and all at once he is related to holy intellect and sun radiance—he is a King.

"The energy that is hidden by water, dark, lying on its back among reeds, becomes a luminous power.... Some invisible force that we know nothing about has put the sophisticated energy of this being into a primitive form and shape, as if into a cage."

Bly doesn't delve deeply into the meaning of this final transformation, except to say:

> The Wild Man part of each man that was once in touch with wilderness and wild animals has sunk below the water of the mind, out of sight, below human memory. Covered with hair now, it looks as if it were an animal itself. The Wild Man in our wedding scene says in effect: "A strong power forced me by enchantment to live under the water until a young man appeared who was ready to undergo the discipline and go through the suffering that you have gone through. Now that you have done that, I can appear as I am—a Lord."

At first the change from Wild Man to King struck me as odd, even troubling. Instead of resolving my puzzlement, Bly's interpretation initially added to it. But I think it goes back to a couple of ideas that he explored earlier in the book. The first is tied to the image of a Sacred King. Like the Wild Man and the Great Goddess, the Sacred King is an archetype who dwells in the mythological or eternal realm. This is where Dionysus resides, along with Zeus, Thor, Osiris, Kali, Artemis, Odin, Shiva, Buddha, Christ, and other gods, including the Lord of the Animals. The once-hidden Wild Man, both reviled and feared, has not only been uncaged, but called upon for help. Released and recalled, he can appear in his more sacred, godlike form.

Of course what's happening in the mythological realm is occurring within humanity's collective unconscious. Even when a culture is determined to hide or repress an eternal idea or form or god, the adventurous among us may dare to enter the dark, shadowy forest of the psyche and, perhaps, discover the Wild Man (or any other number of interior beings) within. Once he's dredged from the pond and summoned from the deep forest, the sacred essence of Iron John—and nature itself—may be revealed, filled with radiance.

The second idea has to do with the intelligence in nature. Though we normally don't recognize it, or we deny the possibility, there are moments when that "holy intellect" is revealed. Some might call it the grand design. And it does hint of the divine. The same is true of radiance. In my own life, there have been times and places (both as a boy and a man) when my awareness has somehow opened up or expanded, and I've sensed a radiant wholeness or holiness. Instead of being sinful or a storehouse of natural resources, the Earth and all its wild nature—in other words, the creation—shines through and is revealed as sacred. But the only way we're going to see and honor that sacredness is if we embrace our own wild nature, no matter how frightening that seems.

This whole notion of a Wild Man, or Wild Woman, can be a tricky one, so it's worth repeating a couple of cautionary notes from *Iron John*. First, the intent is not to *be* the Wild Man, but to be *in touch with* the Wild Man. Attempts to become Iron John or his kind can cause confusion, harm, and even early death. Bly cites the writer Jack Kerouac as an example, and I would also point to actor James Dean, and all sorts of rock musicians, for instance Janis Joplin and Jim Morrison.

Toward the very end of the story, Bly admits that the term "Wild Man" can be inflammatory and he, like many people, is

> . . . not fond of it myself. On first hearing, it promises too much. . . . We need delicacy around both the Wild Man and the Wild Woman, so that we brush them with the wingtip of our minds. It would be disastrous to throw a net over either, or to tranquilize them with jargon, and take them home to our private zoo.

BLY AND OTHERS HAVE CONNECTED the loss of Western civilization's Wild Man with our increased separation from the Earth. Once immersed in wild nature, we gradually retreated from it. And what once was perceived as life-giving and desirable became, in many ways, a threat. Or something to be dominated. It's no wonder, then, that the Wild Man of medieval Europe was ultimately rejected for his uncivilized nature and mythologically banished to the remotest forests, hills, and caves. There he would remain hidden and pose little danger. Over time, he would largely be forgotten.

The history of the United States is replete with evidence of this centuries-long forgetting. Isn't much of our nation's story about "taming" the wilderness, converting—or killing off—Native peoples, exterminating fierce animals, clear-cutting forests, and polluting waters, lands, and the air? Hasn't our culture placed commerce and corporations above the well-being of natural ecosystems and even, in many cases, our own kind? Haven't we boxed wildlands into artificially established, and increasingly diminished, parks and refuges? Don't we insulate ourselves more and more from our natural surroundings, with malls and big-box stores, RVs and SUVs, and the TVs and video games and Internet communiqués that keep us inside? I see the dangers and temptations even in my own outdoor-loving life, with work and classes and other busyness fighting for my attention.

In rejecting and then forgetting the Wild Man, Bly argues, Western men suffered great damage, not only in their relationship with the wider world, but also with themselves, especially their sexual nature: "When the Church and the culture as a whole dropped the gods who spoke for the divine element in male sexual energy—Pan, Dionysus, Hermes, the Wild Man—into oblivion, we as men lost a great deal.... [T]he erotic energy of men lost its ability to move, as they say in music, to the next octave."

Women, too, he adds, have suffered from the Euro-American attitudes and beliefs that have come to favor "the trimmed, the sleek, the cerebral, the noninstinctive, and the bald."

FEW CULTURES, PAST OR PRESENT, have lacked a human-faced hairy monster, giant, or wild man in one form or another, whether mythic or "real." Such shadowy creatures lurk, mostly hidden, across the planet, even—or perhaps especially—in our forgetful Western societies. The best known outside the Pacific Northwest is the Himalayan Yeti, or Abominable Snowman. But the residents of southwest Russia's Caucasus Mountains tell stories of another hairy man, named Quidili; and reports of strange hairy primates have also been reported in western China. Still other hairy monsters inhabit islands, deserts, and even the tropics. In his book *Where Bigfoot Walks*, Robert Pyle lists several: the Cigouave, a Haitian forest beast tied to voodoo; the South Pacific's Oreng-Pendek of Borneo and Sumutra; Malaysia's Orang-Dalam; and East Africa's Agogue. "There are," he adds, "swamp beasts galore, the Moth man, the Gray Man of the Carolinas, and a wide array of troglodytes."

No culture, Pyle muses, "has ever been so confused as ours as to what it really believes. Are we such wonderful observers of the natural world that we should expect to know everything that looms, walks, creeps, or grows outside our doors or beyond the city wall?"

I like that gentle jab. I'm reminded how the simple act of bird feeding and the ensuing visits of chickadees expanded my own small world, which suddenly exploded with songbirds and their melodious voices after forty-three years of inattention. I'm reminded that I largely ignored the spring- and summertime wonders of Anchorage's coastal refuge for more than two decades. And I'm reminded that ecologists now believe we modern humans have discovered only a tiny fraction of the species with whom we share the Earth, while our greatest minds admit how little we understand the workings of our planet, despite the past century's explosion of knowledge and technological advances.

It turns out that Pyle and I agree on a lot, when it comes to wild men and women. For example, it's a mistake to believe that only "primitive" cultures embrace Bigfootlike creatures. Many of humanity's most "civilized" peoples—the Greeks, the

Romans, Europe's medieval Christians—included wild folk in their stories and art, most notably as forms of the Green Man.

Consider, then, the Lord of the Animals, Dionysus, Bacchus, Pan, Faunus, Shiva, Cernunnus, Hermes, Iron John, Sasquatch, Hairy Man, the Great Goddess, Mother Nature, Artemis, Dzonoqua, the Green Man, Wild Man, and Wild Woman. Aren't they all related? "For what are any of these characters," Pyle rightly asks, "but embodiments of nature, the earth, and all that is green and contrary to control?"

The problem for us modern, high-tech, and largely spiritless Westernized Americans is that too often we won't take seriously what we can't see or hold on to or measure: the invisibles of life. Unless, of course, it's written in the Bible. Then it's absolute Truth. Unfortunately, the Bible isn't especially friendly toward wild nature or wild, hairy beings, at least as interpreted by fundamentalist religions. Consider the demonizing of Pan into Satan and Christianity's defeat of paganism. So, in their own ways, both science and the United States' unofficial national religion have worked against the Wild Man.

There are other problems as well. Our culture tends to define myth as a story that's "made up," something fictional or false. Yet for most of our species' history— and from what we can tell, our prehistory, too—myths have been viewed as ways of explaining human nature, our relationships with the larger world, and the origins of humanity and the cosmos. Or as Pyle succinctly puts it, "A myth is simply a system of belief." Seen that way, it can be argued that science has been a powerful myth maker, perhaps even more so than religion, for the past century or two.

Our society also displays the regrettable habit of trivializing powerful symbols through pop culture, commerce, and the media. Just as once-powerful anthems or folk songs become advertising jingles or folk tales become Disneyfied, so the men's movement is diminished by its simplistic stereotyping as groups of middle-aged white men drumming and running naked through the woods. And Bigfoot and other Wild Men are transformed into the cartoon figures featured in tabloids.

Despite all of these sad circumstances, both Pyle and I see reason for hope, as does Robert Bly, who comments in *Iron John*, "When the Wild Man has been preserved inside, a man also feels a genuine friendliness toward the wildness in nature."

Within the U.S., there's substantial evidence that such Earth-friendly attitudes are more widespread than ever, though they haven't always led to wiser ways of living in this world. That's at least partly because of political leaders who reflect hardhearted, bottom-line corporate values more than intuitive, heartfelt, earth-rooted wisdom. (Still, a nature-loving sort has to wonder: how do such people keep getting elected if we're truly becoming a greener, more planet-conscious nation?)

Here I'll pause a moment and reflect on the roots of what seems to be a wild revival in America. For all of our nation's deep-seated tendencies toward conquest, utility, consumption, and consequent destruction, the U.S. has a long tradition of enlightened individuals who have demonstrated "genuine friendliness" toward nature and wilderness. A partial list might start with William Wood in the 1600s and William Bartram in the 1700s; then continue with Henry David Thoreau, John Muir, and John Burroughs in the 1800s; followed by the likes of Aldo Leopold, Robert Marshall, Rachel Carson, Joseph Wood Krutch, Henry Beston, Olaus and Margaret Murie, and Edward Abbey in the early to mid-1900s; and, more recently, Wendell Berry, Terry Tempest Williams, David James Duncan, Rick Bass—the list goes on and on.

As author Thomas Lyon points out in *This Incomparable Land*, it's no coincidence that everyone on this list, and most other members of our nation's "distinctly non-conforming, even heretical, minority," were naturalists and nature writers. "The principal cultural heresy expressed in American nature writing," he explains, "is the refocusing of vision outward from the individual self, and from the corporate self, our species. A radical proposal follows on the widened vision: that the environment, nature, is the ground of a positive and sufficient human joy." It's likely, Lyon adds, that the nature essay "as a distinctive genre" evolved out of the romantic movement in literature and philosophy. After all, the two share many values: an affirmation of the world as congenial to humans; an appreciation for intuitive thought; a scorn for materialism; a love for what is spontaneous, fecund, and life-giving; and a predilection for the simple and primitive.

Not being well versed in the romantic movement (or having forgotten what I was once taught), I can only shake my head in wonderment. Though it wasn't Lyon's intention, he's clearly demonstrated a remarkable parallel between romanticism's ideals and the qualities that Bly attributes to the Wild Man. I wouldn't have made the connection on my own. But having noticed it now, I'm sure it isn't coincidence. The romanticists of the eighteenth and early nineteenth centuries, along with some early American naturalists and nature writers, were among the first to feel—and to celebrate—the initial stirrings of a Western reawakening to the Wild Man.

The reconnection with wild nature that began with the romantic movement was then carried forward by a growing number of nature writers, wilderness advocates, and conservationists, to culminate in what we today call the environmental movement of the past half century, which continues to evolve and grow.

In my more hopeful moments, I see abundant evidence of renewed and "genuine friendliness" toward wild nature all around me: in myself, in many of my friends, in the green activism that stretches across the country, in deep ecology and the Gaia hypothesis, in the confluence of physics and mysticism, in the movement for environmental justice, even in some political quarters. Though the Green Party so far remains a fringe—and, to most citizens, radical—political group, its mere existence is reason for hope. So are the efforts to re-link nature and spirit. This is manifested in part by revived interest in Celtic music and other Celtic traditions, as well as increased respect for indigenous traditions, both in the U.S. and elsewhere. It's also reflected in the teachings of people like Thomas Berry and Matthew Fox. The latter has worked hard to revive Christianity's mystical roots, particularly through creation spirituality, a tradition that "celebrates the original blessing of creation, which includes all beings and all things. It includes the galaxies and the stars, trees, wolves, microorganisms, rocks, mountains, and children. Everything."

While Pyle, like me, applauds the rejoining of spirit and nature and the rise of religions that revere wilderness, he rightly cautions against foolish indulgences, spiritual window shopping, and sentimental longings for an idealized past that likely never existed:

Unfortunately, much of the regreening movement is highly naive about nature and prone to confusing oatmeal with ideas. The headlong rush to embrace everything Native American (to the intense discomfiture and resentment of many Indians); the wholesale adoption of pantheism and animism without any awareness of their motivations, history, or special knowledges; and the conflation of the Green Man (who, like Dzonoqua, is sexually ambiguous) with the "wild man" of muzzy-minded men's groups all detract from the possible potency of these movements.

While I appreciate Pyle's concerns and commend his cautionary note, I hope that he and other critics will reconsider their blanket objections to the misunderstood men's movement. As with those who naively and superficially adopt "Indian ways," Eastern mysticism, or other non-Western traditions, some participants—and perhaps some leaders—in the men's movement have indeed been "muzzy-minded." But as I've already argued, to many of us who have tiptoed into that dark forest, there is much about the Wild Man and the men's movement that rings clear and strong and true. In the same manner, while it's both silly and disrespectful for whites to superficially "go Native"—or Jain, Buddhist, or Druidic—on a whim or with the hope for a shortcut to enlightenment, there's no question that other ways of knowing, including traditional indigenous knowledge, have much to teach us science-biased Westerners about humility, respect for other life-forms, and alternative ways of being in the world. If we learn nothing else from other traditions both past and present, let's hope we learn this: many different paths may indeed lead toward the same destination, the same understanding.

Peering into Pacific Northwest forests, Pyle imagines the possibility of Bigfoot as "an ambassador for a truly green spirituality . . . a model for reintegration" that would put us humans back in accord with wild nature and spirit. I would suggest the same is true for the Wild Man. And this, I think, is a big reason *Iron John* struck such a chord. Many of us men, and at least some women, are eager to embrace that shaggy creature at the bottom of the pond. We sense this may be our last best chance to do so, before we humans make the world unlivable for our kind and many others. As Bly writes, we are starting to remember the Wild Man because now, more than ever, the continued existence of our species, and that of thousands of others, has been put in harm's way by ignorant, dangerous ways of thinking and behaving of people disconnected from the wild Earth.

In the interest of hope, I'll return now to a saying that many of my teachers, role models, and heroes have shared, in slightly different forms. It's a truth that we humans need to remember and apply in our lives, if we accept the credo expressed by Gary Snyder in *The Practice of the Wild* that "we must try to live without causing unnecessary harm, not just to fellow humans but to all beings." So, here it is, then, with my own little twist: we only value and love that which we know; and what we truly love and value we are most likely to protect with the sort of wholehearted ferocity and passion embodied by the Wild Man and Woman.

Only by getting to know wild nature will we learn to embrace and cherish and preserve it, both within ourselves and as manifested in myriad other forms, in the larger, more-than-human world. Such a full embrace is possible, no matter how frightening, because at some deep level, we and all the Others are part of a larger, sacred oneness. All of the world's mystical traditions teach this. Even Christianity maintains that we are all part of the creation: people and trees and hills and butterflies and bacteria. And though it doesn't normally use words like "sacred" or "holy," science now confirms it too.

The good news is that wildness reaches everywhere, from the far wilderness to the innermost pockets of our biggest cities. We can each choose where, in what form, and in what way we get to know the wild. But we must make some effort, if we care at all about healing ourselves, healing the world, keeping things whole. In touching the Wild Man or Wild Woman, we learn to better love the world. And in loving the world, we embrace our own richly wild essence. It's not an easy thing for us modern *Homo sapiens* to understand or practice. But as Gary Snyder says, "I for one, will keep working for wildness day by day," in whatever small way I'm able.

SIXTEEN

Epilogue

First Snow

TWO FROSTED FORMS APPROACH AT A LOPE, THEIR SHAPES softened by a blizzard of tiny, white, hexagonal crystals. Moving closer, they become two women, fluffy piles of snowflakes clinging to hair and running clothes.

"The snow's great, isn't it," one of the runners says as she passes, her comment more of a statement than a question.

"Yeah, it's good fun," I reply, my smile reflecting hers.

For the first time in years, I can say that without reservation, no niggling "but" thoughts running through my head.

But there's the driveway to snowblow and steps to shovel . . .

But I hate thinking about having to drive in this stuff . . .

But I have to make sure the heat tapes are turned on . . .

My relationship with snow changed dramatically when I became a homeowner, especially after moving to Anchorage's Hillside. For most of my life I'd associated snow most closely with fun and outdoor recreation, while largely ignoring the occasional inconvenience, like getting stuck in my car. But up on the Hillside, snow meant work and anxiety more than play.

My semicircular driveway was large enough that I had to buy a snowblower. But even with that, clearing the driveway meant at least an hour's work. Not to mention shoveling or sweeping off the porch and steps and upper deck. There was also the steady monitoring of front and back roofs, making sure the heat tape was on to prevent ice buildup around vents. And leaks into the house.

Life on the Hillside also meant extended winters, heavier snowfalls, colder temperatures, and longer drives on often-slick roads. As time passed, I greeted winter's white shroud with growing apprehension. Instead of welcoming the season's first big snowfall, I inwardly moaned.

Now things have shifted again. Life's circumstances—the end of my marriage to Dulcy, the decision to sell our house—have whisked me off Anchorage's Hillside and plopped me down in the city's northwestern flatlands, an area known appropriately enough as Turnagain.

It's a move I wouldn't have imagined a year ago, when I entered my thirteenth winter among the wooded hills on Anchorage's eastern borders. Heck, I couldn't imagine leaving my Hillside home even after reluctantly deciding to end my eighteen-year relationship with Dulcy, a hard but necessary decision that's still not easily explained.

I proposed buying out her share of the house, so that I could remain in the spot where I'd discovered the joys of bird watching, shared the company of hooting owls and wandering black bears, and nurtured a small patch of feral strawberries. This was also the place where, after eleven years as an Anchorage resident, I deliberately began to learn about my wild neighbors and the local landscape in new and deeper ways.

But as the weeks passed, my mind—and heart—began to see things differently. Finances are what sparked the shift. Taking out a loan to give Dulcy her fair share of our house's value would undoubtedly strain my freelancer's budget.

Those initial financial concerns served as a catalyst for deeper reflections. Selling the house with Dulcy would help bring closure to this chapter in my life. And I could then find a place where my eighty-four-year-old, arthritis-hobbled mom—who's lived with me since 2002—wouldn't have to deal with high stairways.

Still, I agonized long and hard about whether to stay or go. What ultimately became the tipping point in my back-and-forth struggle is this: a move would bring greater congruence between my beliefs and actions. I'd always felt our Hillside house was bigger than we needed. In selling it I could downsize my life. And by moving into a smaller place that's closer to Anchorage's center, I'd expend less energy both at home and on my around-town travels. In short, I'd go more lightly on the Earth.

The lightness I felt on deciding to move signaled its rightness.

My search didn't take long. With the help of a good-hearted friend, I found a new place within a few days. The building itself isn't much to look at, a nicked-up, ground-level duplex built before the 1964 earthquake, with scuffed-up kitchen floor and some peeling paint, inside and out. But the old house felt "right" as soon as I entered it.

More important to me is the house's location: a residential neighborhood with lots of trees and gardens. And songbirds.

Stepping outside the house after my room-to-room walkabout, I entered the front yard, where the finest sort of welcoming committee greeted me. Black-capped chickadees and red-breasted nuthatches chattered brightly in the trees. What could I do but laugh and whistle back my own delight in their presence? As noted elsewhere in these pages, songbirds in general—and chickadees most of all—transformed my life after I'd moved to the Hillside in 1993. To have them appear here seemed the perfect invitation.

I accepted and moved in late September.

When told about my cross-town move, several friends have asked if I miss the Hillside. The answer's been no, even without considering my relationship with snow.

Now an extended fall has given way to winter. But the months ahead don't seem so ominous. My duplex neighbors and I are responsible for keeping the front walk and backyard driveway cleared of snow, but a carport mostly covers the small drive, so it's no big deal. I can get everything shoveled in a half hour or less, front walk included.

Both a grocery store and post office are within walking distance, which is especially handy when the streets are bad. I can also walk or bike to two of my favorite hangouts, Title Wave Books and Café and the Bear Tooth Theater and Pub. What more could a home-based writer ask? I'm also within a mile or two of some long-time friends—and a new sweetheart, Helene, who has quickly become my favorite outdoors companion and a guide of sorts as I get to know this part of Anchorage.

Last but far from least, I'm a long snowball's throw from Anchorage's much-beloved Coastal Trail, a place popular with roller bladers and cyclists in summer, skiers in winter, and walkers and joggers year-round. That means easy access to both summer and winter recreation. And much less driving. It's such a pleasure to go hiking or skiing beyond city streets without having to drive somewhere. I've walked the Coastal Trail, off and on, for years. But I sense that my relationship with it—as an extension of my new neighborhood—is about to take a turn for the better. To borrow from a famous movie line, this could be the start of another beautiful, deepened friendship.

TO CELEBRATE OUR FIRST SUBSTANTIAL snowfall of the season, I pull on jacket, gloves, and wool cap and head out the door and across the front yard, where chickadees zoom back and forth between feeder and trees. A few minutes later I'm passing through open woods blanketed in a soft white shroud, the only tracks those of a small canine. No sooner do I think, *That could be a fox*, than I look up to see a bushy-tailed red fox sprinting through the forest, head turned back my way as it disappears into birch trees and willow bushes. It's only the third I've seen in a quarter century of residing in Anchorage.

During my years on the Hillside, I shared yard and neighborhood with all sorts of wildlife, from songbirds and squirrels to goshawks, moose, weasels, lynx, coyotes, and black bears. I don't anticipate as many different sorts of wild neighbors here in Turnagain (or at least don't expect critters to reveal themselves so willingly in this dog- and people-rich part of town), so I'm cheered to discover a fox inhabits the area.

By 10 a.m. the snow is already three to four inches deep, so upon reaching the Coastal Trail I'm relieved to see lots of boot prints and no ski tracks. I won't be blamed for "messing up" the fresh snow. In fact I meet no skiers during an hour-long walk; only a half dozen runners, a couple people walking dogs, a dad and daughter playing in the powder. Passing a park, I hear the laughter of kids sledding down a small hill.

Walking slowly back to my new home, I lift my face into the falling flakes and allow myself another smile. I feel a vaguely familiar lightness, a playfulness, stirring inside. I'm ready, again, to more fully embrace the idea of Anchorage as winter wonderland. Gray skies above, go ahead and bring it on.

Selected Readings

(Or, books that I love and that have influenced my own writing and, more importantly, my way of living on this Earth.)

Berry, Wendell. *Life Is a Miracle: An Essay Against Modern Superstition.* Washington, D.C.: Counterpoint Press, 2000.

Bly, Robert. *Iron John: A Book About Men.* New York: Addison-Wesley, 1990.

Duncan, David James. *My Story as Told by Water.* San Francisco: Sierra Club Books, 2001.

Eiseley, Loren. *The Immense Journey.* New York: Vintage, 1959.

Fox, Matthew. *Original Blessing.* New York: Jeremy P. Tarcher/Putnam, 2000.

Haines, John. *The Stars, the Snow, the Fire.* St. Paul, MN: Graywolf Press, 1989.

Hillman, James. *The Soul's Code: In Search of Character and Calling.* New York: Random House, 1996.

Kari, James, and James A. Fall. *Shem Pete's Alaska: The Territory of the Upper Cook Inlet Dena'ina,* 2nd ed. Fairbanks: University of Alaska Press, 2003.

Leopold, Aldo. *A Sand County Almanac.* New York: Oxford University Press, 1949.

Lopez, Barry. *Of Wolves and Men.* New York: Charles Scribner's Sons, 1978.

Louv, Richard. *Last Child in the Woods: Saving Our Children from Nature-Deficit Disorder.* New York: Algonquin Books, 2005.

Lyon, Thomas J. *This Incomparable Land: A Guide to American Nature Writing.* Minneapolis: Milkweed Editions, 2001.

Moore, Kathleen Dean. *Holdfast: At Home in the Natural World.* New York: The Lyons Press, 1999.

Mowat, Farley. *Never Cry Wolf.* New York: Little, Brown & Company, 1963.

Nash, Roderick Frazier. *Wilderness and the American Mind.* New Haven: Yale University, 1967.

Nelson, Richard. *Make Prayers to the Raven: A Koyukon View of the Northern Forest.* Chicago: The University of Chicago Press, 1983.

———. *The Island Within.* San Francisco: North Point Press, 1989.

Pyle, Robert Michael. *Where Bigfoot Walks: Crossing the Dark Divide.* New York: Mariner Books, 1995.

Rockwell, David. *Giving Voice to Bear: North American Indian Myths, Rituals, and Images of the Bear.* Niwot, CO: Roberts Rinehart Publishers, 1991.

Sanders, Scott Russell. *Staying Put: Making a Home in a Restless World.* Boston: Beacon Books, 1993.

———. *Hunting for Hope: A Father's Journeys.* Boston: Beacon Press, 1998.

Shepard, Paul. *The Tender Carnivore and the Sacred Game.* New York: Scribner, 1973.

———. *The Only World We've Got: A Paul Shepard Reader.* San Francisco: Sierra Club Books, 1996.

Shepard, Paul, and Barry Sanders. *The Sacred Paw: The Bear in Nature, Myth, and Literature.* New York: Viking Penguin, 1985.

Simpson, Sherry. *The Way Winter Comes: Alaska Stories.* Seattle: Sasquatch Books, 1998.

Snyder, Gary. *The Practice of the Wild: Essays.* San Francisco: North Point Press, 1990.

Stegner, Wallace. *Where the Bluebird Sings to the Lemonade Springs: Living and Writing in the West.* New York: Random House, 1992.

Trimble, Stephen. *Words from the Land: Encounters with Natural History Writing* (especially Trimble's introduction). Salt Lake City: Peregrine Smith Books, 1989.

Turner, Jack. *The Abstract Wild.* Tucson: The University of Arizona Press, 1996.

White, Jonathan. *Talking on the Water: Conversations About Nature and Creativity.* San Francisco: Sierra Club Books, 1994.

Williams, Terry Tempest. *An Unspoken Hunger: Stories from the Field.* New York: Pantheon Books, 1994.

Wood, Nancy. *Spirit Walker.* New York: Doubleday, 1993.